"This excellent book, the fruit of vast learning and passionate commitment, celebrates our complexities, our multiplicity, desiring, and acting. The chapter on Fanon and Existential Phenomenology is a good example of how this book engages with important and timely issues. As well as Fanon, this book calls on feminist perspective, on the civil rights and postcolonial movements, as well as LGBTQIA+ movements. How could anyone with an interest in psychology, psychotherapy, psychoanalysis, philosophy, critical theory, and the political context in which we live not find this book compelling and rewarding?"

Dr Onel Brooks, *psychoanalytic psychotherapist, existential-analytic psychotherapist*

"The shock that his last book *Subversion and Desire* produced was not enough for Manu Bazzano. He is coming back with a new book, even more radically opposed to the psychotherapy orthodoxies. Its polyphonic language, its openings to philosophy, literature, and the arts make the reading of the book instructive and exegetic, a source of great *jouissance*. It establishes the author as first among equals with his distinguished colleagues in queer studies and the queering of psychoanalysis. This is a book that teaches us how not to betray our desire".

Dr Chloe Kolyri, *queer psychoanalyst, lecturer, and author with degrees in medicine, psychiatry, and neurophysiology. A founding member of the Greek anti-psychiatry movement, as well as of the collective on Deleuze-Guattari studies, she has published on queer-gender, Deleuze, and psychoanalysis*

"Few writers and therapists are capable of fearless critique, sharp sociocultural observation, and seeing below the surface of an argument or opinion. In this book, Bazzano demonstrates this rare ability. Reading it leads me to question what I thought I knew or understood about the art and craft of therapy. I felt shaken out of complacency, unsettled, challenged, and stretched. In charting this complex territory, Bazzano has contributed to my development as a therapist. This book instils greater openness and curiosity, providing a key ingredient of compassion".

Dr Rachel Freeth, *therapist, trainer, and author of several books including* Psychiatry and Mental Health: A Guide for Counsellors and Psychotherapists *(2020)*

Difference and Multiplicity

Psychological and psychotherapeutic orientations often neglect the notion that the individual is not one unit, but rather a coalition of affects. Providing a multidisciplinary framework for the practice of psychotherapy and philosophy, this book explores and embraces this multiplicity within the human psyche and challenges the reader to explore and celebrate difference within society.

Chapters reframe the breadth and scope of psychotherapy as an endeavour at the service of both healing and care, while also fostering bold exploration, emphasizing the risk and adventure of being alive. Through clinical studies, first-person accounts, forays into contemporary philosophy, psychoanalysis, psychotherapy, and the arts, this book presents insights that inspire readers to be in the world with courage, compassion, and kindness, with the sense that we do not have to know who we are before becoming active citizens of the world. Bazzano then extends that exploration to the domain of public life by examining contemporary challenges related to climate change, race, gender, ethnicity, and more.

This book is an essential read for therapy practitioners and professionals of related disciplines, who want to expand their knowledge and find different ways to understand and practise their art.

Manu Bazzano, PhD, is a writer, psychotherapist/supervisor, Zen priest, and Butoh dancer. He is a visiting lecturer at Cambridge University and Goldsmiths College, London and founder of Affect Therapy. He facilitates psychotherapy courses and Zen retreats in the UK and abroad. Among his books are *Zen and Therapy: Heretical Perspectives*; *Nietzsche and Psychotherapy*; and *Subversion and Desire: Pathways to Transindividuation*. Website: www.manubazzano.com

Difference and Multiplicity

Adventures in Philosophy and Psychotherapy

Manu Bazzano

Routledge
Taylor & Francis Group

LONDON AND NEW YORK

Designed cover image: © Getty Images

First published 2026
by Routledge
4 Park Square, Milton Park, Abingdon, Oxon OX14 4RN

and by Routledge
605 Third Avenue, New York, NY 10158

Routledge is an imprint of the Taylor & Francis Group, an informa business

British Library Cataloguing-in-Publication Data
A catalogue record for this book is available from the British
Library

ISBN: 978-1-032-86762-5 (hbk)
ISBN: 978-1-032-85300-0 (pbk)
ISBN: 978-1-003-52909-5 (ebk)

DOI: 10.4324/9781003529095

Typeset in Times New Roman
by Apex CoVantage, LLC

For Jim

Contents

Also by Manu Bazzano

Books

Zen Poems
Haiku for Lovers
Buddha is Dead: Nietzsche and the Dawn of European Zen
The Speed of Angels
Spectre of the Stranger: Towards a Phenomenology of Hospitality
After Mindfulness: New Perspectives on Psychology and Meditation
Therapy and the Counter-Tradition (with Julie Webb)
Zen and Therapy: Heretical Perspectives
Re-Visioning Person-Centred Therapy: The Theory and Practice of a Radical Paradigm
Nietzsche and Psychotherapy
Re-Visioning Existential Therapy: Counter-Traditional Perspectives
Subversion and Desire: Pathways to Transindividuation

Butoh performances

The Skin is Faster than the Word
Men Going Down
The Innocence of Becoming
The Angel of History

Music Albums

Walk Inside the Painting (with Daedalo)
Naked Dance
Sex, Religion, and Cosmetics

Introduction

Difference is not diversity. Diversity (often paired with "equality") is all the rage in our neoliberal world. It avows a bland appreciation of equally bland notions such as variety and inclusion. "Variety is the spice of life", we say, barely hiding a yawn. For only a bored/boring person would say that. Meanwhile, glossy promotional brochures of overpriced colleges and universities tell us: "Our institution is *truly* inclusive; we welcome and appreciate a wide range of people of different social and ethnic backgrounds and of different genders and sexual orientations". Diversity is very good – for business. And so is inclusion. Inclusion into what? The answer is straightforward: of Difference within the precincts of the Self-Same. The assumption (philosophically naïve but politically harmful) is that there is a centre, a norm, a dominant mode into which difference is generously, graciously invited – as an outsider. Ah, the generosity of the liberal host, whose generosity is the talk of the town, from whose generous lips generous words tumble out. Beware of those who worship the word "generosity" and its intricate geometries! Beware of those who tell you that the doors of their home are always open! For there will be hell to pay.

Unlike diversity, difference is free from, nor does it buy into, the idolatry of identity in relation to which it is supposed to emerge. It does not presuppose the existence of the Same in relation to which it comes into being. Difference, in other words, is *difference in itself*. It is no longer understood as an empirical link between two terms endowed with their own identity ("*a* is different from *b*"). If there is identity, this is shaped by a prior link between *differentials*.

Multiplicity is not pluralism. It is not caught in the simplistic dualism of One-Many. It does not assume the existence of One, on the foundations of which it then goes on to proliferate into the many.

DOI: 10.4324/9781003529095-1

Pluralism in philosophy gave us Habermas, once Adorno's research assistant and later responsible for selling out the Frankfurt School to the *Bundesrepublik*, for turning a rich legacy of thought and praxis into the compounded banalities of communicational theory, the myth of consensus, the defence of representational democracy – all the insipid shibboleths of current liberalism so dear to mainstream psychotherapy. One could say that Habermas did for Critical Theory what conventional existential therapy has done for existentialism, turning the latter's already wonky tenets – being-towards-death, uncertainty, meaning, freedom, choice, and the hot air balloon of the "human condition" – into even more ridiculous categories and growing detritus, zealously building a zombified range of notions. These are duly varnished through formulaic repetitions within cultish and pricey "existential trainings" which continue to reproduce a veritable regiment of conformists.

Pluralism in psychotherapy gave us more than banal existential therapy. It gave us the Psych Supermarket. Clients/patients came to be seen as customers (when not perceived as unidentified objects in bagging area and dealt with via a set of A.I. pet "therapeutic" solutions). Demagogically invited to choose from different brands, orientations, and approaches, they may be then offered a deal, which on a lucky day could mean two simultaneous approaches for the price of one.

On an intrapsychic level, the psyche is not plural. It is *multiple*. The self is at its very origins not one but many. A plural view of the self has still One at its centre. A multiple self reflects instead the porousness of the world into which we are embedded, as the heart in the organism to paraphrase the subtle and forgotten teachings of Maurice Merleau-Ponty. Both difference and multiplicity are *metaphysical*, Deleuze would say. If that word scares you, dear reader, how about "ontological"? That would mean difference and multiplicity are constitutive of Being, while at the same time corroding Being of its alleged substantiality, edging it towards a field of immanence, towards Becoming and a musical ontology.

*

Written over the last two years, this book incorporates past and present preoccupations and possible shreds and hints of innovation within two practices which continue to be central in my life – philosophy and psychotherapy. " 'Philosophy" can be rightly seen as a grandiloquent term, in an era when many fancy themselves as "philosophers". To think that neither Walter Benjamin nor Fredric Jameson, two thinkers of the highest calibre, ever used the term for describing their work gives pause for thought. The advent of what was simplistically labelled poststructuralism helped us redefine the adventures of philosophy as belonging to *theory*, a term that includes not only dialectic engagement with Heraclitus, Plato, and the entire philosophical canon to this day but also one that encompassed forays into psychoanalysis, the arts, "high" and "low' culture, the everyday, including personal accounts of the writer/practitioner's lived experience, a view of *philosophy as a way of life*. The latter does not entail a moralistic view, as in living up to the standards of chosen and elevated philosophical concepts. This would align philosophy to a branch of religion or rather ersatz religion. I have too much respect for religion, for its degrees of depth and complexity to consider these cheap exploits being anywhere near it. What do I mean by that? Listen to existential therapists harping on about a badly understood idea of "authenticity", applying "meaning" to an unsuspected reality that doesn't give a monkey's about their grandiose bestowing of meaning. Listen to humanistic therapists showing off their badge of fully actualized beings who bestow unconditional positive regard at the drop of a hat, and you'll see what I mean. Listen to psychoanalytic therapists forensically and arrogantly dissecting traumas in the vain hope to heal them, thus bringing patients back to their reserved seats in the traffic jam and their bullshit jobs. That's what I mean. No, philosophy as a way of life has thankfully other manifestations, all of them rich and interesting and as far removed from the cheap moralizing of our deeply puritanical/permissive era as one can imagine. Foucault is in there of course and so is Pierre Hadot, despite the simplistic packages they have been boxed into. There is no better example than my beloved Nietzsche, irreverent virtuoso of philosophy-as-a-way-of-life, with his arresting notion of the *Great Health*, the great mark of which, as he says in the preface to what is still my favourite among all his remarkable texts, the *Joyful Science*, is limitless gratitude after a long and debilitating illness, paired to the keenly felt presence of the world around him, April weather, and the triumph of high spirits.

It's a cold sunny day early afternoon in January as I write this, the month of the two-faced god who looks at past and future, at transitions and imperceptible boundaries. Nietzsche's Great Health is clearly not our insipid "wellness" with its active pursuit of holistic yoga-mindfulness-healthy-habits routines designed to preserve the incurable insularity of the middle-class and to keep the ravenous stupidity of corporate ideology ticking the world over. Great Health stems out of deep illness, that is, a state of profound vulnerability, well beyond the cosy Jungian cliché of the wounded healer; it is a philosophy born out of the endgame; it carries forth the very schoolings of serious illness; it rejoices in the rare joyous spells of energy, strength, serenity, and clarity which unexpectedly open up like the sun through the clouds today, at 3.40 P.M. on a silent Friday afternoon – resisting (out of dignity, out of beneficial pride) giving in to the facile lures of consolation and melancholy conclusions about the so-called "human condition" (Hannah Arendt has a lot to answer for, alongside her existentialist aficionados!). Great health means that, for instance, in the midst of a painful heartbreak, one is able to sing on a cold sunny day a hymn of joyful aloneness and a ballad of praise for abandonment, which is after all our primordial state of being, our state of freedom/destitution, of lush decreation, our final words at the end of the human dance of dust, jawbones, and stars: *Eli, Eli, lama sabachtani.*

It is also inseparably linked to bursts of creative power – in whatever form or shape these may manifest in different people. It has to be, as the creative act is one of the most concentrated expression of power (the generative power implied in *puissance*, rather than the dominating impulse implied in *pouvoir*).

When reciting words such as "actualization" at psychotherapy trainings, they don't tell you that, if you were to seriously pursue it, it will separate you from the shiny puddles of shared values. To become who you are is a dangerous pursuit. It should come with a health warning. If you then happen to be an artist, your blessing and talent will become a curse. You may be thinking, ah the tortured artist cliché! And how late-romantic, how old-fashioned of me, harking back to none other than Otto Rank! If only we'd paid heed to the insights of this astute analyst and writer. But then we would have had to accept that so-called "actualization" (a term I loathe, a wimpy version of Nietzsche's will to power as will-to-become and create oneself) is not for everyone, for most of us want certainties, a cushy job, and exemption from life's vicissitudes. And who can blame us? Most of us coming out of psychotherapy trainings actualize as replicas on the authenticity/congruence/originality assembly line, flawlessly parroting Klein, Rogers, Herr Heidegger, Gendlin, and so forth.

*

My own ongoing illness, becoming more complicated after my first diagnosis in the early months of 2022, continues to teach me how to stay away from the usual siren calls – versions of *hope* – as from the usual bogeymen – versions of *fear*. One chapter is dedicated to the practice of no fear, no hope – difficult, unending, one that I have seen in action from friends who are now very ill and from those who recently passed away. That I can write, scribble, compose, speak, and dance is a sign of good health to me. But let us leave Mr Bazzano: what is it to us that Mr Bazzano has got well again for the time being?

*

I don't like presenting a systematic introduction to my books, and this one is no exception. Readers will choose whether to read it systematically or dip at random into any of the chapters, discovering perhaps themes and threads that are useful to them, even those I might have failed to spot while immersed in the writing. I explicitly advocate and encourage, after Rorty, this sort of "creative misreading", discussed in the *Everyday Uncanny* chapter. In other words, dear reader, don't worry about what I "really meant" by this or that. Notice instead what it does to you, if it affects you in any way, positively or negatively, and if you're willing to take it further, to make use of it for your own life.

Over the last four years I have given myself more fully to an art form that I practised on and off since the late 1990s, and which I consider to be a new way of writing, in Derrida's generous sense – writing with the body, in this case. I am talking about *Butoh*. Some of my performances last year in Italy and London – loosely based on Walter Benjamin's *Angel of History* – were so generously received that I felt emboldened to continue this uncertain and potent terrain. I felt greatly heartened by the positive feedback and encouragement of my Butoh teacher Marie-Gabrielle Rotie, a major international Butoh artist and performer. You will find traces and transcripts of some of these experiences in the *Wayward Angel* chapter.

What has shifted for me since the publication of my last book *Subversion and Desire* is that I am under no illusion: the areas discussed here are *reservations*: segregations or enclaves where one is permitted the cultivation of a style, the sketching of an impression of individual and collective freedom with little bearing on the workings of the neoliberal machine. Sex is one of such segregated places. Some contemporary sexual practices are discussed in two chapters, one of which critically engages with Saketopoulou's notion of *exigent sadism* and present my own formulation of *affirmative masochism*. From BDSM to endless variations, including consensual nonmonogamy (CNM), polyamory, and so forth, these are styles encased within a private logic, rarely if ever spilling over into the sphere of *desire*, of an emancipative force able to substantially change the iniquitous structures of society. In our current historical *conjuncture* (a pertinent term coined by Stuart Hall), desire has become unintelligible, entirely superseded by pleasure. No matter how free, edgy, and innovative one might be in the bedroom, the air-condition dungeon, or the customized sex party, none of these libertarian stances ever translates into revolutionary, progressive, or even merely compassionate politics. On the contrary, they are aligned in the current conjuncture with the libertarianism of our "leaders", desublimating any residual wish one might have to engage in civic action.

The same applies to art, literature, and psychoanalysis/psychotherapy. These domains are reservations because they are essentially dominated by *reactive* forces. Does that entail throwing in the towel? Not in the least. It does mean, however, taking a hint from counter-traditional philosophy, that is, from an *untimely*, rigorous practice of both critique and foresight and be prepared to express uncomfortable, even unpopular ideas with the purpose of clearing the way for the advent of *active* forces – life-affirming, *adventurous* in the true sense of the term. Not the self-centred quest and escapade of neoliberal subjects for whom all experience is a terrain where to plant their little flag of identity. Instead, adventure as *ad-venire*, as being ready to respond to what is *to come*, to the unknown and the uncertain in the perpetual theatre of becoming.

Even before being an invaluable if little understood philosophical concept, *Becoming* is a way of daring to do our unscripted thing in the world with courage, compassion, and kindness, with the feeling that we may not get a second chance, with the sense that we don't have to know who we "truly" are before being active citizens of the world. It seems to be that the organism (the body, with and without organs) does this most of the time effortlessly while the Cartesian dead ringer that has taken over our life takes a long time to get that the season turned a few weeks ago. This applies to practising philosophy, doing psychotherapy, dancing, being in and out of love, making new friends, saying goodbye to what's already dead and gone, and to welcoming the new.

The body kind of knows, not because it keeps some stupid score but because a new inbreath takes up where you left off. A new moment. A new being, if you can bear it. The heart already nurtures your future. The air is full of new scents, and on a musical beach, one morning, you find it in you to forgive those who harmed you, because they didn't know, nor will they ever know the depth of the harm they caused you, caught up as they were, as they still are, in their terrible righteousness, their manicured beards, their soft Calvinist manners, all moral boxes ticked, all right noises made to please the masters, the heads of department, the heads of school, and finally their mum and dad. Meanwhile you are alive to your lips, your eyes, your hands, the voice that wants to speak, and sing, and tell stories to create bridges and affirm the autonomous current of affect that runs through all human and nonhuman bodies, the current of desire that is freedom and joy and social upheaval and revolution. Well yes, that too. There is no time to rest, or to feel sorry about yourself. The field will be soon full of flowers even if your old love has gone. The sun is already so sweet, pale blue and tender like the colour of eternity in the Florentine paintings of my memory. It will be great! There is no time to pause and think and show the world how reflective you are! Forget yourself. Forget the applause, the compliment, the "I love you" texts on WhatsApp. They won't be coming no more, sweetheart. Let your heart break. Be touched by the ten thousand things. See how everything is in motion. Where does that path go inside that Cezanne painting, you ask. Give me your hand my love, let's step in. It was a beautiful ride. It will be an even more beautiful ride ahead.

London, January 10, 2025

Chapter 1

Perversifications

Enchanted afternoon

When the train came to a stop, I phoned Dora to say I was on my way. I'll leave the door unlocked, she said. Left the station at a steady pace, Dino says, the heat in my body caressed by gusts of wind all the way from the sea to this narrow alley, this backstreet beloved of our afternoon walks together. All sounds muted by a heartbeat that felt no longer mine but set in the clouds, eternity participating in my fever. Walked by the semi-abandoned church on the hill, then headed down to her place. A glance at the sea at the end of the square. Stepped inside a hushed living room. Took my shoes off. Made my way to the special room, where I'd never been before. Dora sat motionless in full regalia, black boots, black corset. She looked at me tenderly, nervously. We didn't smile or speak. I undressed – calmly, dutifully. We went straight into sex, both of us thrilled by the novelty and, in my case, also a bit puzzled by the alienation effect caused by the setting. Brecht would have approved, I am tempted to say now with hindsight, but of hindsight the graves are full. What do you mean? I ask. Oh, it's an old proverb, he explains, it means it's easy to be wise after the event. Anyhow, I'll spare you the details, Dino says. I am self-conscious when it comes to sex. Suffice it to say that it was an enchanted afternoon. Time stopped. Nothing else mattered. We were transported into another dimension, and both knew we were closer to each other than ever.

Interrupted love

Reality, or more likely its cheap surrogate, showed up when she spoke of Sybil, the Jungian oracle, Dino says, who gave Dora steady, half-solicited counsel, and whose verdict now avowed that by hanging out with me she precluded the chance of meeting someone who could be *really* there for her.

DOI: 10.4324/9781003529095-2

Amen, Dino says in mock veneration. All the same, he goes on, I felt that everything we experienced on that occasion was tender and true. That the depth of our love was heightened; it spoke of mutual trust, willingness to play, to suspend for a while our tangled knots.

Now I'm not so sure, Dino says. A long silence follows. What's on your mind, I ask eventually. Well, I had second thoughts. I now see that episode as a feast of bondage and abortive unity. I can now see that I was merely an extra in a play. I may be rationalizing of course, divorcing myself from what I felt. It seems to me that some other . . . drive, yearning, *fancy*, took over our love. In that theatrical scenario, I was ushered in to witness and play a marginal role in her psychodrama, a script where the main characters were Gary, her ex and her one true love whom she never truly left (a guy who beat her up regularly, who once raped her, and took her to sex parties), and her father, a classicist manqué. I'm thinking of that time when during a video call out of the blue she started masturbating. I wasn't sure whether to feel flattered or what. I did feel confused and distant, like it wasn't about me, I was an object, but then is it ok for a man to feel objectified?

I see what you mean, Dino, I say. You felt excluded, you didn't matter, though I am not sure about your conclusion. It sounds, if I may say so, reactive. Sounds like you had expectations that were not met, and this made it difficult perhaps to experience in a more open way what was unfolding. I am reminded of that quote by Georges Bataille, an author you may know: "I wanted experience to lead where it would, not to some end point given in advance".[1]

Yes, he replies, I understand that, and can't say I like where I'm going with this. How so? I ask. What was special about that particular encounter? Dino says. Was it the am dram set-up, the sex? I mean, sex with her was OK, but I had far more exciting encounters with lovers in the past, lovers who were truly generous, unlike Dora who is merely fond of saying the word *generosity*. To talk of generosity while doing diddly squat is sentimental. It's sentimental, as some people do, to wax lyrical about the munificence of the singular eucalyptus tree, burning so as to be beneficial to the species, while ignoring that this generosity is circumscribed to their own and that eucalyptus trees also dry out the soil draining all the other plants of water. Anyway, who cares, right? I'm just trying to say that the exhilarating thing between us was love. When I met her, I stopped having sex with anyone else, including my partner. This is still the case; would you believe it! I never told her this. Don't ask me why. Maybe I kind of felt that it would freak her out in some way, that she would experience it as pressure or something.

I don't really know. How ridiculous I have become! Between us, love was the thing; it permeated everything. I do wonder sometimes whether I've ever loved anybody the way I loved her. Go and say that to her friends. But I also wonder whether feeling special was for her a more tenacious need than love. I don't know. In the end, she couldn't really do love, so we did high drama instead. Sure, experimentation is great, and so is pleasure. But pleasure is not desire; it isn't about freedom; it is often re-enactment of unresolved stuff, compulsion to repeat static set-ups where the other has no say, cannot affect her, the protagonist, in any meaningful way. Sounds cruel, but to me that is a fatuous pantomime! Am I embittered? OK, maybe I am, so what? It was like, hey, I'm bored, why don't we go to a West End theatre to watch *Slave Play* like cool people do! Then I'll write a *PowerPoint* presentation listing all the cutting-edge bits for my dissertation. Never got my money back for that worthless ticket I never used. It's like, I am bored, darling! Spank me again, Dino says to no one in particular, with a smirk on his face, before I go to the polls to vote for the Tories. You sound sad, I suggest, and a bit angry too perhaps? Yeah, I *am* angry. For all her love of transparency, she had quite a secret arsenal of BDSM stuff in her closet. Transparency my foot! Forgot to tell you that once, the morning after a lovely evening spent together, she said to me over breakfast while we were having a really nice time: "You're just like Gary after all. You too are a bad guy; you hang out with me but you're with someone else". All this, as expressed, is a matter-of-fact, sweet, passive-aggressive tone. Now, I'm no saint, but I was stunned. I had my bit of fun and haven't been, you know, a paragon of virtue. Does it mean that I'm just the same as a guy who beats women up and rapes them? OK maybe I am! Need to think about that one. But no, I really don't think so. But I let it go. I had to. Mainly I'm sad, that's true. I mean, look at me. Another day is one more day away from her. The other week I allowed myself to drift. I remembered all the things I treasured about our love. Funny how sex wasn't really part of these. Moments of serenity, laughter, tenderness, the two doves by the living room window one December afternoon; our laughter carried by the wind in spring as we walked up our beloved path, past the school; the picnic on the summer grass; the autumn light flooding her kitchen; the hushed tender talk after love looking at the ceiling. What does it matter if we live or die? Dino asks the room. We have loved; that's more than enough. True, we were inept at shielding this precious love from the bad weather of our own demands and inanities, from people's judgements and envy.

Today it's her birthday. I woke up feeling tearful; I *so* wanted to call her and say how my heart aches for her, how much I want her to be well. If I did, we'd be back into the misery whirlpool. In all these years, she rarely showed some understanding of what she does in the relationship, you know, her *part* in it. I *am* sad. At our interrupted love. I am dismayed at our inability to take care of something so rare and wonderful and precious, and overindulge instead in endless, pointless misery. When I get like this, I bring myself to earth by recalling that alongside her endearing, bumbling pseudo-philosophical pretensions and muddled yearnings, alongside her abysmal ignorance, her passive aggression (have I mentioned her passive aggression?), her babydoll, gun moll schtick, she is a gloopy, short, double-chinned, middle-aged woman with little fat hands and a middling imagination, blissfully oblivious of her talent for cruelty. I bring myself to earth remembering her creepy, cheap seductions born of desperation. I come down to earth remembering that she was never in flight from her privileged, boring milieu as I naïvely thought at first, and that her forays into drugs, sex and hip yoga were not lines of flight but exotic furniture. And by recalling that when we were briefly apart, she got pregnant after angry sex with the electrician who'd come to look for exposed wires and cracking insulations. Unbelievable! Straight out of a cheap porn flick! That's what you get I guess from dating someone younger. I do wonder sometimes whether for Dora's generation, sex is a violent exercise a little less meaningful than tennis.

Angry sex? I ask. Yes, Dino says, that's what she told me. Did she have the child? No, she had an abortion and then told me about it when we hooked up again, and I wept quietly when we were lying together in the dark on a December evening, feeling her pain. The real schmuck, the sensitive guy! Done a lot of weeping in this relationship. Mark my words, Manu, I'll stop wasting my time. She often mentioned having a kind of sixth sense, Dino says, an intuition of how people close to her felt when they were absent, something her friends obligingly confirmed. But unless you have compassion for people, unless wisdom plays a role in your so-called deep intuition, what good is it? Did her sixth sense extend to the deep pain I felt, to the sleepless nights, to the sheer despair I often went through during our relationship? Nope. Like a needle in a compass, her intuition pointed solely towards her and her needs. Well, there is a name for that: middle-class new-agey hippy shit.

I see what you mean, Dino, I say. Wonder if this has to do with, you know, different degrees of subjectivity. My impression is that her subjectivity, the way she perceives herself, is similar to a particular stage, for instance like the Romantic poets who walk alone by the raging sea or in the Cumbrian hills and feel, really *feel* their inner life filling up with rich and complex thoughts and emotions, so they can say: "That's me, I exist". Some would say that's not enough. Hope you don't mind me be so didactic, but let's see where it goes, is that OK? Yes, says Dino, carry on, I like it. So, some would say something else is needed, namely the presence of another and/ or others who acknowledge/recognize me and whom I acknowledge/recognize. That's when subjectivity really comes to the fore. That's trickier obviously, as the other has the power to unsettle/overwhelm/inspire/love/hate me. And I also have the power to do the same over the other. This sounds all very neat, but it gets even trickier for women. They inherited millennia of subjugation to men, and in this necessary encounter with the other may at times slide into unhealthy submission and/or enmeshment – typically forgetting themselves and their need so as to make men happy. They may then revert, understandably, to more interior forms of subjectivity, where the other is not really allowed in. I am talking, of course, of your particular situation, that is, a heterosexual relationship. Because of this unbalance, it is difficult for any historically subaltern group to move through this other, perhaps deeper stage of subjectivity. Sorry to sound like a professor. Carry on, Dino says with a smile. The thing is, this stage of subjectivity, essential in my view, can happen through honest conflict as much as through love. But when it comes to romantic relationships, then the question is, "Is there enough love to contain the rough ride? Is there a big enough love that can contain both love and hate?" and I am not sure that this is the case between you two. There is more to this, there is society and the world without which subjectivity is stuck in the "beautiful soul" trap, but I stop there on this.

All the same, I carry on, going back to the electrician if you don't mind, aren't you being unfair? You describe what she had with this guy as demeaning. Maybe they had a relationship. Who's anyone to judge? Anyhow, you are in a relationship of many years. Every night she has to deal with the fact that you hold someone else in your arms. Yes, I see. Well, I guess they did have a relationship, Dino says. She described it as "He comes to fuck me from time to time". Felt stabbed in the chest when she said that – probably what she intended. I guess you can call that a relationship, sure. Again, I am the schmuck here, getting stupidly worked up about love and shit like that.

I'm not sure Dino, isn't this jealousy speaking? Nothing wrong with that, but it sounds like an ungenerous part of you. Do you remember the work we did with different parts of the psyche? I do, and I *am* being unfair, but things like that help me sober up when I'm caught up in reminiscing about what we had, because that brings up unbearable pain. Anyway, we did what we could, and it was good while it lasted, our interrupted love. But we are too different. For one thing, I have no rich daddy to fall back on, no family to go to on Christmas day. She often complained about being alone, but has no idea of what is like, you know, like you and I did, to come to a foreign country, in my case with 5 quid in my pocket and attempt to make a living. No idea whatsoever. Plus, I wonder though if she really ever understood what living hell she created for me. Never before in my life I felt positively suicidal as I did last year. I don't think she ever got that. I bet she's now telling herself that I was the one who left. But what can anyone do when the other makes your life hell? Did she even *love* me? Or was it more about her need to feel special? But she *was* special! She still *is*! I swear to God, Manu, this is the *last* time I'll ever mention her! Why is it that people are incapable of receiving love, Dino says covering his face, why is it so hard to see how much they are loved, cherished, *adored*? *Je t'adore*, I whispered to her one night in spring, and meant it, holding her beautiful face in my hands and looking into those loving eyes of hers. It pains me so much that I wasn't able to affect her in any meaningful way. And without that, Dinos says, love is tourism. It leaves us unchanged, stuck, forever enamoured of our boring neuroses. I'm ranting, I know, but I wonder if she ever understood how much pain I was in. She wanted me to take flight (implicitly, passively), to fly to her, but never dreamt of sketching a landing strip, without which my already eroded bones would have smashed to smithereens. I now realize, Dino says, that I rarely felt so lonely as in the few nights we slept together. No proximity, no holding each other, she was gone deep in her sleep while I gazed at the white ceiling. Maybe it's all in my head, maybe like the other Dora, you know, the one linked with the godfather of psychoanalysis, she'll simply say "Nah, I am not in love with my father. I don't have daddy issues. I don't crave his approval! Thank you and goodbye". I give up! She was incapable of holding me in moments of vulnerability. Her upbringing I guess. Nor did she *really* want me. Had she come to my room on that last fateful night, things would be different now. Had she not passively complied to my suggestion for a break; had she responded to my last fraught effort to save our love from sinking; had she fought a little for us, maybe things would be different now. How do you stay in a relationship with someone who doesn't *do* anything? Little did I know then of her penchant for triangulations, of her tendency to serially attach herself to men perceived as having some kind of power and a bad boy persona, burdened with the task of acting out their own shadow as well as hers so that she can go on playing the innocent. Little did I know that my hunch was right that night, that she was already considering a replacement, that she was going to kiss another willy, to paraphrase her baby-doll lingo. Little did I know she would hook up with a naïve, pussy-starved opportunist play-acting as my friend, banking on the faded glamour of his bygone "wild" persona, ducking his anger issues by fussily donning an oriental costume – and whose problem she has now become. Little did I know she would defecate in the pool where I swam, polluting my place of refuge and solace, creating more pain, making me finally realize the monstrous extent of her narcissism. I can hear her protesting "I had no choice! We had no choice!" – the *cri de cœur* of the indolent and the clueless the world over. Some defecate because they are frightened, others because they are livid and their bowel movement is a covert way to wage war.

When it gets dark on these winter afternoons, I miss her badly. In those moments I feel inconsolable and find myself speaking to this part of me like you suggested. I tell it that it's OK to feel that way. It's OK to cry. You loved her. You still do, and these tears are only right. Let them come. You know, Manu, I so wanted to please her, I did all I could to invite her gradually into a great part of my world. It was risky. It seemed to me it could work, that it would slowly open a path that was uncertain but that would give more of a chance to our love; we could have done creative work together. But it didn't work; she stomped her feet on this delicate ground, wanting more. And more. Not once did she say *come and meet my family and friends*, or *let's have a weekend together, let's go to this place I know, the two of us*. Oh well, Dino says. Her friends will be happy now; those pins stuck in the voodoo doll of our frail love have finally worked. Some of my so-called friends too breathe a sigh of relief, now that I'm ready to join the English *Quiet Desperation Club*.

Last week I dreamt I was drowning. She sat on the bank watching me, repeating her pet phrases: *Not a moment goes by. It means a lot. It means a great deal. Ditto;* and the most useless phrase of all: *I love you.* As the waves began to engulf me, she was driven to act: first she made the salute of a captain whose ship is sinking, then picked up an enormous diary and flicking the pages shouted something in my direction. The howling wind made it difficult to understand at first, but I thought I heard *Ditto!* The funny thing is that in my dream I felt heartened by that. *Not a moment goes by!* Maybe that's what you mean by my naivety. I am drowning, and the fact that she looks at her schedule to find a window to fit me in will somehow save me. And that all those *I love yous* she showered me with in nearly five years will save me from drowning. That's naïve alright. Ah, best not to wait for love to save you, I say. All the same, I know in my heart how much pain she was in. I know her loneliness. I know that she did love me. I also know that her pride is stronger than any love she might have felt. And that her love was sincere, an awe-inspiring feeling that forgot to take into account one essential thing: the existence of another, as you say, i.e., Yours Truly. *Not a moment goes by!* But how can I forget the joy we felt? There's nothing like it in the whole wide world, nothing! Never more! And those long tender goodbyes . . . *Nevermore*! croaks the raven. I gave her all I had. It wasn't enough. I even found her next fuck-buddy, pardon me, her (instant) next "great love"; she couldn't even do that, she couldn't find another somewhere else, on her own steam! Oh Manu, what can I say? That song, how does it go? *I gave her everything but it was never enough . . .* something like that . . . *I gave her my heart but she wanted my soul.*

Affirmative masochism

Dino spoke repeatedly of interrupted love. For weeks after our session, I went back to his phrase. It sounded uncanningly familiar, and it took me awhile to realize the association: Leopold Sacher-Masoch's novel *Venus in Furs*.[2] Allow me a brief detour. Considering how fashionable Sade is, I assume very few people would agree that the inflated attention paid to Sade from the Surrealists to this day occurred at the expense of the infinitely more interesting writer Sacher-Masoch, whose works are invaluable well beyond his common association with what is still largely deemed a pathology, namely "masochism", irreparably associated with Sade and "sadism". Masoch was born and lived for the first 12 years of his life in Lemberg, capital of Galicia, what is now Lviv, the beautiful Ukrainian city I had the good fortune to visit in occasion of a psychotherapy conference in 2019. Putin's invasion of Ukraine three years later meant that the affectionate and fecund conversations initiated with many dear colleagues and the plans we made for more events to take place there were interrupted. I remember my surprise when I came across Masoch's statue in Serbska Street just off Rynok Square, in the heart of the Old Town. Which is why I felt compelled to state, during my talk next day to a receptive audience of 300 Ukrainian therapists and trainees, that psychotherapy trainings would be more complete if they featured readings such as *Venus in Furs*. For it was patently wrong as well as crude of Austrian psychiatrist Kraft-Ebing to banalize and mythologize Masoch in his *Psychopathia Sexualis* by coining the term "masochism", and to point at the writer as the poet of masochism himself afflicted with the alleged anomaly.[3] It may take another 60 years and properly absorbing the work of Gilles Deleuze to reframe *Venus in Furs* in terms of contractual relations and contracted alliances with an emphasis on persuasion and education, all geared towards honouring mutual vows and promises by signing a contract. Not unlike therapy. Two features in the writings of Masoch (utopian thinker, socialist, humanist, and campaigner against anti-semitism) would make a welcome adjunct to the mawkish sentimentality of mainstream, attachment-driven relational therapy: (a) the recognition of the contractual and highly ritualized nature of human encounters, whether contract and ritual are explicit or implicit and (b) the acknowledgement of the intensity of life (whose other name is *affect*) that rages all around the layers of language and the worthy exertions of cognition.

It appears to me that, paradoxically, what was missing in the scenario Dino described in our session is the embracing of a more alert "masochistic" stance – a stance of receptivity that is vital to eros itself and to being in love, and one that alone escapes the gimmicks and titillations of an acquisitive, avaricious attitude to sex. Some would say that I am adopting a moral stance. Maybe so, but not a moralistic one. In our neoliberal world, we are told that we are free to do what we want. Far be it from me to interfere with that ostensibly sound principle. If, however, someone wants to link explorations of this kind to *eros* rather than soulless hydraulics; if one is ready to be momentarily caught in eros's net, they may then experience something akin to what I have called *affirmative masochism*,[4] namely, *a state of being divorced from the ubiquitous narcissism of our culture* and one that is *open to radical receptivity to the other*. Psychically, this implies a subversion of the patriarchal norm. The father archetype is not merely wrestled with but altogether bypassed in favour of a *Marian* vision where it is the Virgin who nails Christ to the cross. This is nothing less, in Deleuze's words, than "Masoch's version of the 'death of God'". Mary warrants the *parthenogenetic* (asexual) second birth of the son in the resurrection. In this scenario,

> it is not the son who dies so much as God the Father, that is the likeness of the father in the son. The cross represents the maternal image of death, the mirror in which the narcissistic self of Christ (Cain) apprehends his ideal self (Christ resurrected).[5]

With Masoch, we are in the domain of desire rather than pleasure. We are miles away from the anodyne tickles and titillations of BDSM-themed commodities, where we ourselves become commodities, worshipping at the cartoonish altar of a pleasure born out of lack and the false need to bolster the Cartesian self's flimsy credentials. We come close instead to something akin to heresy in a metaphysical and even religious sense. The ritualistic set-up conjured up in *Venus in Furs* presupposes nothing less than a subversive theology. This seditious worldview is the backdrop of all the rituals and contracts between the two protagonists Severin and Wanda. In a letter to his brother Charles on January 8, 1869, Masoch describes Christ as the man who inaugurates a world without the father. Christ is no longer the son of God but the new man, "the Man on the Cross who knows no sexual love, no property, no fatherland, no cause, no work".[6] In this scenario, both the father and God are removed.

The above is diametrically opposite to the setting Dora summoned Dino in – one where *the father is the only character*, dominating his own slave-play in three guises: (a) as Dora's own biological father, whom his wife tricked into having another child, Dora, whom he did not want; (b) as the phantom of her ex, Gary, the alleged batterer – whom she strangely, unreservedly defended against Dino; (c) the introjected dark father, that is a combination of Dora's own unacknowledged, reactive will to power manifesting as frantic claim to specialness, paired to the unconscious compulsion to inflict emotional pain to Dino (despite his serious health condition), plus the introjected affective ambience – the emotional wasteland of her English upper-middle class upbringing.

Pére-version

We are dealing here not with perversion – that is subversive, decentring of patriarchy, founded on a polymorphous view of sexuality – but instead with what Lacan calls *pére-version*, a plea for a return to a version of the father archetype (*pére*) and paternal authority, an appeal to the re-instatement of conventional sexuality in disguise, based on repression and desublimation.[7] Pére-version is a despairing call for daddy to come to help. But the father figure, showing up in Kafka's unpublished story "Give It Up!" as a policeman, replies: "You are asking me the way? Give it up, give it up!". The authority figure, whose task is to preserve the order of things, is incapable of giving direction.[8] If one were to transfer this set-up into the boudoir, the result would be comical as well as profoundly sad.

The above reading is possibly unfair to Dora and partial to Dino. I am aware of erring at times on the side of counter-transferential identification with Dino, partly to do with our similar cultural background. Like Dino, I too have been shitting blood in the morning on a regular basis, something that, unlike Dino, who seems to be still ensnared by these, has sobered me up in relation to both the narcissistic vagaries of romantic love and the existentialist platitudes on uncertainty and finitude, very groovy-sounding unless you are in the throes of reality.

In any case, my possible identification with him didn't prevent me from pointing out in no uncertain terms that his thinking in relation to Dora seemed rather naïve. How could he not assume, I asked him, that conflicts would inevitably arise, and that love could not take care of everything? How could he ever expect that Dora would not want more from him? True, she danced an ambivalent jig throughout, never daring to state her desire plainly even to herself, but that does not excuse Dino's lack of reflection and concern, even, at times, his gullibility.

Like him, I too was diagnosed with a serious health condition, and I confess to being puzzled by Dora's apparent lack of both empathy and sympathy. I also wondered whether, by often making the air unbreathable for Dino, Dora didn't allow him any choice but leaving, thus avoiding having to make the decision she may have wanted to make, namely, ending the relationship with an ailing man, no longer an attractive proposition for someone like her, younger, at a different stage in her life, and seemingly keen to pursue pleasure, money, and sex, rather than the bristlier landscapes of love and desire. And who is to blame her? At any rate, it seems to me that the theatrical scenario Dora staged for Dino is nevertheless instructive; it epitomizes all that is unpersuasive about current BDSM narratives. The patriarchy sits undisturbed in its cosy dungeons after all the play-acting, the cracking of designer whips, and various pantomime versions of a weekender's *petite mort*. Conversely, what emerges in Masoch's case is far more troubling *and* transformative: contractual submission places interrupted love at the very centre. Interrupted love is a central aspect of masochism. In the parallel world of this highly ritualized scenario, fantasy comes to the fore; it interrupts both Logos and the Law. It enables a person's identification with both "incest and second birth", saving them from the danger of castration while turning the latter "into the symbolic condition of success".[9] In the ritual encounter, a person undergoes a second birth, which originates from the woman alone. Three acts of sedition are involved here, as Deleuze explains:

> [t]he first magnifies the mother, by attributing to her the phallus instrumental to rebirth; the second excludes the father, since he has no part in this rebirth; and the third relates to sexual pleasure, which is interrupted, deprived of its genitality and transformed into the pleasure of being reborn.[10]

Mere genitality here becomes transfigured into the erotic, provided we understand eros outside the narrow confines of the Protestant and puritan views of sexuality (which dominate conventional psychotherapy across all orientations), as something we must manage and/or something that affords temporary discharge from the ever-present demands of Capital, Logos, and the Father. This move is aligned to both *sublimation* and *defusion*. Briefly stated: *sublimation* is not inimical to the pleasure principle; it is not repression but its opposite, that is, allowing sexual energy to circulate beyond genitality and manifest as an *active*, creative force in and out of the encounter instead of stagnating as *repressive desublimation*[11] – the flattening out of art, love, and politics via the phoney catharses of moronic sex. Similarly, *defusion* (not to be confused with the same term employed in Acceptance and Commitment Therapy) does not repress the sexual principle but aids the formation of a "freely mobile energy"[12] by keeping at bay the absolutist presence of Thanatos.

The impossibility of knowledge

The heart has its reasons which reason knows nothing of, Pascal wrote in the seventeenth century. The heart wants what it wants, Emily Dickinson echoed two centuries later. Thousands of songs and poems followed – a few of them coming close to the depth of those statements. Add eros and its upheavals to the stirrings of the heart, and they become all the more charged, those declarations, all the more truthful in describing the unpredictability of love. We are caught under the net. Ensnared within a prison we begin to cherish. In love with the wrong person: one who is already attached, or one whose compulsion to drama overrides any consideration for the other; or one whose chronic passivity is misconstrued as openness.

Faced with a prolonged, pathos-filled path to traverse before an event jolts us out of the sorcerer's spell and makes us free again. In Iris Murdoch's novels, this essential moment of sobriety is both liberating and painful. The once-beloved is now suddenly perceived as living and breathing in a different light, as a separate person who is not part of me. The once-beloved must be learnt anew. Or forgotten. Either way, when can we ever say we know or have known another? Perhaps – Murdoch suggests – only after we have realized the impossibility of knowledge; only when we have renounced the desire for it and even ceased to cherish our need for it. What we then achieve is not knowledge but co-existence, a being-with – in itself one of the manifestations of love.[13]

Can sexuality ever be divorced from love? Is it passé to think of love as the core (at times unspoken) of sex and its toils? The vagaries of contemporary dating in the life of clients and patients tell ambivalent stories at best. In clinical work as in everyday life, we soon learn how our mind can often be our own hell – a dungeon of torments and darkness, as Byron wrote echoing John Milton.[14] And what about the "joys of sex" feted in gourmet lovemaking manuals all those years back? How does love fare in a current cultural and psychic landscape of stimulating and creative challenges to notions of gender and to what constitutes the norm? Finally, could (aspects of) psychoanalysis help us navigate the unsteady terrain of love and sex? Some interesting pointers come from unexpected sources – for instance the poetry of Byron.

Perversifications

In his dramatic poem *Manfred*, Byron describes the protagonist trapped in a mountain as the mist rises. He is advised to wait before starting his descent. He rejects the advice, giving Byron the chance to dwell less on physical dangers than in describing a psyche ensnared in trying to figure out how danger comes to be perceived in a mind caught up in vexatious memories. Intense, entangled absorption on thought bamboozles the reader, obliging her to be very attentive while "making it hard to sustain attention".[15] Byron appears to tease us into fast reading even though tactics are at work aimed at capturing our attention so as to "prevent the reader falling too easily for the narrative's dominant sexiness".[16] In his study *Byron and the Poetics of Adversity*, Jerome McGann[17] calls these moments of confrontation *perversifications*, born out of an adamant, dead-serious stance of confronting the readers and inflict misperception and confusion on them. These are high-lighted by the fact that *Manfred* presents an intricate melange of spirits and destinies, a multitude of personified voices closely linked to the work of poetry itself. Claire Bucknell writes:

> Supernatural power, the ability to shapeshift, alter fates, change the weather, comes to be associated with the inventiveness of song, with rapidly metamorphosing rhymes . . . and dancing, careless rhythms.[18]

Perversification of rhyme and rhythm allows for difference and multiplicity to come to the fore, for dissimilar experiences to be voiced. Shifts in poetry are abrupt but create unexpected associations. In the poem/travelogue *Childe Harold*, we find both personal and collective catastrophe, the elegy for love lost and for the fall of an entire nation.

An insight in early psychoanalysis (now summarily discarded) reminded us that in order to approach the unconscious, a methodology is required that is similar to its opaque workings – hence the royal place assigned to dreams. Likewise in aspects of Byron's poetry and, I would add, in approaching the thorny domain of eros. Perversification in psychotherapeutic work similarly asserts the polymorphous perverse as the foundation of sexuality.

The puritanism of polyamory

Mary is troubled by a recurring thought. I wonder, she says, if I am becoming old-fashioned. How so? I ask. Well, for instance half of my younger friends are on the polyamory trail. At first, of course I supported their "quest", but soon began to notice the royal mess they get in. I mean, people can do what they like. The last thing I am is a moralizer, but I question this form of freedom. I mean, is it freedom? Or an attempt to manage the unmanageable? Is this, you know, *Eros Management Ltd*? Or a new kind of consumer choice? Do you mean, I ask, a little perplexed, having more than a partner in love is like shopping? She laughs. Well, it would seem that way, don't you think? I mean what is love? Big question, right? I don't know, but I'm clear about the fact that it is not about, you know, satisfying my needs. Half of my needs are false anyway, haven't we learnt that from Marx?

Well, I say, when you state that love is not about satisfying one's needs, it sounds a bit one-sided. Surely both aspects are valid: satisfying some of our needs *and* being open to love. But maybe without the first bit, it becomes too idealized. I mean, love can be many things, right? Of course, Mary says, looking a bit surprised. I guess I'm making a polemical point. There is a sort of crass pragmatism in polyamorous discourse that really grates with me. Like what? I ask. OK so, I'll hang out with Sam because he knows all about Foucault, and maybe some of his cleverness will rub off me. I spend time with Ron because my oh my he is hot in bed and attentive to my erogenous zones, and what he does with his tongue opens up new pathways in my brain. Then there is Alejandro; he is just a fabulous dresser and makes me laugh and I get such a kick when I'm seen with him. And of course there is Joanna, with whom I explore my gay side and who is keen to go to sex parties where I get a chance to stretch my boundaries and discover unknown landscapes within my very interesting inner world, she says rolling her eyes. But is it satisfying? No. I'm still to find a polyamorous individual who is not a bundle of messed-up fake needs and desires. Yes, of course, the same can be said for all those self-satisfied monogamous people out there who think they have found the holy grail and look down on others who are not in their position.

I laugh. Mary beams at me, stirred up. Sure it is both. Of course, monogamy would present us with different problems. I am not saying that monogamy is where is at. And yet. Bear with me, she goes on, I am beginning to think that this polyamory stuff is just too American, a mix of bourgeois philistinism and Californian ideology. And I wonder whether love is something else, something, well, higher. Not about meeting my needs but a chance to give myself fully to another, to trust another wholeheartedly, and to be able to recognize and say simply, my love, I can't live without you. I am also unconvinced, Mary adds, about this need to control, manage, and make everything under the sun transparent. A lot of pressure, she says, and perhaps even a bit of coercion?

What Mary said, particularly the last point, reminded me of a book by Anne Dufourmantelle, *In Defense of Secrets*, where she makes a broader case in favour of opacity.[19] She writes of the dignity of the secret, trampled by a worldview that values scientific truth at the expense of mystery, sacrifice, and the sacred, a worldview that fails to recognize the unknowability of many of our deeper experiences. She questions the facile view of opposing truth and the secret. Reading the book saddened me for many reasons, both personal and professional. I found it sad that psychoanalysis has relegated the secret to a grey zone between the symbolic and the real and that psychotherapy, an art founded on the intimate communication of secrets, has become invested in the sub-Heideggerian acting out of *aletheia*, the unveiling of a debatable "truth" that far from being true is a conditioned product of contemporary political fears and pseudo-ethical anxieties.

As an aside, and as someone who has been cancelled twice in 2024 (for a terrible mistake I made way back and that I have atoned and paid for in blood, as those who know me are aware),[20] I confess to feeling troubled by the monochrome, absolutist views of some of my colleagues and comrades. They make all the right noises: they are keen to liberate mental health; they want to bridge the gap between the individual and society; they foster worthy political causes; they critique neoliberalism; they quote Sartre and De Beauvoir. But their zealous pursuit of truth and virtue betrays the soft tyranny of their entrenched puritanism. I do not wish on anyone the truly horrible experience of finding oneself at the receiving end of their righteousness, vengefulness, and venom. For those who can bear it, this is nevertheless instructive. For instance I finally understood what those two magnificent works, Nathaniel Hawthorne's *The Scarlet Letter* and Arthur Miller's *The Crucible*, are all about.

Could it be that polyamory – for all its valuable questioning of monogamy and its obvious trappings, for all its courageous utopian stance towards openness and new forms of loving and being with others – risks reasserting the patriarchal norm in its disguised form, as Logos overruling eros, its unruliness, its ambiguities through a sort of hysterical need for consensus? The most popular texts on the subject are entirely within the conventional, sanitized frame of Attachment Theory (AT). They validate and inflate rather than critique the fossilized classifications known as attachment styles. They substantiate most of AT's conservative epigons, from polyvagal theory to emotional trigger work to emotionally focused therapy (EFT). They focus on idealized notions of *security* and seem to be motivated by an ethos of cognitive control over the profound and mysterious working of eros.[21]

I have written elsewhere a more extensive critique of AT.[22] Here, I will only say that AT has managed to sanitize the entire psychic landscape and exile eros out of the consulting room, a point on which several queer theorists/psychoanalysts concur. It is therefore instructive to find that such a conventional, deeply conservative frame should constitute the basis for theorizing practices such as CNM and polyamory.

Could it be that polyamory – with its insistence on honesty, transparency, and cognitive/managerial control of one's own and one's partner's sexuality – is at heart puritanical? Clearly, this is not the Puritanism of seventeenth-century Salem. Nevertheless, an analogous zeal in imposing and prescribing what is perceived as right in matters of sexuality is found in contemporary attitudes to relationship.

***

When the train came to a stop, Dino says, I got off and hopped on the first train back.

Notes

1 Georges Bataille, *Inner Experience*. Albany, NY: State University of New York Press, 1988.
2 Leopold von Sacher-Masoch, 'Venus in Furs', in *Masochism*. New York: Zone Books, 1991.
3 Richard Von Krafft-Ebing, *Psychopathia Sexualis*. London: Forgotten Books, 2019.
4 Manu Bazzano, 'Men Going Down', in *Subversion and Desire: Pathways to Transindividuation*, Abingdon, OX: Routledge, 2023, pp. 161–178, 161.
5 Cited in Gilles Deleuze, 'Coldness and Cruelty', in *Masochism*. New York: Zone Books, 1991, p. 97.
6 Gilles Deleuze, 'Coldness and Cruelty', in *Masochism*. New York: Zone Books, 1991, p. 100.
7 Jacques-Alain Miller, 'Perversion', in *Reading Seminars I and II: Lacan's Return to Freud*, ed. Richard Felstein et al. Albany: State University of New York Press, 1996.
8 Franz Kafka, *The Complete Stories*. New York: Schocken Books, 1971.
9 Gilles Deleuze, 'Coldness and Cruelty', in *Masochism*. New York: Zone Books, 1991, p. 94.
10 Gilles Deleuze, 'Coldness and Cruelty', in *Masochism*. New York: Zone Books, 1991, p. 96.
11 Herbert Marcuse, *One Dimensional Man: Studies in the Ideology of Advanced Industrial Society*. London: Routledge, 2002.
12 Gilles Deleuze, 'Coldness and Cruelty', in *Masochism*. New York: Zone Books, 1991, p. 116.
13 Iris Murdoch, *Under the Net*. London: Vintage, 2002.
14 Lord Byron, 'The Prisoner of Chillon', https://www.poetryfoundation.org/poems/43842/the-prisoner-of-chillon. Retrieved 7 December 2024, written in 1816.
15 Clare Bucknell, 'His Own Dark Mind', *London Review of Books*, Vol. 45, No. 23, November 2023, https://www.lrb.co.uk/the-paper/v45/n23/clare-bucknell/his-own-dark-mind. Retrieved 1 December 2023.

16 Clare Bucknell, 'His Own Dark Mind', *London Review of Books*, Vol. 45, No. 23, November 2023, https://www.lrb.co.uk/the-paper/v45/n23/clare-bucknell/his-own-dark-mind. Retrieved 1 December 2023.

17 Jerome McGann, *Byron and the Poetics of Adversity*. Cambridge, MA: Cambridge University Press, 2022.

18 Clare Bucknell, 'His Own Dark Mind', *London Review of Books*, Vol. 45, No. 23, November 2023, https://www.lrb.co.uk/the-paper/v45/n23/clare-bucknell/his-own-dark-mind. Retrieved 1 December 2023.

19 Anne Dufourmantelle, *In Defense of Secrets*, trans. Lindsay Turner. New York: Fordham University Press, 2021.

20 I have written more extensively on this issue in 'Men Going Down', in *Subversion and Desire: Pathways to Transindividuation*. Abingdon, OX: Routledge, 2023, pp. 161–178.

21 See for instance Jessica Fern, *Polysecure: Attachment, Trauma and Consensual Nonmonogamy*. Vancouver, BC: Thornapple Press, 2020.

22 Manu Bazzano, 'After Attachment Theory', in *Subversion and Desire: Pathways to Transindividuation*. Abingdon, OX: Routledge, 2023, pp. 59–73.

Chapter 2

On transindividuation

Introduction

There have been numerous attempts within the "psych world" to heal the seemingly unrestorable fracture between the individual and society – with mixed, often unconvincing results. In the 1930s and the 1960s, the attempt was to bridge the public and the private, the sphere of politics and economy with the realm of desire and libidinal economy. It often meant, and for some of us still does, bringing together Marx and Freud, a discourse of social emancipation with one of individual freedom. This mode of inquiry has been largely abandoned, not only because of the onslaught of neoliberal ideology in the world of psychology but also because it failed to understand two fundamental mistakes: (a) the error of psychologism, which only sees the individual and the inter-individual, and (b) the error of sociologism, which only sees the inter-social. We have overlooked that the reality of the individual is vaster than the individual; that it includes important pre-individual facets. What would it mean to leave behind the false division of individual and society and recognize the systematic unity of psychic *and* collective individuation? What would it mean to give birth to a real collective? This chapter will explore these questions drawing on the work of Spinoza, Simondon, and Freud, expounding on one innovative proposition as yet unexplored in psychotherapy: *transindividuation*.

Of the advantages and disadvantages of phenomenology

It is not controversial to suggest that, given psychotherapy's historical allegiance with individualistic narratives, a finer attunement to social context and progressive socio-political praxis and ideas would bolster its

DOI: 10.4324/9781003529095-3

efficacy and help ground its practice. At least this is what I had thought until a few years back when I published an article in a counselling and psychotherapy monthly. The piece articulated a critique of Donald Trump's politics and its nefarious consequences on notions of identity, masculinity, and mental health. A few letters from therapists expressed dismay at my assumptions that there would be no Trump supporter in their midst.[1] It was a wake-up call. It upset the patent simplicity of my assumptions and alerted me to the likely emergence of an insidious cultural shift within the psych world, an area arguably wedded from its inception to an emancipatory ethos. The letters may have of course voiced the views of a minority, yet a seemingly unshakeable belief persists even within the more "progressive" quarters of psychotherapy and counselling, namely the conviction that there is a factual division between the individual and society. Even when a particular theoretical frame and ensuing practice aim at bridging the divide, the belief persists unscathed. After all, one can only bridge two entities thought of as distinctly separate. Even when the divide is summarily bypassed, the belief is still there. Deep rooted in the (philosophical, psychological, religious, secular) tradition; entwined to our flesh, bones, and thoughts, the notion of an atomized subjectivity, of a self and/or a separate soul is not easily resolved. "The thought of subjectivity – Merleau-Ponty memorably noted – is one of these solids that philosophy will have to digest". He went on: "let us say that once 'infected' by certain ways of thinking, philosophy can no longer annul them but must cure itself of them by inventing better ones".[2] His own answer was to invent the notion of the body-subject and, through the bodily notion of the subject, access the *flesh* of the world. This is not the place to delve into the exquisite intricacies of Merleau-Ponty's phenomenology, something I have attempted elsewhere.[3] It may be enough to note how marginal and embryonic the latter has remained within both existential and psychoanalytic traditions, despite avowed acknowledgement of its significance in therapy training handouts and ceremonial citations in doctoral dissertations. The importance of Merleau-Pontian phenomenology consists in remaining anchored to subjectivity and providing an interesting solution to this ancient dilemma. The anchoring is admirable: it does not stoop to the ontological bypass choreographed by the Heideggerian *Dasein*, seen at times by Merleau-Ponty as an attempt to retrieve "our relationship with Being such as [it was] prior to self-consciousness", an idea which relies on "primordial ontology",[4] to a nostalgic return to the lost Arcadia of a pre-Socratic existence preceding the birth of subjectivity-as-we-know-it.

At the same time, remaining anchored to Cartesian/Husserlian subjectivity arguably limits Merleau-Ponty's phenomenology. This is relevant to our current investigation, as it appears to substantiate the artificial divide between individual subjectivity and society. One way out of this impasse is posed by the notion of *transindividuation* as formulated by Gilbert Simondon,[5] a pupil of Canguilhem and Merleau-Ponty, whose work provides invaluable insights – especially in relation to the themes of individuation[6] and technology.[7]

What is transindividuation?

Transindividuation is a new theory of individuation. The conventional notion of individuation only takes into account the individual, only "an aspect, a phase of a process",[8] whereas transindividuation inscribes the individual within a much wider process. It goes beyond the individuated "I", conventionally understood as an already formed entity. It understands the individual as "contemporaneous with its individuation, and individuation contemporaneous with the principle". The principle of individuation, that is, "must be truly genetic, and not simply a principle of reflection".[9]

Within this perspective, individuation must be at all times associated with the pre-individual, which is for Simondon a source of metastable states. Another way of saying this is that there is no actualization worth of its name without a close link to a virtual field of potentialities.

Transindividuation also goes beyond the equally conventional notion of the interindividuated "We". It is a process of "co-individuation within a pre-individuated milieu and in which both the 'I' and the 'We' are transformed through one another".[10] In that sense, transindividuation constitutes the foundation for all social change. Bernard Stiegler explains:

> We ourselves, as humans, are a type of individuation that is very specific, as our individuation is not only . . . an individuation of the living organism, of life, but an individuation of the psyche as well, so it is operating as both conscious and unconscious processes. And Simondon says that the individuation of the psyche is always already an individuation of a group of psyches, because a psyche is never alone. It always operates in relation to another psyche. At the limit itself, himself, or herself, a psyche in this situation is a very specific doubling of oneself in narcissism and a type of dialectical relationship to oneself.[11]

Crucially, in relation to psychotherapy, transindividuation takes on board the dimension of the *emergent*, which Simondon calls the pre-individual, a "differentiate field . . . a bundle of potential functions localized, as a differentiated region, within a larger field of potential".[12]

This is not as abstract at it may sound but is related to how each separate area is involved in solving problems that cannot be addressed without further individuations. One concrete example of this is anxiety, a topic of direct concern for psychotherapists, discussed by Simondon in a chapter on psychic individuation.[13] In anxiety, the human organism feels weighed down by its existence "as if it had to carry itself – a burden of the earth, *ákthos aroúres* as Homer says, but also a burden to itself".[14] In anxiety, we feel as if existing as a problem posed to ourselves, and this division is felt "into pre-individual nature and individuated being".[15] In anxiety, the subject attempts to "resolve itself without going through the collective".[16] It wants to come to the level of its unity "by way of a resolution without mediation or delay". In this sense, anxiety is "an emotion without action, a feeling without perception". It is "pure reverberation of the being within itself".[17] If anxiety could be sufficiently shored up, it would bring about a new individuation, a true transformation. But this process – which implies the disbandment of prior structures to the point of annihilation of the seemingly solid and unitary individuated being – would require *resorting to other domains of individuation*, unthinkable without a conceptual frame such as transindividuation. In Simondon's words:

> The individual being flees itself, deserts itself. And yet in this desertion there is a sort of underlying drive to go recompose oneself elsewhere and otherwise by reincorporating the world such that everything can be lived.[18]

Self and society

The widespread belief that politics deals with external reality, while psychotherapy attends to the private domain is misleading. Or at the very least it constitutes too neat a demarcation between the outside and the inside. Still, the very real challenge for psychotherapists is summoning a convincing ontological perspective that may take us out of the impasse generated by this deeply ingrained division. The objective could then be described as becoming better equipped in submitting universally accepted notions such as this to closer scrutiny. This could mean approaching psychotherapy and counselling as *axiological* practices, that is, practices of evaluation, making the most of utilizing Nietzsche's hammer – a method of inquiry by which one weighs at first the balance of active and reactive forces at play[19] – be it within an organism, an entity, an institution, and so forth and then, if necessary, attempts to resolve the balance in favour of *active* forces – of natural, psychical, spiritual forces that are not governed by the spirit of revenge against life-and-death. In order to do this, we may need at times to design new concepts or at least articulate novel interpretations to old ideas, in the hope of releasing the deadlock in a particular field of practice and inquiry. One of these concepts is *transindividuation*, a new idea in psychotherapy which aims to problematize and expand on the notion of individuation. Not only is the latter term disappearing fast from current psychotherapeutic discourse in favour of the politically compliant notion of integration. If and when it gets mentioned, individuation is restricted to the *necessary but insufficient* first step of finding an internal locus of evaluation,[20] of becoming more "authentic"[21] (Grene, 1954), of aligning the ego with a capitalized *Self*.[22]

Transindividuation (and the closely related notion of the *transindividual*) is new in psychotherapy and the psych world. Surfacing (partially, obliquely) in Spinoza, Marx, and Freud, it was consistently conveyed by Simondon,[23] whose ideas cross the borders of several fields of inquiry, and is now more widely discussed in the area of the humanities and philosophy of science.[24] Partly drawing on Balibar,[25] I will outline some traits of transindividuation as they appear in Marx, Spinoza, and Freud, before focusing on Simondon.

Disassembling, reassembling

For Spinoza, social human nature is an uneven amalgam (what the historical Buddha called *skandhas* or aggregates) of different components – *not of body and mind*, as most of us still assume in obeisance to Spinoza's contemporary Descartes – but *of moods and deeds*, some of which follow reason while others ensue from passion. As a result, and in a way that reminds one of Plato, the affective configuration of a particular individuality and its concurrence of rational and affective forces in the *polis* intersect, connect, and reflect one another. In this sense, subjectivity is already transindividual.

At its core, Spinoza's thought aims at explicating different "modes of communication" which at times organize themselves "at the level of affects, and sometimes at the level of rational ideas".[26] It remains to be seen whether rational ideas are themselves affects, but that belongs to a different exploration. What is relevant here is that for Spinoza, the finite mode of subjectivity is relational *and* transindividual. His is a counter-traditional, aporetic ontology, to be sure: we come to be incessantly disassembled and reassembled, are traversed by affects, and partake them with others within the ever-changing wider sphere of society. The ethical task in these circumstances – which is where psychotherapy becomes useful – is to be able to turn the inherent passivity of the "passions" into action and more widely (following Nietzsche) to turn passive forces into active ones. Entertaining this view could mean doing more than merely critiquing the double bind of individualism and holism in the direction of creating a structure of feeling and expression, as well as developing a set of active interventions on individual and societal level. We are affected, we affect, and this double movement changes us, changes others. Being involved in this process may alert us to the fact that viewing ourselves as separate individuals is an attractive illusion and a second-rate mode of being in the world, a *private* i.e., deprived existence depriving us of the rich transindividual nature of our individuality.

The society effect

In his sixth thesis on Feuerbach, Marx critiques Feuerbach's attempt to resolve the conundrum of human nature or human essence (*das menschliche Wesen*) by assimilating it into the essence of religion. He affirms human nature as constituted "in its effective reality" by the "ensemble of social relations"[27] rather than as the universally accepted abstraction of the single person. This may be considered as "a point of departure for an ontology or relations":[28] individuality understood neither as a separate, originary substance (be it the atomized soul of Christianity or its close Cartesian version of the *cogito*) nor is it "reducible to the totality which encompasses it"[29] be it the abstract Heideggeresque "relatedness" now *de rigueur* in conventional existential therapy[30] or in the more concrete sense of a society or community. For Marx, however, society and community under capitalism are akin to simulacra; they hide the reality of alienated relation, a realm where alienation is the main form of relating. Capitalism does not engender nor foster a *society* as such but merely, in the words of Louis Althusser, a *society effect*.[31] In Marx's own words:

> To the producers the social relations between their private labours appear as what they are, i.e. they *do not appear as direct social relations between persons in their work*, but rather as material relations between persons and social relations between things.[32]

The implication is that in our societies, there are no direct social relations between individuals; all social relations go through money and the commodity form (this applies to therapy as well). They are assembled "*at a distance*, in the element of commodity exchange and of the value-form"; they are "relations of equivalence between commodities themselves".[33] The advent of capitalism in the history of our species is unprecedented in that sense: "a religion which offers no reform of existence but its complete destruction", in the words of Walter Benjamin.[34]

It is hard to resist the humanistic temptation of indulging in noble lamentations and bungled biddings to restore the notional Eden of pre-capitalist "authentic" human relations sullied by alienated structures. It is equally hard to distance oneself from the orthodox Marxist views which tend to regard capital as an eternal structure and fail to take into account its various permutations: first neoliberalism, with its cunning embracing of the Stoics, its contradictory appeal to the alleged freedom of the market while acquiescing to its impersonal sovereignty.[35] More recently, through global ownership and control of information, capital has arguably morphed into something else, something worse – a mutation which calls for communal responses and acts of resistance, given that "the production of counter-hegemonic knowledge can really only be comradely and collaborative".[36] Could counselling and psychotherapy ever be part of this counter-hegemonic knowledge and practice? For this to happen, a different notion of individuality is needed alongside changed ways of understanding its link to society.

Alienated social relations – the product of capitalism, neoliberalism, and the vectoralism of global information of our day – create agents who never meet as simple human beings. Our personhood depends on economic exchange as well as on our juridical existence: "the economic *informs* the juridical and the juridical activates the economic",[37] and it is from this double structure that we find in Marx something akin to transindividuation. The double structure denies the two dominant ontologies: (a) the *individualistic* notion of atomized subjectivity and (b) the *holistic* notion that sees relatedness as a given and individuality an incontestable part of it. What is common to Simondonian transindividuation here is that, paradoxically, the alienated double structure described by Marx alerts us to the fact that subjectivity is more complex and variegated than it is normally believed. By clarifying the phantasmagorical, even hallucinatory nature of social relations, it also opens the door to another way of conceiving subjectivity outside the obligatory routes of individualism and holism.

The group of one

In his 1921 book *Group Psychology and the Analysis of the Ego*, Freud focuses on the emergence of the "I" in relation to society, examining this correlation in ways that remain irreducible to the tenets of both psychology and sociology.[38] By placing the unconscious at the centre, the conventional understanding of individual and social domains within which we often find ourselves entrapped is significantly altered. Rather than existing separately, they are reversible functions belonging to a single formation – a thesis that culminates in the *Postscript* where individualization is presented as a particular aspect of group formation. The "group of many" is the institutional group, and the "group of two" is constituted either by the love relationship or by the "hypnotic relationship" where the person delegates to the other (a teacher, a worldview, perhaps a therapist) their own examination of experience. Then – in a manner that anticipates the theories of multiplicity that followed – we are presented with the group of one (*Masse zu eins, Einsamkeit*), "the isolated individual as an intrinsically fragile, aleatory effect of a certain negative modality",[39] a modality hinting at a traumatic rupture between the individual and the group, a rupture which is *constitutive* of individuality. The "transindividual" aspect of this equation is that individual psychology is negated as a self-existing structure, but this negation does not translate into a primacy of the social/sociological component. The individual is then understood in transindividual terms, as the amalgam (aggregate, *ensemble*) of four group formations: (1) the institutional, (2) the atomized self, (3) the transferential version of amorous relations, and (4) the transferential version of hypnotic relations. This representation escapes the trappings of both individualism and holism in ways that are tangentially similar to other visions of transindividuality, particularly Spinoza's; it presents a view of society not as a structure made up of individuals but of *relations*.

Internalizing the outer, externalizing the inner

As his oeuvre is being translated into English and other languages, the timeliness of Gilbert Simondon's work is slowly beginning to be recognized – notably within Deleuzian studies, including psychoanalytic studies,[40] but also in the field of technology studies.[41] It influenced Marcuse, whose exploration of alienation and reification in capitalist societies took into account Simondon's writings on technology – not solely in terms of the technocratic net within which we are inescapably entrapped but also in terms of technology's potentially liberative function as an opening to other forms of rationality.[42]

Transindividuation points at the intrinsic inherent unity of inner psychical individuation and collective individuation. Unlike the inter-individual, it does not bring into relation two or more individuals understood as distinct, separate units with clear-cut internal and external borders. Normally we either resort to the insights of psychology and psychotherapy which for the most part tend to understand and relate almost exclusively to interiority; or we rely on sociology which on the whole only understands the inter-individual. Transindividuality is a way out of this impasse. What is particular about transindividuality is that it carries a charge of pre-individual reality. Before the coming into being of individuality, there is a pre-individual process which is normally overlooked. These pre-individual elements then become simplified and summarily translated into what we call "me". In the process, some of them become dormant, some are activated, some are forgotten, and some die out. Even those that die out constitute a reservoir which can contribute to further individuation and actualization – if, that is, we consider individuation and actualization as *organismic* rather than ego-bound processes. Failing to take into account the pre-individual domain means forfeiting individuation and actualization. It means abandoning the possibility of partaking to the birth of a real collective dimension and settling instead with a stale scenario of inter-relations between monads: the much-celebrated dyad of I and Thou agreeing, disagreeing, dialoguing from their respective fortresses, chronically deprived of the vibrancy, expansiveness, and surprise of the transindividual dimension. By forgetting, as we routinely tend to do, that the subject is vaster than the individual, we remain forever stuck within a linear and often sluggish movement which knows little of the leaps and bounds possible when we are more attuned to the pre-individual domain. By forgetting the pre-individual and transindividual domain, we forego a vital link with a field of potentiality and virtuality. Only the recognition of the pre-individual dimension allows real collectivity rather than a clash, a merging, or a guarded dance of egos. The paradox at the heart of the transindividual is that it unfolds parallel to the elaboration of the individual person's psychology and that it does so unknowingly by touching upon, traversing, affecting/being affected by other layers and domains which together, whether or not actively recognized, constitute an "I" that is more than "I", a movement that internalises the outer and externalises the inner.

Concluding remarks

Transindividuation questions the separation between interior life and external life. Even before coming into being as an individual, there is a current of pre-individual elements. Incorporating this notion into our understanding of the relation between individual and society could mean becoming better equipped at imagining a community that does not step on individual needs and desires and at imagining an individuality that does not neglect the importance of community.

Normally, we hold an individualistic notion of liberty – in our neoliberal world, the freedom to do what one pleases, the freedom not to pay taxes, to grab what we can while we can, the freedom of a lone monad deludedly disconnected from its inherent situatedness. Similarly, we hold a rather drab idea of equality – the equality of quantifiable social roles and personas, the equality of uniformity. Could liberty and equality go together? Could we have individual freedom alongside equality? Equality and freedom are both denied precisely in the same conditions, because "there is no example of conditions that supress or repress freedom that do no supress or limit – that is, do not abolish – equality and vice versa".[43] Moving beyond the habitual and arbitrary division between individual and society may prove effective in honouring both domains as sides of the same coin. Spinoza is again the main inspiration here. "I" am a "we", he would say.[44] Our intimate individual desires and the independence of our thought are already communal. In a similar vein, politics also has to do with the association of affects and learning – an aspect that is as important as its more established emphasis on the distribution of power.

In this sense, psychotherapy potentially plays a pivotal role here – if, that is, it succeeds in bypassing the politics of euphoric security, the ecstasy of the status quo, the perpetuation of a skewed notion of individual psyche.

*

Notes

1 Manu Bazzano, 'Sons of our Fathers', *Therapy Today*, https://www.bacp. co.uk/bacp-journals/therapy today/2019/november-2019/sons-of-our-fathers/. Retrieved 21 April 2024.
2 Maurice Merleau-Ponty, *Signs*. Evanston, IL: Northwestern University Press, 1964, p. 154.
3 Manu Bazzano, 'The Poetry of the World: A Tribute to the Phenomenology of Merleau-Ponty', in *Re-visioning Existential Therapy: Counter-traditional Perspectives*, ed. M. Bazzano. Abingdon, OX: Routledge, 2020, pp. 168–177.
4 Maurice Merleau-Ponty, *Signs*. Evanston, IL: Northwestern University Press, 1964, p. 154.
5 Gilbert Simondon, *Individuation in Light of Notions of Form and Information*, trans. Taylor Adkins. Minneapolis, MN: University of Minnesota Press, 2020.
6 Dominique Lecourt, 'The Question of the Individual in Georges Canguilhem and Gilbert Simondon', in *Gilbert Simondon: Being and Technology*, trans. Arne de Boever, ed. A. De Boever, A. Murray, J. Roffe, and A. Woodward. Edinburgh: Edinburgh University Press, 2012, pp. 176–184, 177.
7 Arne De Boever, Alex Murray, Jon Roffe, and Ashley Woodward, eds., *Gilbert Simondon: Being and Technology*. Edinburgh University Press, 2012.
8 Bernard Stiegler and Irit Rogoff, 'Transindividuation', *e-flux Journal*, March 2010, https://www.e-flux.com/journal/14/61314/transindividuation/#:~:text=It%20is% 20the%20process%20of,are%20also%20processes%20of%20individuations. Retrieved 2 August 2024.
9 Gilles Deleuze, *Desert Islands and Other Texts 1953–1974*. Los Angeles, CA: Semiotext(e), 2004, p. 86.
10 Gilles Deleuze, *Desert Islands and Other Texts 1953–1974*. Los Angeles, CA: Semiotext(e), 2004.
11 Bernard Stiegler and Irit Rogoff, 'Transindividuation', *e-flux Journal*, March 2010, https://www.e-flux.com/journal/14/61314/transindividuation/#:~:text=It%20is% 20the%20process%20of,are%20also%20processes%20of%20individuations. Retrieved 2 August 2024.
12 Brian Massumi, 'The Autonomy of Affect', in *Deleuze: A Critical Reader*, ed. P. Patton. Oxford, OX: Blackwell, 1996, pp. 217–239, 227.

13 Gilbert Simondon, *Individuation in Light of Notions of Form and Information*, trans. Taylor Adkins. University of Minnesota Press, 2020, pp. 257–318.
14 Gilbert Simondon, *Individuation in Light of Notions of Form and Information*, trans. Taylor Adkins. University of Minnesota Press, 2020, p. 283.
15 Gilbert Simondon, *Individuation in Light of Notions of Form and Information*, trans. Taylor Adkins. University of Minnesota Press, 2020, p. 283.
16 Gilbert Simondon, *Individuation in Light of Notions of Form and Information*, trans. Taylor Adkins. University of Minnesota Press, 2020, p. 283.
17 Gilbert Simondon, *Individuation in Light of Notions of Form and Information*, trans. Taylor Adkins. University of Minnesota Press, 2020, p. 284.
18 Gilbert Simondon, *Individuation in Light of Notions of Form and Information*, trans. Taylor Adkins. University of Minnesota Press, 2020, p. 284.
19 Manu Bazzano, *Nietzsche and Psychotherapy*. Abingdon, OX: Routledge, 2019.
20 Carl R. Rogers, *Client-Centred Therapy*. London: Constable, 1951.
21 Marjoree Grene, 'Authenticity: An Existential Virtue', *Ethics*, Vol. 62, No. 4, 1952, pp. 266–274.
22 Carl G. Jung, *On the Nature of the Psyche*. Abingdon, OX: Routledge, 2001.
23 Gilbert Simondon, *Individuation in Light of Notions of Form and Information*, trans. Taylor Adkins. University of Minnesota Press, 2020.
24 For example, Arne De Boever, Alex Murray, Jon Roffe, and Ashley Woodward, eds., *Gilbert Simondon: Being and Technology*. Edinburgh University Press, 2012.
25 Etienne Balibar, *Equaliberty: Political Essays*, trans. James Ingram. Durham: Duke University Press, 2014.
26 Etienne Balibar, *Spinoza, the Transindividual*, trans. Mark G. E. Kelly. Edinburgh University Press, 2020, p. 158.
27 Karl Marx and Friedrich Engels. *On Religion*. Mineola, NY: Dover Publications, 2008, p. 71.
28 Etienne Balibar, *Spinoza, the Transindividual*, trans. Mark G. E. Kelly. Edinburgh University Press, 2020, p. 144.
29 Etienne Balibar, *Spinoza, the Transindividual*, trans. Mark G. E. Kelly. Edinburgh University Press, 2020, p. 144.
30 For instance Ernesto Spinelli, *Practising Existential Therapy: The Relational World*. London: Sage, 2014.
31 Louis Althusser and Etienne Balibar, *Reading Capital*. London: Verso, 1985.
32 Karl Marx, *Capital*, Vol. 1, trans. Ben Fowkes. London: Penguin, 1976, pp. 165–166, emphasis added.
33 Etienne Balibar, *Spinoza, the Transindividual*, trans. Mark G. E. Kelly. Edinburgh University Press, 2020, p. 149, italics in the original.
34 Walter Benjamin, 'Capitalism as Religion', in *Selected Writings, Vol. 1: 1913–1926*. Cambridge, MA: Harvard University Press, 2004, p. 289.
35 Jessica Whyte, *The Morals of the Market: Human Rights and the Rise of Neoliberalism*. London: Verso, 2019.

36 McKenzie Wark, *Capital Is Dead: Is This Something Worse?* London: Verso, 2019, p. 19.
37 Etienne Balibar, *Spinoza, the Transindividual*, trans. Mark G. E. Kelly. Edinburgh: Edinburgh University Press, 2020, p. 152, emphasis in the original.
38 Sigmund Freud, *Group Psychology and Other Writings*. London: White Press, 2004.
39 Etienne Balibar, *Spinoza, the Transindividual*, trans. Mark G. E. Kelly. Edinburgh: Edinburgh University Press, 2020, p. 168.
40 For instance Chloe Kolyri, *Gender as a Lure. Psychoanalysis, Politics and Art.* Athens: Patakis, 2017.
41 Arne De Boever, Alex Murray, Jon Roffe, and Ashley Woodward, eds., *Gilbert Simondon: Being and Technology.* Edinburgh University Press, 2012.
42 Andrew Feenberg, *Technosystem: The Social Life of Reason.* Cambridge, MA: Harvard University Press, 2018.
43 Etienne Balibar, *Equaliberty: Political Essays*, trans. James Ingram. Durham: Duke University Press, 2014, p. 49.
44 Baruch Spinoza, *Ethics*. Princeton, NJ: Princeton University Press, 1996.

Chapter 3

The everyday uncanny

For Chloe Kolyri

*

Wide awake in the dead of night one week before going to Vizitsa, in the Mount Pelion region of Greece for a Symposium on the theme of *Life*, I realize I am nothing. I summoned infinity, and infinity accepted my invitation. It showed up unexpectedly at 3.10 A.M., and although my heart was beating and I could hear and feel inbreath and outbreath, I knew that I was nothing and that in a few days at Vizitsa, I would have nothing to say and that I will be saying it in 40 minutes. This may have nothing to do with the irruption of infinity but with the wreckage of endings piling up, the last one compounding all others, every heartbreak reopens all the others, all the failed goodbyes *adios hasta luego addio adio* bye bye baby bye bye. And I didn't have a chance to say goodbye. No, I didn't have a chance to say bye bye baby, bye bye.

On the third day, I rose again. I drew a cross with my tongue on the barren soil to honour Gerard Nouveau who may have written Rimbaud's *Les Illuminations*. A sleepless night waiting in vain for the beloved to come to me, the beloved asleep next door, enwrapped in her cocoon of dreams, the beloved who sleeps the sleep of the righteous. The first light of dawn, a hasty departure on tiptoe to avoid the banality of goodbyes, a last glance at her light blue slippers by the front door. In the pungent air of a summer dawn, I manage to crack a joke or two with the driver who puts on a song that goes *Ils me dirent, "résigne toi"/Mais je n'ai pas peur/J'ai repris mon âme/J'ai changé cent fois de nom/Mais j'ai tant d'amis.*

I embraced the summer dawn, wrote Rimbaud/Nouveau, but how to narrate the dawn of the world under a wounded sky? A child in the streets

DOI: 10.4324/9781003529095-4

of Berlin – Ah Benjamin! The child. The street. The dawn. Together they compose a decisive scene: the dawn of the homeless child. The child who experienced the street at dawn – primordial dawn in the open space of the revolution.

*

Thanks to Vassiliki Roussou, I have learnt of Dyonìsios Solomós' poem *O Pórphyrios*, *The Shark*, inspired by a newspaper account of the tragic death of a young English soldier whose remains were washed ashore the day after he was killed by a shark as he swam in the Corfu's harbour on July 19, 1847. July 19 marks another ending. A picnic on the summer grass, echoes of laughter and joy now muted. Happy are the wasted hours pursuing a dream of love running through our fingers. Another summer come and gone, and the wasted hours are still the best: I loved you then, the poet said, and it would be a small price to die having heard that you loved me, having felt your kiss flowing through my very soul. How romantic you are. Sure, but with a capital R. There would have been no subjectivity to speak of without the Romantics, that very same subjectivity that will sooner or later must be attenuated so as to feel the forces traversing this body/mind – immanent forces, natural forces, nothing to do with the Platonist archetypes conjured up by that bourgeois doctor Carl Gustav Jung. The gift of passion brings us closer to the creature; *with all its eyes* it sees *the Open*. Had not hoped that life could be so good. Expiring, the soul fills with joy.

*

I want to speak of *events*. First, here is a *non-event*, recounted by Charles Dickens. A disreputable man is found on the street as he lies dying. Suddenly, those taking care of him manifest eagerness, respect, even love, for his slightest sign of life. Everybody bustles about to save him, to the point where, in his deepest coma, this wicked man himself senses something soft and sweet engulfing him. But to the degree that he comes back to life, his saviours turn colder, and he becomes once again mean and crude.[1]

In the political arena, reactionary upheavals; racist, homophobic, transphobic reactions; and counter-revolutions are also non-events. *Event*, from the Latin *evenire*, means to come, to happen, what is around the corner, the *new*. Unlike the non-event, the event heralds the new. The event transfigures the subject, and the enigmatic message it carries within itself ignites others.

*

I don't really like Charles Dickens and was happy to discover that I am not the only one. His contemporary, James Fitzjames Stephen, lawyer, judge, and literary critic, didn't like him either. While acknowledging Dickens' great ability in maintaining a steady stream of wit and warmth in his writing, he found that it relied a little too much on caricature and oversimplification instead of genuine representation of the world.[2] Even more worryingly, like a particular brand of politician, Dickens is good at adapting his own mind, in Stephen's view, to the prevalent feeling among the public, particularly of course the middle classes. This is music to my ears, and it confirms my lovingly held prejudice that, to this day, a successful novelist is by and large one who is able to pander to the prevailing mood of the middle classes. Unlike, say, the minoritarian literature of writers like Kafka, championed by Deleuze and Guattari, Dickens firmly belongs to majoritarian discourse and majoritarian literature. He is highly proficient, Stephen maintains, at cashing in on the discontents of polite society and on the fierce and feeble sentiments aroused by the world's sins and woes and on taking on a sorrowful subject and rubbing people's nose in it.[3] To make the reader *feel* becomes the be all and end all, a romanticization of passive affects that remain stale and do not turn (as Spinoza encourages us to do) into *active affection* and an *ethics of joy*. Eliciting the arousal of pleasant shallow feelings has a few likely outlets, all of them inept, none of them either critiquing or opposing the order of things. As with watching documentaries on the *Shoah* while remaining complicit to the present-day genocide in Gaza, it may bring about a mood of self-ennoblement at being oh so sensitive, so affected by the suffering of the world. It may beget an urge to give to charity, or drop a couple of coins in the cup of a homeless person at the corner, to feel one's heart swell with the sense of being on the side of the good and the righteous while doing diddly-squat. Dickens's response to Stephen's critique was good-natured, full of that complacency and irritating bonhomie, typical of the beautiful souls – see for instance dogmatic person-centred practitioners whose exhibitionistic offering of unconditional positive regard tends to disdain honest conflict while fulfilling the task of displaying moral superiority. There is no pleasure, Stephen comments, in confronting someone who refuses to hit back and who pathetically explains that it is not in their nature to fight. While noble in appearance, this stance expresses superiority and contempt.

Call it counterintuitive if you must, but the adversarial position I am advocating here would require a thorough reassessment of what is meant by "intersubjectivity" and the "relational". Personally, I am not fond of either notions, but I find it surprising to realize how far removed they have become from the origins of intersubjectivity, that is from Hegelian *Anerkennung*, the acknowledgement/recognition which is born of encounter with one's own and the other's otherness rather than out of the presumption of pre-given, "ontological" correspondence or affinity. In short, I believe mainstream psychotherapy's ethos is helplessly Dickensian. It elicits passive affects while at the same time augmenting a kind of euphoric security.

What is the Dickensian ethos? For Stephen, it is a mixture of sermonising, sentimentality, and moralizing. Mainstream psychotherapy does just that in the name of so-called "integration". Something appears to be happening, but nothing really does. There is no transformation to speak of. At the most, some kind of positive cosmetic change.

If we follow the above argument to the letter, the thing to do is then to draw exclusively on minoritarian discourses, to get our inspiration from the avant-garde. Personally, this stance has great appeal. At times, however, I wonder whether a more strategic position may be needed. For instance if I were to adhere exclusively to the avant-garde, I would have quit being a psychotherapist a long time ago. The dominant, mainstream mode in psychotherapy is, frankly, hopeless, for it is entirely steeped in the spirit of revenge – what Nietzsche calls in his beloved French *ressentiment*. Unlike art (minoritarian art in particular), science and the will to knowledge in general (psychology included) are animated by *ressentiment*, by the need to grasp, order, and make right the inherently transformative and creative chaos of existence. It could be argued that psychoanalysis is immune to this because it is not psychology. This is only partly true. Mainstream psychoanalysis lost its way a long time ago when it joined the chorus that clamours for the fumigation of the unconscious and describes its aim as making the unconscious conscious. The view presented by early Freud of the unconscious as a "*reservoir* of representations of instinctual life which finds its more vivid exemplar and illustration in dreams"[4] has long been buried. In doing so, psychoanalysis has by and large become another brand of neoliberal psychology. The invitation here, following Nietzsche's *psychology of the mask* and *axiology*, is twofold: (a) to subvert the direction of psychotherapy while wearing the psychotherapist's mask in the same way in which heretical, counter-traditional philosophers wore the mask of the religious person in order to avoid being burned at the stake and (b) to practise axiologically, that is weighing up the presence of reactive and active forces in clinical work (or in Spinozian terms, of passive and active affects) in favour of active affects and an *ethics of joy*.

*

How can we turn a non-event into an event, for instance in the world of philosophy and psychotherapy? One way is by practising *active misreading*. According to psychotherapist and Zen teacher Jeremy Woodcock, this is akin to "not being pinned down by another's meanings but launched into one's own musings, a point of departure rather than a place of arrival" (personal communication, 2024).

An example of active misreading would be to misread Dickens against Dickens, hijacking the moral of the story and bypassing its sentimental, cut-price morality in favour of more searching interpretations. It implies, more generally, practising philosophy *against* philosophy and practising psychotherapy *against* psychotherapy. Also: by reading Proust against Proust. Proust's pursuit was Platonic through and through, but the text itself scatters everything that would comprise a "whole" or a "unity". *The unity, if any, is the unity of multiplicity.* The doer is implicated in the deed, or with Nietzsche, there is no doer behind the deed. The subject is encircled in the predicate, the verb, the action. The world is a *chaosmos* where the alleged hierarchy of organic and inorganic things no longer holds. Life is perpetually moving, metamorphosing, or emigrating from one condition to another.

I am effectively advocating the creative *misreading* of a text. The task of the attentive reader, Rorty argues, is to *impose* a language on the text which may bear little relations to the author's language and then to remain open to the possibilities that emerge.[5]

An example of creative misreading is working associatively with a dream – a process of holding literal and canonical interpretations lightly, in favour of the cluster of affects crystallizing around and within the oneiric terrain. We need to find a little more in any given text than the author (or their habitual audience) has found there. For the active misreader, the traditional difference between discovery and creation is meaningless. Nietzsche would agree, and so would William James. Active readers are interested in extracting and even appropriating something of value in a text so as to bring the discourse forward, *to dream the dream further* instead of being bogged down in the futile attempt of "getting it right". We all see what happens to followers who are a little too keen on getting it right. They turn a writer or a practitioner into a guru. They literalize the teaching and tenets of a practice to the point where they become sacred fossils. Brandishing the holy relics, they then turn to their unsuspecting colleagues, pointing their fingers and saying "You are not *truly* person-centred/psychoanalytic/focusing/existential/ (delete as appropriate). Look, Rogers/Gendlin/Freud/Heidegger (delete as appropriate) spells the truth very clearly and you are deviating from it; you are perverting it".

To rely, however, as Rorty seems to do, on a mere act of will when practising active misreading ignores the valuable insights from counter-traditional psychoanalysis and in particular Laplanche's notion of the enigmatic message. It is possible to misread an author with the sole aim of appropriating their work and bending it to one's own project. But this is a limited, even superficial endeavour. To misread also means to misread the literal content of what is being expressed, in favour of an attunement to the reader's imaginative and affective response. The latter gets an inkling of the enigmatic message carried within the content. The message, mysterious to the author and to the recipient, is nevertheless passed on; it advances and germinates. The poet may have not meant literally what I feel and understand in response to a particular poem, but what the poem evokes in me is implied within its creation. It surpasses the literal meaning. Paradoxically, by misreading it, the dual activity of effectively responding to the work and then creatively misreading it carries forward the enigmatic message.

*

What makes an event possible? Events emerge in a chaosmos, a chaotic multiplicity but "inseparable from a screen that makes something – something rather than nothing".[6] The event momentarily breaks the screen. The screen – Timaeus calls it the receptacle (*hupodoche*), the nurse of all becomings – Is of course essential. The receptacle must be unconditioned by what appears in it; there are impressions in it, Timaeus says, that will be stamped from the seeing of variegated things.[7] This view is marred by a craving for permanence, similar to what is found in spiritual practitioners

who emphasize the *witness*, the ethereal little "me" surveying the rise and
fall of phenomena, a consoling consciousness weathering the erosions of
time. But consciousness arises solely out of phenomena, out of becoming,
like a child from the mother. It is not a divine supervisor overseeing the
flux of phenomena, nor does it sententiously bestow meaning on things like
existential therapists are compelled to do.

The event has several characteristics (four, says Deleuze, ventriloquizing and expanding on Leibniz, Whitehead, and Henri Michaux). A basic
way of looking at what may constitute an event is to see it in relation to
the mystical experience. In *The Art of the West*, writing about the Baroque
(a theme dear to both Deleuze and Leibniz), the French art historian Henri
Foucillon[8] indicates that the Baroque Gothic saw the acknowledgement of
the mystical experience, understood by Michel de Certeau[9] (albeit in exclusively Christian terms) as an individual explanation of one's crossing to
and from an inexpressibly universal event, which sets the body in a state
of ecstasy or trance and which has left marks, scars, or other physical evidence that substantiate the individual's journey. To be clear, the experience
in question is a disaster for the subject encased in its chrysalis. It is a fall,
catastrophe, the end of the world as we know it. What's more, it cannot be
proved, measured, or quantified; it cannot be narrated to a friend, a lover, an
audience. It may have no empirical or historical foundation. It is, however,
the virtual perception of a movement that is simultaneously all-embracing
and scattering.

The mystical experience does not occupy a high place in a hierarchy
of events. There is no hierarchy to begin with. What's more, the mystical
experience is fraught with a thousand traps and misconceptions. Suffice it
to say that it is only one of the ways in which the event manifests itself.
What is relevant to our discussion is that the event brings forth singulariza-
tion or *singularity*. The notion of singularity comes with a beguiling historical background, exquisitely described by Tom Conley.[10] Cartography in the
Middle Ages reflected a view of events that relied on the *speculum humane
salvationis*, the mirror of human salvation, a notion eventually explicated
in an anonymous book of the same title published in the early fourteenth
century: a reflection of totality, of the totality of God or existence in the
human eye. This mode of understanding began to change in the late fif-
teenth century with the bewildering experience of alterity which oceanic
colonial travellers found in their encounters, an experience which was no
longer contained within the speculum mundi. Registering the disorienting

and unconceivable array of difference had to bring about a transformation of perspective. "For a brief time – Conley writes – the world itself was taken to be a mass of islands and continents, of insular shapes that contained a possibly infinite measure of singularities".[11]

Infinity invades the room, an infinite number of atoms and molecules. The mystical fall is a mathematical dimension, the dimension of the Baroque. To come anywhere near this dimension, we would need to wave a melancholy goodbye to existentialism, phenomenology, and their Ptolemaic rebounds to the experiencing subject and its bag of tricks. We would need to remember the unbridgeable chasm between two diametrically opposed notions of *res extensa*: the one conceived by Descartes and the one conceived by Leibniz. In Descartes (as with the majority of psychoanalytic, existential, and phenomenological approaches that are happily stuck with Cartesianism), the world is delineated from the centre of the *cogito* in a straight line and can be divided into thinly separated parts. The emerging cartography retraces the quincunx, "a two-dimensional system of gridding and squaring that places a center (the ego) at the intersection of the diagonals of a surrounding square".[12] Each time the ego-self moves into space, it alters one of the corners of the rectangle of its boundary, turning it into a new centre, until space is conquered. The design of this mental matrix is Ptolemaic, and it perfectly chimes with Ptolemaic cartographies such as *Mappamundi*, the Medieval map of the world and the one outlining the Christian Empire.

For Leibniz, as for Deleuze and other counter-traditional thinkers, the self cannot be delineated in such crude fashion. At any given moment, it spins amid forces that traverse the body and constitute the body, its motions and pliability. Unlike the Cartesian scenario and the mental matrix of Ptolemaic cartography replicated in mainstream psychotherapy, this is not a combat zone but a play of folds. While a communication of sorts does exist within Ptolemaic cartography between the individual body and the world, this is still the limited perspective of Leonardo da Vinci's *Man in a Circle and Square*. It is still moored to the Roman *umbilicus mundi*, the outdated *omphalos*, the navel of the world. Other maps are needed – maps that rewrite the world as chaosmos, a terrain where bodies are themselves entwined within the circuit. Not only do we need other maps. We also need other languages and boldly pursue the path opened by imaginative writers: "riverrun, past Eve and Adam's, from swerve of shore to bend of bay":[13] the beginning of *Finnegans Wake*, a work that reframes and expands the body-subject, from umbilicus mundi to a new form that includes radio signals and dream signals. As James O Connor writes:

> While the dreamers are connected by dream radio, their bodies are themselves bound into the circuit; there are no headsets, no wires that are not already parts of their bodies. Machines and flesh share functions. The dreamer does not merely listen. The dreamer is the signal, the message, and the noise. The dreamer sends and receives.[14]

*

Deleuze writes about the event's four attributes and its three or more characteristics. Here, I like to focus on what he calls *satisfaction*, the final phase of self-enjoyment, marking the way in which "the subject is filled with itself and attains a richer and richer private life, when prehension is filled with its own data". We find description of this in biblical, neo-Platonic, and English empiricist literature: "The plant sings of the glory of God" – Deleuze writes – "It feels in this prehension the self-enjoyment of its own becoming".[15]

The above bears a striking resemblance with Zen, and in particular with Dōgen's fascicle *Bendōwa* (negotiating the Way), written in mid-autumn 1231, the second work after his return from China. He mentions "disporting oneself freely" in samadhi (concentrated meditative practice),[16] emphasizing the interconnectedness of self and environment, both experiencing realization in the sphere of *jijuyū sammai*, a state of absorption in which the practitioner receives *and* applies the joy of awakening in oneself. Dōgen writes:

> Although both the mind of the person seated in zazen and its environment enter realization and leave realization within the stillness of samadhi, . . . it does not disturb a single mote of dust, or obstruct a single phenomenon.[17]

The view of the universe that emerges from these writings is of a very generous place where everything aids everything else. "Trees and grasses, wall and fence expound and exalt the Dharma for the sake of ordinary people, sages, and all living beings" Dōgen writes. "Ordinary people, sages, and all living beings in turn preach and exalt the Dharma for the sake of trees, grasses, wall and fence".[18] I don't think it implausible to link *jijuyū sammai* to *jouissance*. The cultural context is clearly different, with the latter circling around a sexual/intellectual/political experience of rapture, but the central element of *joy* remains at the centre – a joy that circumvents prescriptive narratives of lack and pleasure and that does not depend on another. In Leibniz's ontology, as mediated by Deleuze, this is

> [a] satisfaction with which the monad fills itself when it expresses the world, a musical Joy of contracting its vibrations, of calculating them without knowing their harmonics or of drawing force enough to go further and further ahead in order to produce something new.[19]

In order to produce something new. A question that is found in Leibniz and that will be central to Bergson and Whitehead. It is also one of the loci where, I believe, the western philosophical counter-tradition and Zen meet. The aim is no longer, as with traditional spiritual narratives, to attain eternity but to break through the frame of the objective world so that new pathways are found that allow for innovation. Leibniz's best of all worlds is "neither the least abominable nor the least ugly".[20] It is no longer the one that replicates the eternal, but the one that makes innovation possible.

*

The starting point for the presentation that informs this chapter was Charles Dickens's story *Our Mutual Friend*, the tale of a man who collapses on the street. The day before I delivered my talk/performance, the very same thing happened to me.

Up early on this Friday morning 30 August, in the small mountain village of Vizitsa in the Mount Pelion region of Greece. Beautiful, surrounded by forests and with an exquisite traditional architecture. A convivial breakfast of Greek yogurt, homemade jam, boiled eggs, toast and coffee in a garden filled with hilarity and tenderness with my wonderful new friends, an assorted group of psychoanalysts and philosophers, many of them from Thessaloniki. Philosophy is born in friendship.

In my room listening to an old favourite, Rain Tree Crow's *Blackwater*. "Come lead me through the morning for the land that I long to see again" David Sylvian croons adorably to a backdrop of Richard Barbieri's strings and Steve Jansen's inimitable percussive brushes. Is that song about journeying to the underworld, I wonder. It certainly is about lost love, "see her cry, see the face I loved". From the open window the sound of bells and chanting from the nearby orthodox Church. Far in the distance, the sea, the Pagasitikos bay glimpsed through the beautiful roofs.

I bring up on my laptop Margarita Karkayanni's paper on Nietzsche's Genealogy which she'll deliver in a couple of hours. Intriguing title: Life as the Will to Nothing in the Third Treatise of the Genealogy of Morals. Can't wait to listen to the talk (in Greek), following the word-by-word translation courtesy of Google I just uploaded. To me Margarita is three people gradually becoming one: (a) the interesting face I couldn't help noticing, peering from a black and white photo on the Symposium conference's webpage; (b) the person who spoke to me during a break on the first day and told me about sailing, about Crete where she lives part of the year, and of the depth and beauty of the sea (reasons for which I eventually referred to her as the Marine Lover of Friedrich Nietzsche, after Irigaray's book of the same title); (c) the person who introduced Michalis Tegos's stimulating talk on Alain Badiou yesterday morning. It takes me a while to realize that she is one and the same person. Walking towards the outdoor venue, as the heat slowly starts to rise, I feel increasingly heavy, dizzy, and unsteady on my feet. I call the specialist nurse in London but there is no reply. I decide to go up the café and order an iced coffee. It makes things worse, and I now have the distinct feeling that the ground is disappearing from under my feet. Ioannis, someone I exchanged a few words with the day before, is sitting at the next table with a couple of friends. I nod in his direction. He must have realized that something is not right. Are you OK? I'm not OK I say, I feel very sick and I can barely speak. He tells me to lie on the café's bench and holds my feet up, then runs and comes back two minutes later with Nikos. They know what to do; Ioannis is a psychiatrist with medical training, while Nikos is the cool-headed anaesthetist I was introduced the night before, partner of Vassiliki, the psychoanalyst friend who'd introduced me to Solomós's poem *The Shark*. Before I understand what's happening I am in a car. We are heading to the hospital in Volos, on the coast, some forty minutes from Vizitsa. We stop a couple of times as I keep throwing up. I feel better in between, and at that moment the radio plays Nina Simone's *I feel good* and I find the strength to smile and hum the tune. The song had brought to mind the end of Wenders's film *Perfect Days*. I remember thinking, maybe this is it. And I feel good; the trees of an intense green, the mediterranean blue vault overseeing a splendid late summer day. Not a bad way to go, I think, so I try to sing, and my two friends sing with me.

The doctor keeps me in A&E for three hours – kind, good-humoured, supportive. I lay under a metal blanket, an astronaut hovering between waking and sleeping, surveying dark mazes and chiaroscuros in Hades. Nikos moves things along without fuss and kindly urges the doctor. After the scan and the scan print out (which became part of my performance next day), we leave. The light of the early afternoon is magical and while Nikos goes to pick up the car Ioannis beckons me to come closer. Look, he says. At the end of the road, the sea. I weep with happiness.

On the way back, a surge of joy, love, and gratitude for these two wonderful men, for their presence of mind, their good heart and generosity. I feel happy to be alive. This time, the radio is playing James Brown's *Sex Machine*, 'Get up (get on up!)'. That's all I wanted, Nikos said, for you to get up and be well again, Manu! That brought tears to my eyes. Then uproarious laughter from all three when I add: "not sure though about being a sex machine right now". "We owe a visit to Chiron's cave, centaur and healer – Ioannis says – it's just near here. He must have lent us a hand".

The scary moment passed. I feel all the more grateful for the magnificence of life. "Life and death are of supreme importance – we chant at night during a zen retreat – time swiftly passes by and opportunity is lost. Let us strive to awaken. Let us not squander our life".

*

In their interpretations of Leibniz, both Deleuze and Benjamin highlight the notion of *expression*, that is, the way in which a monad reflects the phenomenal world. The structure of expression emphasizes the immanent nature of the world in each of its modest constituents. Benjamin utilizes this in relation to how "each work of art includes its 'fore and-after-history'" in the same way as for Leibniz, "every monad is 'pregnant' with its past, present, and future histories".[21] In a similar fashion, Deleuze is inspired by Leibniz's idea of the *complete individual concept*, present in each individual substance and encompassing all past, present, and future predicates. Leibniz famously gives the example of Alexander the Great: God is able to glance at Alexander and survey his entire history and destiny. He can see that he conquered Darius, that he studied with Aristotle, that he would march to India and more. Within Alexander's individual substance is found Alexander's complete individual concept. Deleuze reframes this in a radically secular fashion which however takes on transcendental and theological aspects: he reformulates it as the presence of the virtual immanent to (i.e. *within*) our phenomenal world.

A useful notion here, found in Benjamin and only indirectly linked to Deleuze, is *apokatastasis*. For Benjamin, "only a redeemed mankind . . . is granted the fullness of its past – which is to say, only for a redeemed mankind the past has become citable in all its moments".[22] A Greek term for restoration (as well as redemption), originally used by the Stoics to represent the cycle of cosmology, apokatastasis was taken up by Christian theologians with reference to Jewish eschatology, namely St. Peter's speech in Acts 3.21, describing Christ whom heaven must hold until the times of that restoration of all things (*achri chronōn apokatastaseōs pantōn*) and by Origen of Alexandria, who applied it to mean the salvation of all souls.

As part of his tenacious critique of dominant, teleological notion of progress, in the *Arcades Project* Benjamin develops apokatastasis in a secular direction, describing it as part of a "methodological proposal for the cultural-historical dialectic".[23] He later relates it to the notion of the eternal return found in both Nietzsche and August Blanqui. Even though Deleuze does not engage with apokatastasis, the eternal return is nevertheless central in his work, expedient in unlocking new concepts of intensities, affects, and the virtual.[24]

Expression, discussed earlier, is the spatial equivalent of eternal return: in Deleuze's case, this is evident in the notion of a multiplicity of worlds simultaneously existing; in Benjamin, as infinity of ideas, each containing an image of this world. Similarly with Benjamin's historical-materialist version of *forma fluens*, a notion I found useful in developing postqualitative research.[25][26]

In both cases, there is affirmation of becoming, a challenge to both dialectical and transcendental thinking. Despite their differences, these two thinkers share a healthy scepticism of historical progress, and both support an anti-historicist, fragmented notion of life as impermanent, revealing by accident its mystery through allegory, through a glance in a crowded street, through love at last sight.

Redemption, at least in Benjamin, is closely allied to catastrophe or at least to the intimation of catastrophe, be it individual or collective demise.

*

The day after my near collapse, heavy rain and thunder in the early hours. I don't know what life is but I am complicit with its beauty and terror.

I slowly resurface, and after a low-key day, in the evening I begin to feel ready for my talk/performance. To get in the mood, I put on a Joy Division T-shirt and a Versace tie. I am scheduled last, after a talk by Vassiliki Roussou and a generous appreciation of my book *Subversion and Desire* from Yannis Riga and my dearest friend Chloe Kolyri. My turn comes. I start the Butoh ash walk forward while speaking and reading. It's gone dark and I can't read my notes. Surprisingly, as I move slowly among the audience, one after another torches from people's mobile phones lit up, allowing me to read. I'm lying on the ground, singing softly: *E lontano, lontano nel mondo, una sera sarai con un altro, e ad un tratto chissá come e perché ti troverai a parlargli di me, di un amore ormai troppo lontano.* (Far away somewhere, one night you'll be with another and all of a sudden who knows why you'll find yourself telling him about me, about a too distant love). I move backward, speaking of redemption and catastrophe, of ecstasy and relinquishment, of dark soundless nights. Manos enriches my performance intervening with a humorous tune, and Maria does it by singing the aria *Lasciatemi morire* (let me die) from Monteverdi, the same Maria who found me alone in the small church that morning and whispered in my ear a religious song in Greek. Responses to my talk are thoughtful, sensitive, searching. Later in the square, by the plane tree thought to be over 1000 years old, hanging out with Kakia and Margarita over supper, I learn that their supervisor had been none other than Gillian Rose. This stops me in my tracks. Gillian Rose! A delightfully difficult, heartbreaking/heart-opening philosopher, author of masterpieces: *Love's Work*, her account of facing terminal cancer; *The Broken Middle*, on Kierkegaard; *The Melancholy Science*, on Adorno. Later Kakia tells me:

> Gillian was a fiery, spiritual, magical force of nature, and we had indeed a wonderful relationship. I felt so lucky to have met her, and used to call her the woman of my dreams. Her fatal disease was definitely a major shock for all of us, but her presence has been so strong that, at the time, I hardly thought that she really left us. I don't say this as a denial or self-protection, neither as a naive faith in the afterlife, but rather as an elusive, though real sensation of her abiding power.
>
> (Goudeli, personal communication, 2025)

Then we all get up to dance to a traditional tune, Maria is singing accompanied by a group of musicians, we join Chloe in her beautiful dance, our inspiring friend and mentor and instigator Chloe Kolyri. Minutes later, the whole village is flooded by torrential rain.

Sunday it's goodbyes, and why are we made in such a way that we're always on the verge of leaving? Next morning, in the room of the weirdest hotel in the world, I read the translation of Chloe Kolyri's appreciation of my book *Subversion and Desire*. In reading it, she says, she followed a circadian path and found – I blushed as I read it – that I am planting a bomb and creating "a new psychotherapy". The subject, she goes on to say, is not something fixed and determined but exists universally as both living and non-living, in a state of metastability. On the one hand, every organism tends to fall into a state of stability, on the other hand, its internal appetite [orexis] wants to keep it open to resistance and desire. If the tendency to rigidity were completed, a final sedimented form would emerge that would be of no interest to Life and which, for this reason, would overtake it. As an active, creative misreader in Rorty's sense, Chloe understood better than I ever could what I am writing – particularly about vacillation, which she describes as a magical and moving point, as an awakening from the certainties of rational consciousness.

This is home, I find myself thinking. The South – of Europe, of the psyche, a multiple soul populated by many gods, neither one god nor the puritanical non-god of the secular North. At home, I can afford to fall and vacillate, knowing/unknowing that I am held and loved and understood, that I can fall and continue to fall and discover that I can no longer fall as in the wayward angel in the poem Christina Katsari sent me days later.

As I step out a preternatural light floods the cobbles streets in central Athens. I spend precious, too short time with Margarita, Marine Lover of Friedrich Nietzsche, both of us perched on a stool outside a café sipping a foamy cappuccino right in the middle of the Monday morning bustle. I keep asking her about Gillian Rose, and about her projects, and will she write a chapter in the Affect book? I am delighted to hear she will.

On my way to the airport a while later, the cab's radio unexpectedly plays Bowie's camp version of the Velvet Underground's *Waiting for the Man*. Life is good.

Notes

1 This chapter is in part a transcript of a talk/performance given at the *Speeches on the Mount* conference on the theme of Life on August 31, 2024 in Vizitsa, Mount Pelion. I wanted to retain some link to the unrepeatable event, and for that reason it retains at times an informal, discursive style.

2 Charles Dickens, *Our Mutual Friend*. Ware, Herts: Wordsworth Editions, 1997.

3 J. Fitzjames Stephen, *The Writings of James Fitzjames Stephen: On the Novel and Journalism*, ed. Christopher Ricks. New York: Oxford University Press.

4 Adam Phillips, 'Getting the Life You Want', *London Review of Books*, 20 June 2024, pp. 41–46, emphasis added.

5 Richard Rorty, *The Rorty Reader*, ed. Christopher J. Voparil and Richard J. Bernstein. Hoboken, NJ: Wiley-Blackwell, 2010.

6 Gilles Deleuze, *The Fold: Leibniz and the Baroque*. London: Continuum, 2006, p. 86.

7 Plato, *Timaeus and Critias*, trans. Robin Waterfield. Oxford, OX: Oxford University Press, 2008.

8 Henri Foucillon, *The Art of the West*, 2 vols. London: Phaidon, 1970.

9 Michel de Certeau, *The Mystic Fable: The Sixteenth and Seventeenth Centuries*, ed. Luce Giard, trans. Daniel Smith. Chicago: University of Chicago Press, 2015.

10 Tom Conley, 'Singularity', in *The Deleuze Dictionary*, ed. Adrian Parr. University of Edinburgh Press, 2010, pp. 254–256.

11 Tom Conley, 'Singularity', in *The Deleuze Dictionary*, ed. Adrian Parr. University of Edinburgh Press, 2010, pp. 254–256.

12 Tom Conley, 'Singularity', in *The Deleuze Dictionary*, ed. Adrian Parr. University of Edinburgh Press, 2010, p. 254.

13 Tom Conley, 'A Plea for Leibniz', in Gilles Deleuze, *The Fold: Leibniz and the Baroque*. London: Continuum, 2006, pp. ix–xxi, xviii.

14 James Joyce, *Finnegans Wake*. London: Faber & Faber, 1975, p. 3.

15 James O. Connor, 'Radio Free Joyce', in *Sound States: Innovative Poetics and Acoustic Technologies*, ed. Adelaide Morris. Chappel Hill, NC: University of North Carolina Press, 1997, pp. 27–31, 21.

16 Gilles Deleuze, *The Fold: Leibniz and the Baroque*. London: Continuum, 2006, pp. 88–89.

17 Eihei Dōgen, *The Heart of Dōgen's Shōbōgenzō*, trans. Norman Waddel and Masao Abe. New York: State University of New York Press, 2002.

18 Eihei Dōgen, *The Heart of Dōgen's Shōbōgenzō*, trans. Norman Waddel and Masao Abe. New York: State University of New York Press, 2002, p. 13.

19 Eihei Dōgen, *The Heart of Dōgen's Shōbōgenzō*, trans. Norman Waddel and Masao Abe. New York: State University of New York Press, 2002, p. 13.

20 Gilles Deleuze, *The Fold: Leibniz and the Baroque*. London: Continuum, 2006, p. 79.

21 Gilles Deleuze, *The Fold: Leibniz and the Baroque*. London: Continuum, 2006, p. 79.
22 Walter Benjamin, *Selected Writings*, Vol. 4, ed. Howard Eiland and Michael W. Jennings. Cambridge and London: Belknap Press, 2006, p. 390.
23 Noa Levin, 'Spectres of Eternal Return: Benjamin and Deleuze Read Leibniz', *Filozofski vestnik*, Vol. XLII, No. 2, 2021, pp. 305–329, https://doi.org/10.3986/fv.42.2.14, p. 309.
24 Walter Benjamin, *The Arcades Project*, trans. H. Eiland and K. McLaughlin. Cambridge, MA: The Belknap Press, 1999, p. 459.
25 Gilles Deleuze, *Nietzsche and Philosophy*. New York: Columbia University Press, 2008.
26 Manu Bazzano, 'Making Love to Your Data', *Therapy Today,* March 2021, pp. 42–45.

Chapter 4

No hope, no fear

For Prabs

*

During the filming of David Bowie's *Lazarus*, one of the songs on his final album *Black Star*, the doctors informed him that the cancer he'd been suffering from was terminal and that they would discontinue treatment. The video features Bowie in close-up on his deathbed with a blindfold and buttons stitched over his eyes, aware of the impending death and seized by a desire to make art for one last time. In the last scene, Bowie walks backwards and locks himself in a dark, empty wardrobe. The image, at once moving, desperate, and full of vitality, reminded me of a historical precedent from five centuries earlier. One of the ambitions of Renaissance poet and Dean of St Paul's Cathedral in London, John Donne, was to die in the pulpit, and he almost managed it. On February 25, 1631, seriously ill, he got out of bed to preach his last sermon, the famous *Death Duel*.[1] His appearance was dreadful and caused alarm in the congregation. Dr Donne has preached his own funeral service, a contemporary commented. He didn't die in the pulpit but found another way to turn his death into a work of art. He obtained a large wooden urn and a board, then undressed, put on the shroud, with knots tied to his head and feet, and climbed onto the urn where he kept his balance while an artist drew his life-size portrait. This was then hung next to his bed, to remind him what the future had in store, and to show his courage in facing it. Like Bowie, Donne staged his own demise five centuries earlier, coming close to accomplishing that mastery of death which suicides arguably seek.

*

Our session is early today, 8 A.M. on a Tuesday morning on a mid-November day. Unusually warm, the sky dense with clouds, autumn's beauty a blessing. At the start of every session, Rafael closes his eyes for a

DOI: 10.4324/9781003529095-5

few minutes before speaking. This time it takes him longer. I keep my eyes half-closed, waiting for him to speak.

Ruby is away, he finally says. She left last Thursday to some exotic place in search of "nature", away from her demanding job. Won't be back for a while. I have no problem with us being apart. In fact, I think it's good for us. Still, I don't know what got into me. It's like, I don't *really* know Ruby even though we've been together on and off for nearly four years now. I remember that night when I couldn't sleep. She was so far away in her slumber. When morning came and I had to go, she stayed there in that other world – remote, inaccessible. As I stepped out, under late summer's soft drizzle, I felt an unbridgeable distance. How will I ever see the world, even for a moment, through her eyes? I asked myself.

The next bit is a bit embarrassing, Rafael says. You see, where she is now, the kind of place, the sort of holiday, how can I say, it doesn't square up with all our deep talks and with what I know of her. Realizing that I don't really know her derails me. I felt so down this morning. I thought that if I were to, you know, *exit* this life, that wouldn't be such a crazy idea after all. I feel ashamed of being so shaken up by my realization that I don't know her. Last time after love we cried our hearts out reading Tsvetaeva's poem to Rilke who was dead by then. It went something like this: *What's it like there Rainer, how are you feeling? How does a poet's first viewing of the universe match with his last glance at the planet, this planet you only visited once?* We read the poem looking at the white ceiling, so together, so alone in the world and for a rare brief moment surrendered to our love. *How was your trip Rainer? How did it tear, did you bear, did it burst your heart open? Was your very breath sweet or worse? Was it sweet?* Reading Tsvetaeva through the tears, we held each other like there's no tomorrow, Rafael says, as if the whole sky had flooded the room; as if nothing else mattered. *How's writing in the new place Rainer? If you're there, there must be poetry, because you are poetry. How's writing in the new life, not even able to rest your elbow on? Drop me a line, I miss your handwriting.*

I should calm down, Rafael says. She is so good, so polite and I'm a drama queen; Southern soul and all that. She sent me friendly messages on *WhatsApp* as she usually does and photos of the dogs in the house of friends where she stays. Then I had a meltdown after a difficult night. I felt so utterly desolate. It was like all we had had been brushed aside, that it didn't matter; that my name is on her list of chores if you see what I mean. I'm a fallen leaf in the wind. I rang her; she held me tenderly. On *WhatsApp*!

In the background, chairs lined with the Union Jack. Getting out the door to come to our session, I thought "what's the point?" I have lived, loved, tasted the honey and the vinegar, the sweetbitter and the bittersweet. What is the point of going on?

I watched a Norwegian film the other night, Rafael says, *Oslo, August 31*. The protagonist, Anders, is a 30-something junkie, a talented but disheartened writer. He visits his old haunts after a successful spell in rehab. Memories of an old love spoilt by his addiction. Failed attempts at finding her. His state of mind is such that throughout the film, you don't know whether this is the first day of his new life or his last day on Earth. The last scene affected me deeply, Rafael says, then pauses. He is crying softly now. Sorry, he says. So . . . what was I saying? Well, Anders visits his sister's empty apartment. Sits at the piano, plays a classical tune. Then expertly prepares what it's going to be his last fix. He draws the curtain, sits on the bed, and after injecting himself, he gently reclines on the bed. The film ends as it started. With loving, lingering shots of Oslo, the town Anders had loved.

We sit in silence. I don't know who Ruby is, he says. Nor do I know who I am. It's weird. When we are apart, which is most of the times, she holds a part of me I don't know. And in her absence, I hold a part of her she doesn't know.

*

I do not endorse literal suicide. But I'm in favour of *symbolic* suicide – the difficult detachment from the *role* we play in the world, something I partly learnt from reading the philosopher Jan Patočka. Friend of Husserl and former student of Heidegger, he was forced to retire prematurely from Charles University in Prague for his political convictions (including the signing of the human rights manifesto *Charta 77*). Patočka died of a brain haemorrhage following gruelling police interrogations in hospital. Platonic philosophers – he writes in his *Heretical Essays* – defeat death because they don't run away from it but look at it as directly as one can. They call their practice *melete thanatou*, concern for death – inseparable from genuine concern for life. Looking death in the face is an act of freedom, which requires leaving behind the undifferentiated mode of the herd, the latest manifestation of which is technological proliferation.[2] It requires what Plato calls, responding to Cebes and Simmias in *Phaedo*, a truth gathered into itself alone.[3]

This meditative attempt to recognize the reality of death implies a move towards interiority, a gathering of our mind/heart.

Technological civilization is not *per se* evil, as some would have us believe. Fleeing to imaginary Arcadias won't help. It is just that technological civilization's understanding of subjectivity is trivial: it is stuck at the level of *persona*, our social role. Like many, I like my posts being liked on social media. On a good day, I even perversely relish the shabby provocations of rabid, ignorant trolls who attack my writings without having read them. Technological civilization turbo-charged this fixation with the persona but did not initiate it. Idealization of our role and simulacrum had a long gestation with the Italian Renaissance through the bourgeois revolution two centuries later, when its ideals of *liberty, equality, and fraternity* merged with an irredeemably blighted notion of individuality whose only claim remains to this day inert. For it merely calls for the measurable equality of *roles*, rather than the equality of real bodies or body-subjects. For Patočka, a necessary re-connection with our vital force occurs, paradoxically, via a *withdrawal* of being. There are echoes here with Zen, a tradition I had the privilege and honour to study and practise for many years, and that still constitutes the very backbone of my existence. An intensive silent retreat in this tradition is called *sesshin*, "gathering of one's mind/heart". In Patočka's terms, this move subordinates the undifferentiated dimension (what he calls the orgiastic; what Heidegger calls *das Man*) to a difficult stance of radical interiority and freedom/responsibility. This shift *may* happen when acknowledging the certainty of death or when examining the persistence of suicidal thoughts in difficult moments in our life. It does *not*, however, unveil "the truth". Instead, it journeys from one enigma to another. The enigma – of my own being, of my unknowability to myself, of the sheer insolvability of human interactions – deepens. This enigma is the *secret*, from *se-cernere*, to set apart from the frantic triviality we often immerse ourselves in our everyday.

Those who elect *symbolic* suicide aim to restore the secrecy/sacredness of their subjectivizing individuality and of their loves. They personify a refusal to have one's heart scrutinized by the auditor, the lawyer, the moralist, the policeman – and the therapist. Unless the therapist is a fellow explorer instead of a stand-in for the auditor/lawyer/moralist/policeman. A shift towards secret/sacred interiority folds on itself; it is auto-affection. It is, for Spinoza, an *intensive mode*, turning the natural passivity of affects into *active*, affirmative affections. Becoming less subjected to potentially destructive encounters, we can afford to be traversed by the intensity of the vital force itself. This is what *care of self* means – the cultivation of intense affections that do not rely on the actions of other bodies but are traversed by power itself. Or, paraphrasing Spinoza: a mode of existence which is less dependent on forces invading us from outside and is increasingly filled by the insight of the interior life as part of infinity. This is highly pragmatic too; it means creating a habitable zone where we can breathe, think for ourselves, *live* – away from the coercion of state, parishes, and coteries. It means having a taste of what in Zen it is called *jijuyu-zanmai*, at times translated as self-generated joy.[4] The transformative shift into this active mode of affection may for some of us unfasten suddenly at times when we are facing the reality of death and gazing at its shimmering abyss. Far from the existentialist heroics of staring at the sun, this is closer to owning one's inherent human frailty, discomfiture, and faltering – finding in these an opening towards creation and communication. Deleuze remarked how strange it is of great thinkers such as Nietzsche to have within them both fragility *and* the utmost power to create which is one sign of Great Health.[5] The frail health that eventually prompted Deleuze to suicide was that very same force that made his groundbreaking, luminous work possible.

As with other artists and poets attuned to the inner life, John Donne championed its sovereignty over and above the pretensions and presumptions of coercive institutions. His controversial treatise *Biathanatos* echoes Epictetus – for whom the essential thing is remembering that the door out of existence is always open – and Schopenhauer – who muses that Hamlet's soliloquy may well be the meditation of a criminal. Donne's treatise defends suicidal thoughts from societal impositions, claiming that Jesus himself – a controversial argument already present in Thomas Aquinas – was in essence a suicide. Authoritarians are often anti-suicide, except of course when enthusiastically sending the young to be slaughtered in criminal and pointless wars. Rationalists and moralists parrot the Aristotle of the *Nichomachean Ethics*, for whom suicide is a citizen's neglect of his/her obligation to the commonwealth.[6]

*

At your funeral I thought of our last conversations. You'd drift, doze, then wake up, and apologize. We'd both look at the tree outside your bedroom window, autumn well on its way. We both wished we'd met earlier in our lives. You drank with relish the hot chocolate I brought you. It gave me pleasure to see you enjoying it even though you'd drift, forget to drink, then take another sip. "How was your night?" "I spare you the details".

To me you were a true sailor. We spoke about Joseph Conrad and you remembered something he had written somewhere: you've never been at sea unless you've been 1000 miles away from any shore. You did just that. You experienced that and understood what he meant.

We both shared a love of Ovid, the poet of exile. You showed me the following passage from book 15 of Ovid's *Metamorphosis* and asked me to read it out to you. I did, and you then told me off, prompting me to read it better, with greater emphasis.

Now since the sea's great surges sweep me on, all canvas spread, hear me! Listen! In all creation nothing endures, all is in endless flux, each wandering shape a pilgrim passing by. And time itself glides on in ceaseless flow, a rolling stream – and streams are never still, nor softly creeping hours. As wave is driven by wave, and each, pursued, pursues the wave ahead, so time flies on and follows; flies, and follows, always for ever new. What was before is left behind; what never was is now; and every passing moment is renewed.[7]

I felt calm next to you and so loved our conversations. On the day before you died, I felt you had no fear and no hope. No hope, no fear – a desirable way to live and die.

Notes

1 John Donne, *Death's Duel. Or, A Consolation to the Soul against the Dying Life and Living Death of the Body*, 1631, https://www.online-literature.com/donne/3915/. Retrieved 12 November 2024.

2 Jan Patočka, *Heretical Essays in the Philosophy of History*. Chicago, IL: Open Court, 1999.

3 Plato, *Phaedo*, trans. David Gallop. Oxford, OX: Oxford Classics, 2009.

4 Norman Waddell and Masao Abe, *The Heart of Dōgen's Shōbōgenzō*. New York: State University of New York Press, 2002.

5 Gilles Deleuze and Claire Parnet, *Dialogues*, trans. Hugh Tomlinson and Barbara Habberjam. New York: Columbia University Press, 1987.

6 Aristotle, *Nichomachean Ethics*, trans. David Ross. Oxford, MA: Oxford World's Classics, 2009.

7 Ovid, *Metamorphoses*, trans. Arthur Golding. London: Penguin, 2002, XV, pp. 176–186.

Chapter 5

A phenomenology of difference

The body, not the "subject"

Fanon's active engagement with Sartre is well documented if seldom examined in current writings and practices nominally informed by existential phenomenology. His seminal text *Black Skin, White Masks* (whose original title was, interestingly, *Essay on the Disalienation of the Black*), published when he was only 27,[1] brings to life several Sartrean tropes, including authenticity, bad faith, and the subject's power/ability of being-for-others. Virtually unknown, let alone examined within majoritarian existential therapy, is Fanon's fruitful dialogue with Merleau-Ponty, and this despite the thriving literature on the subject.[2]

Fanon's route to Merleau-Pontian phenomenology is significant for any practitioner interested in embodied difference. Born in 1925 in the island of Martinique in the Eastern Caribbean Sea, as a young man, Fanon became a pupil at the Lycée Victor-Schoelcher of the poet, educator, and founder of the *Negritude* movement Aimé Césaire, a key literary and anti-colonialist political figure who famously referred to the process of colonization as *thingification*, the commodification of human beings. Originally published in 1955, his *Discourse on Colonialism*[3] is still relevant today. This is because, as Jasbir Puar points out, current culture is still characterized by "a lack of engagement with postcolonial theory" which leaves racial dynamics "unexplored".[4] This is also true of psychotherapy culture – including majoritarian existential therapy. One of Fanon's merits is to have developed and expanded the anti-colonialist direction of Césaire's work. He saw Negritude as "the emotional if not the logical antithesis of that insult which the white man flung at humanity"[5] – a shift in thought and praxis which necessitates in his view the expansion of mere cultural identity (in this case *racialized* cultural identity) into the context of wider political struggle,

DOI: 10.4324/9781003529095-6

including a struggle for national liberation.⁶ As a young Black man in the early 1940s, Fanon experienced first-hand the violence and bigotry of the collaborationist Vichy regime, accelerating a contextual, racial-historical understanding of *lived experience* (what phenomenologists call *Erlebnis*) – not as universal factuality but as an occurrence *specific* to the Black person under the yoke of colonialism and racism. Factuality is only *one* aspect of facticity, and the one that is more relevant here is *contingency*. Factual lived experience is subjected to historico-political contingencies. These are felt at the level of the skin. Consequently, it is inaccurate to speak of subjective experience in terms of a universal subject, as the philosophical tradition has done since time immemorial. It has done so not because the tradition is marred by some sort of epistemological impediment, but because the language of universality is historically closely allied to Empire and to its *legacy of violence*, in Caroline Elkins's turn of phrase.⁷

It would be likewise inaccurate to bound psychological/psychotherapeutic explorations to a unitary (Cartesian, Husserlian) self, a variation of which is the notion of a self-existing, fundamentally self-bound "psychic apparatus" as the Freudian tradition has it (despite its own genial, now largely discarded hypothesis of the unconscious). It would also be inaccurate, while we're on the subject, to speak of "relatedness" as a *given* in human interactions (rather than as an aspiration) if one then breezily bypasses both the asymmetry of human interactions and the contingency integral to facticity.

What is the alternative to the debateable notion of the (universal) *self*? The answer is straightforward: *the body*. In particular, the lived experience of the *subjugated* body. The pathos and passion of bodies itemized, reviled, and subjected to the violence of the state and of dominant culture – to the xenophobia, racism, misogyny, homophobia, transphobia, and aporophobia (hatred of the poor and contempt for the homeless) circulated by majoritarian views and orchestrated by our societies of control. Fanon's books were not written for the powerful but for the "wretched of the earth". His learning and praxis, as a psychiatrist and political activist, were *not* motivated by the desire to curry favour from institutions. His focus was elsewhere.

We do not learn of the vicissitudes of the psyche and the tribulations of experience by passively reciting the constructs of an arbitrary existential "canon" dished out in the classrooms of costly and cultish existential training schools. We may want to pay close attention instead to those who know in their marrow "ontological insecurity" and "existential uncertainty":

not as the tropes of a "universal human condition" but more concretely as unemployment, displacement, illness, exile, exclusion, poverty, as tragic/ ecstatic upheavals of bodies subjected to hatred, prejudice, and all sorts of normative phobias.

We may want to pay close attention to those who edge close to anguish and dread, who in their experience of deep existential crisis feel on their skin the fragility and fragmentation of the human subject. We may want to listen to those who, having seen through the vain promises of neoliberal ideology, may need assistance in affirming their lived experience and in actively resisting the psychological control exerted by a monological psych world bent on replicating *ad infinitum* the view that the only thing that matters is profit, and that the only way to know how well one is doing is by measuring the success of the self-entrepreneurial model peddled by neoliberal psychology.

The counter-traditional line of thought I am conjuring up here, anchored in contingency, specificity, and the asymmetry of human interactions, is redolent of the more critical takes on the implications of the Hegelian master/slave dialectic[8] and has been extensively developed by an overlooked but stimulating perspective: feminist *standpoint theory*.

Standpoint theory and disembodied research

For Sandra Harding,[9] who coined the term, standpoint theory is several things at once. It is an inquiry into the nature of epistemology, a way of asking *who* can produce dependable knowledge and *how* knowledge can be supported. It is a philosophy of science, asking which are the best practices and goals for scientific research. It is also a sociology of science, looking closely at the different conditions which generate particular forms of knowledge. As a methodology, it has a rich and interesting lineage: from Marx, who suggested that the surest way to learn about the class system is by examining the life of a worker rather than the life of a member of the elite, to feminists who 100-plus years later applied the same method to the life of women. This methodology can be organically applied to any new group that at different historical turns bears the brunt of injustice and oppression – think of the civil rights and postcolonial movements, of LGBTQIA+ movements, and so forth.

For Brenda J. Allen,[10] knowledge is born out of *power relations* between dominant and nondominant groups. The latter – Fanon's "wretched" or "damned" of the Earth – are the ones who can provide a more extensive and incarnate knowledge of a reality dominated by power dynamics. An analysis of power dynamics, let alone of contingent/embodied *Erlebnis*, is invariably lacking in a majoritarian world of "research", hellbent on turning knowledge into another *product* in the market, particularly since the 1980 Bayh-Dole Act in the United States and Thatcher's REF (Research Excellence Framework) in the United Kingdom[11] – a nihilistic cultural turn encouraging universities to become what they have now become: *businesses*, and little else besides.

These situational – hence implicitly existential and phenomenological – perspectives find echoes in contemporary philosophies who rebuke so-called "pluralism", that is, the multiplication of the subject in order to "accommodate all sorts of differences (i.e. a politics of inclusion)", intersecting the subject "with every variable of identity imaginable, split to account for the unknown realms of the subconscious, infused it with greater individual rights".[12]

For those of us who care about the lived experience of subjected bodies – of Black, queer, transgender bodies; of poor, foreign, exiled bodies; of bodies non-aligned, noncompliant to majoritarian views and the dogmas *du jour*. For those who want their practice to become *praxis* – that is, allied to active rather than reactive forces and as such "a political force in the wider, transformational sense of the term"[13] – the writings of Frantz Fanon are a rich and stimulating source of inspiration.

Disalienation

The trajectory of Fanon's life and thought progressed from the Caribbean to Europe to North Africa to sub-Saharan Africa, each time significantly altering his perspective – a journey documented in his posthumously published *Toward the African Revolution*.[14]

Crucial to our discussion are the two years (1947–1948) he spent at the University of Lyon attending Merleau-Ponty's lectures on language and communication, before qualifying three years later as a psychiatrist under the supervision of the radical Catalan psychiatrist and artist Francesc Tosquelles, who emphasized the key role of culture and society in experiences of mental distress. Tosquelles is a key figure in a lineage of critical psychiatry whose methodology will be inspiring to those who believe in the transformative power of psychotherapeutic group work.[15] Tosquelles was the founder of *institutional psychotherapy*, an approach initially drawing on Marx and Lacan, and whose contributors included Oury, Fanon, Canguilhem, and Guattari. Institutional psychotherapy implemented a radical restructuring of mental health clinics and asylums, with patients actively involved in managing the facilities. At Saint-Alban hospital, where Fanon did his medical residency, Tosquelles, Oury, and others transformed a crumbling and underfunded hospital, where patients lived in horrible conditions, into a thriving place. Would this sort of experimentation even be conceivable in our current climate?

This aspect of Fanon's trajectory places his psychiatric training and understanding of mental distress firmly within a socio-political context. It constitutes the crucial backdrop to how he will subsequently approach Merleau-Pontian phenomenology and develop his own notion of *disalienation*. Fanon understood alienation as "a creation of middle-class society". He explains:

> What I call middle-class society is any society that becomes rigidified in predetermined forms, forbidding all evolution, all gains, all progress, all discovery. I call middle-class a closed society in which life has no taste, in which the air is tainted, in which ideas and people are corrupt. And I think that a person who takes a stand against this death is in a sense a revolutionary.[16]

Disalienation is the process by which the othering taking place when confronted with a group can be understood and worked through. A society that perpetuates racism and alienates the other is stuck, uncreative, and ends up simply preserving stale modes of being in the world. Disalienation leaves space for the possibility of decent human interactions – a possibility Fanon phrases as a question in the very last words of *Black Skin, White Masks*:

> Superiority? Inferiority? Why not the quite simple attempt to touch the other, to feel the other, to explain the other to myself?[17]

Fanon and Merleau-Ponty

In *Phenomenology of Perception*, Merleau-Ponty writes:

> We must learn to find the communication between one consciousness and another in one and the same world. In reality, the other is not shut

up inside my perspective of the world, because this perspective itself has no definite limits, because it slips spontaneously into the other's, and because both are brought together in the one single world in which we all participate as anonymous subjects of perception.[18]

Despite his subsequent critique, Fanon's approach in *Black Skin, White Masks* is phenomenological and sympathetic to Merleau-Ponty's radical reflexivity. In "The Lived Experience of the Black", a chapter in *Black Skin, White Masks*, his dialogue with Merleau-Ponty comes to the fore. It is here that Fanon replaces Merleau-Ponty's *corporeal schema* with two sequential notions: (a) the *historico-racial schema* and (b) the *racial-epidermal schema*. Merleau-Ponty's corporeal schema has to do with agency and synergy – how bodies position themselves in relation to the world and objects within it.

We grasp external space through our bodily situation. A corporeal . . . schema gives us at every moment a global, practical, and implicit notion of the relation between our body and things, of our hold on them. A system of possible movements . . . radiates from us to our environment. Our body is not in space like things; it inhabits or haunts space. It applies itself to space like a hand to an instrument, and when we wish to move about, we do not move the body as we move an object. We transport it without instruments as if by magic, since it is ours and because through it, we have direct access to space. For us, the body . . . is our expression in the world, the visible form of our intentions.[19]

The permeability of body and world is not fixed, nor can it be set apart from history and contingency. The world alters this body. This body alters the world. The world affects this body. This body affects the world. They rearrange one another in "perpetual contribution".[20] Our bodies, placed within a historical horizon, can change and subvert the horizon. The following example illustrates what is meant by corporeal schema and the perpetual contribution between the body and the world:

No-one could separate the history of the guitar from its players. Somebody comes along, "learns" the guitar and manipulates it as never before, and the history of guitar music is altered. With fingers and stance, their body communicates with the guitar through a pre-thetic schema that opens up the parameters of possibility (and therefore the history) of the instrument, at the same time as transforming the player's life. Moreover, even those who will not change the history of guitar music themselves are liable to be "altered" as their practice develops and that music communicates itself through their increasingly expressive being.[21]

The musical metaphor is apt. At a conference of Black writers and artists in Rome in the late 1950s, Fanon resorted to music in order to describe his vision of a revolutionary culture and later developed this idea further.

> *On National Culture* – later published as a chapter of *The Wretched of the Earth* – [Fanon] celebrated the defiant "new humanism" of bebop, which had grown out of "the inevitable, though gradual, defeat" of segregation. Having cast off their role as entertainers for the white man, bebop musicians were shaping their own destiny as artists. In "fifty years or so," Fanon predicted, the "type of jazz lament hiccupped by a poor, miserable 'Negro' will be defended by only those whites believing in a frozen image of a certain type of relationship and a certain form of negritude." Black American jazz, with its commitment to artistic independence and innovation, was, for Fanon, an exemplary practice of cultural freedom, a model for the wretched of the earth in their efforts to invent a new, emancipated identity.[22]

Merleau-Ponty's notion of the corporeal schema points to ways in which the affective, pre-cognitive interchange between body and world may unfasten creative possibilities – including freedom, understood as active participation in the transformation of its expressive horizons. The body's involvement with the world redraws its horizons while simultaneously being itself redrawn and transmuted. Implicit in this scenario is the following insight: *one of history's essential traits is difference.* Bodies are traversed by cultural-affective and, at times, enigmatic messages across years, decades, and centuries. Through their active response – by turning passive affectivity into active engagement – they assert the present historical time as *difference.* They deny the determinism of *fate* in favour of the pliability of *destiny* – an important distinction for any psychotherapy committed to transformation and for a polity engaged with change. Fate is unmovable, but destiny implies direction, detours, digressions. Destiny implies *agency.* And if it is true that one of history main's traits is difference, it follows that there is *no originary age* to a culture. Harking back to a time of non-obfuscated "Being" misses the enigma and potency of the present. A culture wanting to assert its "originary" nature will inevitably *suppress* difference, a stance which has caused and continues to cause harm on a devastating scale.

Merleau-Ponty's version of phenomenology is unique. It leaves the path open to emancipation and to appreciation of difference. His emphasis on difference is pivotal in attempting to re-claim the value of phenomenology today, at a time when conflicts around difference are the order of the day. The so-called "culture wars" often arise out of a compulsion to maintain rigid notions of identity and its attendant accoutrements – to prop at any cost the empire of the self-same. But in order to direct phenomenology away from its beguilement with the universal human subject, closer attention is needed to critics of phenomenology such as Fanon. In *The Lived Experience of the Black*, Fanon writes:

> Ontology . . . does not permit us to understand the being of the black person. For not only must the black person be black; they must be black in relation to the white man.[23]

Anticipating the objection to the above statement (namely, that the opposite is also true), Fanon's response is that it would be a *false* objection. Unlike the white person, whose experience dictates both normativity and universality, Black people "have no ontological resistance in the eyes of the white man". Instead,

> [they] have been given two frames of reference within which they have had to place themselves. Their metaphysics . . . their customs and the sources on which they were based, were wiped out because they were in conflict with a civilization that they did not know and that imposed itself on them.[24]

Reflecting back on his early years in Martinique, Fanon observed that the Black person "among his own . . . does not know at what moment his inferiority comes into being through the other". It was only later, when meeting the white man's gaze, that he became painfully aware of something else. Explicitly referring to Merleau-Ponty's bodily schema, he writes:

> And then the occasion arose when I had to meet the white man's eyes. An unfamiliar weight burdened me. The real world challenged my claims. In the white world the man of colour encounters difficulties in the development of his bodily schema. Consciousness of the body is solely a negating activity. It is a *third-person consciousness*. The body is surrounded by an atmosphere of certain uncertainty.[25]

What Fanon calls *third-person consciousness* turns the body into a thing, perceived in the abstract, as an object. He goes on to explain:

> I know that if I want to smoke, I shall have to reach out my right arm and take the pack of cigarettes lying at the other end of the table. The matches, however, are in the drawer on the left, and I shall have to lean back slightly. And all these movements are made not out of habit but out of implicit knowledge. A slow composition of myself as a body in the middle of a spatial and temporal world –such seems to be the schema. It does not impose itself on me; it is, rather, a definitive structuring of the self and of the world-definitive because it creates a real dialectic between my body and the world.[26]

The above description of the *schéma corporel* retraces favourably Merleau-Ponty's vision of the permeability of body and world. Difficulties arise, however, when trying to adapt the bodily schema to interracial interactions. Here a different model is needed. Disputing the classical view of early twentieth-century neurologist Lhermitte, whom he quotes in the following passage, Fanon turns the corporeal schema into the *historico-racial schema*:

> Below the corporeal schema I created a historico-racial one. The elements that I used were provided to me not by "residual sensations and perceptions primarily of a tactile, vestibular, kinaesthetic, and visual order," but by the other, the White, who has woven me out of a thousand details, anecdotes and stories.[27]

It is not race that creates racism; it is the other way around. In and of itself, race is an empty construct; but the impact of racist hatred and prejudice on the person has to be taken fully into account. Fanon replaces Merleau-Ponty's individual accounts of subjectivity with sociohistorical relations of power.[28] The sociogenetic account does not assume the existence of a linear link between the person, the family, and the state which is a given within the ontogenetic, individual-centred perspective.

For Fanon, Merleau-Ponty's bodily schema cannot reflect the experience of the Black person in Europe: it is inextricably wedded, despite its open-endedness, to the universalizing demands of the white European male subject. These demands are also central to those majoritarian existential phenomenological analyses, now canonical in traditional existential therapy in the Anglophone world, which draw primarily on Husserl and

Heidegger and are largely devoid of a situated, historico-contingent, and emancipatory discourse.

What can be learnt from Fanon are the entangled layers encroaching on the alleged universality of embodied subjectivity when it comes to Black experience – *and* to other differential, subaltern experiences. Not only that "zone of nonbeing, an extraordinarily sterile and arid region, an utterly naked declivity"[29] to which the black subject is relegated. Not only the visible body targeted by racism, a body "marked by otherness that is forced into relentlessly surveyed objecthood",[30] but also the body "in its innermost interiority" and the body in its "ostensibly universal aspects"[31] – all moulded by racialization.

A famous example in Fanon's writing recounts of him being singled out as a child by a white child, who said to his mother, *Tiens, Mama! Un nègre!* (Look, Mother! A Negro!). The sequence of his bodily response, he was to reflect many years later, made the bodily schema crumble:

> "Look, a Negro!" It was an external stimulus that flicked over me as I passed by. I made a tight smile. "Look, a Negro!" It was true. It amused me. "Look, a Negro!" The circle was drawing a bit tighter. I made no secret of my amusement. "Mama, see the Negro! I'm frightened" Frightened! Frightened! Now they were beginning to be afraid of me. I made up my mind to laugh myself to tears, but laughter had become impossible. I could no longer laugh, because I already knew that there were legends, stories, history, and above all historicity, which I had learned about from Jaspers. Then, assailed at various points, the corporeal schema crumbled, its place taken by a racial-epidermal schema.[32]

Scapegoats

For Fanon, "it is necessary to grow a new skin, to develop new thoughts, to set afoot a new human being".[33] Fanon's insights on situated experience may help navigate our way through the turmoil of the "culture wars". But it would be misguided to reframe his impassioned account of Black experience in terms of postmodernist identity politics. For Fanon, cultural identity is inextricably situated – within a political context of national liberation and with a generous helping of a universalism of *solidarity*:

> If a man is known by his acts, then we will say that the most urgent thing today for the intellectual is to build his nation. If this building is true, that

is, if it interprets the manifest will of the people and reveals the eager African peoples, then the building of a nation is of necessity accompanied by the discovery and encouragement of universalizing values. Far from keeping aloof from other nations, therefore, it is national liberation which leads the nation to play its part on the stage of history. It is at the heart of national consciousness that international consciousness lives and grows. And this twofold emerging is ultimately only the source of all culture.[34]

Clearly, a universalism of solidarity is at variance with what the Peruvian sociologist Aníbal Quijano[35] calls the *coloniality of power*, a brand of universalism common to the white, cis-het European tradition. Something else is needed than mere imitation of European values, for that would be "almost an obscene caricature".[36] Invention and discovery are needed, "if we want humanity to advance a step further, if we want to bring it up to a different level than that which Europe has shown it".[37] Like sexual difference, "race as a category makes its fraudulent appeal to anatomy or physiology to 'wind up' the question".[38] To appeal to either race or sexual difference "as a physiological or moral absolute (often both together) is . . . simply a way of bringing all discussion . . . to a standstill".[39]

If psychoanalysis taught us anything, it is that personal identity is complex, multilayered, unpliable to the positivist need of turning it into a *thing*. The same may apply to national identity. Migrants attempting to cross borders are scapegoated for disrupting the identity of a nation. Trans are scapegoated for disrupting a supposedly solid sexual identity. Our fear is then legitimated and goaded to turn into legalized loathing of "irregular" or "illegal" migrants. Something similar applies to transphobia. "I can punch you, and take all of my hate/into your body".[40]

The hatred and prejudice hurled at trans in the so-called culture wars must give pause for thought. The false appeal to anatomy and/or physiology assumes the existence of a perfect category of women. In a playful, moving, and learnt chapter of her epistolary memoir, *Love and Money, Sex and Death*, McKenzie Wark[41] reports a dialogue between herself and another trans woman friend in a Manhattan restaurant. They have been chatting animatedly and humorously trying to guess the sexual orientations and attitudes of people sitting at other tables, about their appearances and concealments. Then the conversation turns to "theory":

"In Plato's philosophy" – I'm getting pretentious, but you like it when I play the Theory Game – "it's not just that the sign of the thing falls short of the thing itself. The thing itself also falls short, in turn, of the pure idea or form of the thing. Behind appearances are things. But things, too, are just a kind of mere appearance: behind things are their forms. These cannot be touched, or tasted, or seen. They are knowable only to thought itself".

"But who cares about Plato?" you dismiss me with a wave.

. . .

"So, have you been having any pleasure of the flesh lately – *with anyone I know*?". . . You are on to me, I'd better try to hold your attention by throwing a conversational curveball.

"Secular Western culture inherited a residue of Platonism via Christianity. Even some kind of Marxists imagine a world of false appearances. For them, it's capitalism. The overthrow of capitalism restores 'man' to the possibility of an authentic life: no more advertising . . . and bye-bye to alienation. Man is restored to himself as himself".

"Men. Hmph. I don't know what anyone sees in them".[42]

The conversation goes on, meandering back and forth from the personal to the political, to a light highbrow talk that is both affecting and thought-provoking.

I launch another move: "OK, so this is also how a certain brand of feminism thinks about the figure of woman. That she just *is*. There's hand waving about biological chromosomes, but those are things that are outside the everyday realm of human perception. Woman is a Platonic ideal that 'real' women just embody by default as variations upon perfection. They then inevitably join misogynists in their distrust of femme signs as deception, and the trap as the lowest deceiver of all".

"That's fucked up", you declare.

"Agreed. In this Platonic world, no sensible thing can do justice to the pure realm of the true. No readable representation can do justice even to things, let alone to the pure and true idea.[43]

Exploring one's own sexuality and sexual difference is a constant process: this is what I have learnt thus far by listening to transgender activists, therapists, and clients. I've also learnt that the line of solidarity of those at the receiving end of prejudice and oppression is not a given but something which has to be generated at every step, defended, and cultivated. It might have been a given decades ago, but it has been lost with the advent of identity politics. Even "intersectionality", *cris the coeur* of Hillary Clinton's 2016 presidential campaign and a darling idea of the liberal *belles ames*, is but a pale substitute for solidarity. In its place, Jasbir Puar suggests a notion borrowed from Deleuze and Guattari: *assemblage*. Whereas intersectionality implies entity, identity, distinct subjects, assemblage is instead a collection of multiplicities, "an affective conglomeration that recognizes other contingencies of belonging . . . that might not fall so easily into . . . reactive community formations".[44]

While the *intersectional* version of identity is a *hermeneutic of positionality*, suggesting that various manifestations – gender, race, nation, age, class, religion, sexuality – can be analysed separately, the notion of *assemblage* questions identity itself; it responds to interlacing energies that mix and disperse linear notions of "time, space and body against . . . coherency . . . and permanency".[45] Intersectionality requires a fixed notion of identity, in accord with the state machinery of census, demography, racial profiling, surveillance. "Difference" is then framed into a taxonomy (or is that *taxidermy*?) – a gridlock which leaves the fixed structures of personal and collective identities unexamined. With these structures left untouched, with the constant movement of assemblages suppressed, the possibility of social change weakens. This view says that *position* comes first, then *movement*; but in fact it is the other way around.

The *Combahee River Collective*, a Black-feminist-lesbian-socialist organization active in Boston, Massachusetts, from 1974 to 1980, linked identity politics to collective liberation. They advanced a critique of both masculine forms of liberation politics *and* feminist approaches that ignored race and class. They asserted that liberation for oppressed people must be anti-capitalist and anti-imperialist.[46] One thing is an identity politics of resistance, quite another is what identity politics has become: the ideology of the neoliberal elite.[47]

"Stay romantic"

In September 2023, I attended an event on Gender, Identity, and Sexuality, part of the Focusing-PCE Symposium in Athens. It was facilitated, among others, by Anna Apergi-Konstantinidi, president of the *Greek Transgender Support Association* (GTSA), and Parvy Palmou, Gestalt practitioner and head of the *Department of Health for Trans and Intersex Families*.[48] I found the event informative, unsettling, and deeply affecting. At some point, I asked Anna whether my desire (that the struggle for transgender rights was one with the movement against all forms of oppression) was a romantic notion. She gave me a big smile. The short reply that followed moved me to tears. She said: "Stay romantic".

*

Notes

1 Frantz Fanon, *Black Skin, White Masks*, trans. Charles Lam Markmann. London: Pluto Press, 1986. Originally published in 1952.
2 See, for instance: (a) Jeremy Weate, 'Fanon, Merleau-Ponty, and the Difference of Phenomenology', in *Race*, ed. Robert Bernasconi. Oxford: Blackwell, 2001, pp. 169–183; (b) Dilan Mahendran, 'The Facticity of Blackness: A Non-conceptual Approach to the Study of Race and Racism in Fanon's and Merleau-Ponty's Phenomenology', *Human Architecture: Journal of the Sociology of Self-Knowledge*, Vol. 5, No. 3, 2007, pp. 191–203; (c) Gayle Salomon, 'The Place Where Life Hides Away: Merleau-Ponty, Fanon, and the Location of Bodily Being', *Difference: A Journal of Feminist Studies,* Vol. 17, No. 2, 2006, pp. 96–112; (d) M. Pish, 'Frantz Fanon's Critique of Maurice Merleau-Ponty's Corporeal Schema', *Suny Digital Repository, Open Access,* 2016, https://dspace.sunyconnect.suny.edu/handle/1951/67610. Retrieved 10 October 2023; (e) S. Whitney, 'Affective Intentionality and Affective Injustice: Merleau-Ponty and Fanon on the Body Schema as a Theory of Affect', *Southern Journal of Philosophy*, Vol. 56, No. 4, 2018, pp. 488–515; (f) B. Stawarska and A. Ring, 'Black Speaking Subjects: Frantz Fanon's Critique of Coloniality of Language in Merleau-Ponty's Phenomenology', *Open Editions Journal*, Vol. 45, No. 1, 2023, pp. 64–86; (g) Leswin Laubscher, Derek Hook, and Miraj U. Desai, eds., *Fanon, Phenomenology, and Psychology*. New York: Routledge, 2021.
3 Aimé Césaire, *Discourses on Colonialism*, trans. Joan Pinkham. New York: Monthly Review Press, 2001.
4 Jasbir K. Puar, *Terrorist Assemblages: Homonationalism in Queer Times*. London and Durham: Duke University Press, 2007, p. 48.
5 Frantz Fanon, *The Wretched of the Earth*. New York: Grove Press, 1963, p. 212.
6 Immanuel Wallerstein, 'Reading Fanon in the 21st Century'. *New Left Review*, No. 57, May/June 2009, https://newleftreview.org/issues/ii57/articles/immanuel-wallerstein-reading-fanon-in-the-21st-century. Retrieved 18 October 2023.
7 Caroline Elkins, *Legacy of Violence: A History of the British Empire*. London: Bodley Head, 2022.
8 Theodor Adorno, *Hegel: Three Studies*, trans S. W. Nicholsen. Cambridge, MA: MIT Press, 1993.

 9 Sandra Harding, *Sciences from below: Feminisms, Postcolonialities, and Modernities*. Durham: Duke University Press, 2008.
10 Brenda J Allen, *Difference Matters: Communicating Social Identity*. Long Grove, IL: Waveland Press, 2023.
11 William Davies, 'Stay away from Politics', *London Review of Books*, Vol. 45, No. 18, 21 September 2023, pp. 11–14.
12 Jasbir K. Puar, *Terrorist Assemblages: Homonationalism in Queer Times*. London and Durham: Duke University Press, 2007, p. 206.
13 Manu Bazzano, *Subversion and Desire: Pathways to Transindividuation*. Abingdon, OX: Routledge, 2023, p. 193.
14 Frantz Fanon, *Toward the African Revolution*, trans. Haakon Chevalier. New York: Grove Books, 1994.
15 Camille Robcis, *Disalienation: Politics, Philosophy, and Radical Psychiatry in Postwar France*. Chicago, IL: University of Chicago Press, 2021.
16 Frantz Fanon, *Black Skin, White Masks*, trans. Charles Lam Markmann. London: Pluto Press 1986. Originally published in 1952, pp. 224–225.
17 Frantz Fanon, *Black Skin, White Masks*, trans. Charles Lam Markmann. London: Pluto Press 1986. Originally published in 1952, p. 231.
18 Maurice Merleau-Ponty, *Phenomenology of Perception*. London: Routledge, 2012, p. 253.
19 Maurice Merleau Ponty, *The Primacy of Perception*. Evanston, IL: Northwestern University Press, 1964, p. 5.
20 Maurice Merleau-Ponty, *Phenomenology of Perception*. London: Routledge, 2012, p. 54
21 Jeremy Weate, 'Fanon, Merleau-Ponty, and the Difference of Phenomenology', in *Race*, ed. Robert Bernasconi. Oxford: Blackwell, 2001.
22 Adam Shatz, 'Rapping with Fanon', *New York Review of Books*, 2019, https://www.nybooks.com/online/2019/01/22/rapping-with-fanon/. Retrieved 1 November 2023.
23 Frantz Fanon, *Black Skin, White Masks*, trans. Charles Lam Markmann. London: Pluto Press 1986. Originally published in 1952, p. 110.
24 Frantz Fanon, *Black Skin, White Masks*, trans. Charles Lam Markmann. London: Pluto Press 1986. Originally published in 1952, p. 110.
25 Frantz Fanon, *Black Skin, White Masks*, trans. Charles Lam Markmann. London: Pluto Press 1986. Originally published in 1952, pp. 110–111, italics in the original.
26 Frantz Fanon, *Black Skin, White Masks*, trans. Charles Lam Markmann. London: Pluto Press 1986. Originally published in 1952, p. 111.
27 Frantz Fanon, *Black Skin, White Masks*, trans. Charles Lam Markmann. London: Pluto Press 1986. Originally published in 1952, p. 111.
28 B. Stawarska, A. Ring, 'Black Speaking Subjects: Frantz Fanon's Critique of Coloniality of Language in Merleau-Ponty's Phenomenology', *Open Editions Journal*, Vol. 45, No. 1, 2023, pp. 64–86.

29 Frantz Fanon, *Black Skin, White Masks*, trans. Charles Lam Markmann. London: Pluto Press 1986. Originally published in 1952, p. 10.
30 Gayle Salomon, 'The Place Where Life Hides Away: Merleau-Ponty, Fanon, and the Location of Bodily Being', *Difference: A Journal of Feminist Studies*, Vol. 17, No. 2, 2006, p. 96.
31 Gayle Salomon, 'The Place Where Life Hides Away: Merleau-Ponty, Fanon, and the Location of Bodily Being', *Difference: A Journal of Feminist Studies*, Vol. 17, No. 2, 2006, p. 96.
32 Frantz Fanon, *Black Skin, White Masks*, trans. Charles Lam Markmann. London: Pluto Press 1986. Originally published in 1952, p. 112.
33 Frantz Fanon, *The Wretched of the Earth*. New York: Grove Press, 1963, p. 314.
34 Frantz Fanon, *The Wretched of the Earth*. New York: Grove Press, 1963, p. 247.
35 Anibal Quijano, *Coloniality of Power, Eurocentrism and Latin America*. London and Durham: Duke University Press, 2000.
36 Frantz Fanon, *The Wretched of the Earth*. New York: Grove Press, 1963, p. 365.
37 Frantz Fanon, *The Wretched of the Earth*. New York: Grove Press, 1963, p. 365.
38 Jacqueline Rose, 'The Analyst', *New York Review of Books*, Vol. LXX, No. 14, 21 September 2023, pp. 49–51, 50.
39 Jacqueline Rose, 'The Analyst', *New York Review of Books*, Vol. LXX, No. 14, 21 September 2023.
40 Anonhi and the Johnsons, 'Scapegoat', in *My Back Was the Bridge for You to Cross*. Music album. Bloomington, IN: Secretly Canadian, 2023.
41 Mckenzie Wark, *Love and Money, Sex and Death*. London: Verso, 2023.
42 Mckenzie Wark, *Love and Money, Sex and Death*. London: Verso, 2023, pp. 95–96, italics in the original.
43 Mckenzie Wark, *Love and Money, Sex and Death*. London: Verso, 2023, p. 98, italics in the original.
44 Jasbir K. Puar, *Terrorist Assemblages: Homonationalism in Queer Times*. London and Durham: Duke University Press, 2007, p. 211.
45 Jasbir K. Puar, *Terrorist Assemblages: Homonationalism in Queer Times*. London and Durham: Duke University Press, 2007, p. 212.
46 'The Combahee River Collective Statement', 1977, https://www.blackpast.org/african-american-history/combahee-river-collective-statement-1977/. Retrieved 3 November 2023.
47 Samir Gandesha, *Identity Politics: Dialectics of Liberation or Paradox of Empowerment?* 4th Gillian Rose Memorial Lecture, Centre for Research in Modern European Philosophy, 19 October 2023, UCL.
48 Pavlos Zarogiannis (chair), 'Gender, Identity, and Sexuality as Multiplicities: Heteroglossia and Polyphony', *PCE & Focusing Symposium*, Ionic Center, Athens, 22 September 2023.

Chapter 6

On ascetic sadism

Overwhelm

I don't come across often a book as daring as Saketopoulou's *Sexuality beyond Consent*, dedicated in Greek to the author's grandmother, "the first feminist in my life".[1] It is an *untimely* book, in Nietzsche's manifold sense of the term. Unfashionable. Unsettling. Occasioning the visceral responses elicited by (rare) art and (rare) sexual encounters. Exceeding instruction. Defamiliarizing. Quickening. Drafting a portal to invigorating experience.

There was a time when I revered *Erlebnis*, the "lived experience" of phenomenologists. Until a closer look at Husserl's canonical version made me realize that it boils down to mental episodes and events whose aim is the artificial unification of internal consciousness. A sad realization. Within hermeneutics, the subject retains copyright on experience. Sat smugly in its colonial showroom, proud of trophies pilfered through package holidays into a "wild" and "natural" unconscious, sailing risky waters in its Ark, armed with the first disposable *Arché* at hand – Attachment Theory, inter-subjectivity, the symbolic order.

But experience is *experiment*. It relates to the dynamic, "enigmatic quality that extends beyond what the subject intends or aims for". It involves "an interaction with an object *outside* the self – a person, a work of art, an encounter – and the interior process it sparks".[2]

Outside is key – a move inspired by Laplanche. *Where it was, I shall be*, Freud famously declared – an ambivalent stance with the ego wearing the dual costumes of conquistador and explorer. Laplanche's edit is less ambivalent: "Where it was, *the other* shall be". I would add: "Where it was, *others* shall be": The "it" can't be reduced to the unitary *will* of Schopenhauer (an indigestible influence in Freud), nor can it be generalized as the phenomenologists' "world". The "it" is multiple. It is *multiplicity*.

DOI: 10.4324/9781003529095-7

For Laplanche, the core of psychical life is *ex*-centric, "Copernican", centrifugal, incited by the enigma (not a riddle, not a mystery) inadvertently transmitted to the infant by primary caregivers. However, the subversive potential of Laplanche's shift has yet to be realized. The psychoanalytic gaze, transfixed by Oedipus, has consistently neglected the Sphinx. Now, that would be an exciting project: constructing a psychoanalysis/psychotherapy of the Sphinx. Riffing on, augmenting, *queering* Laplanche, it would be nice to say that Saketopoulou attempts to veer our gaze towards the Sphinx, towards an unsettling endeavour, one worth pursuing because potentially transformative. But even though her investigation is refreshingly unsettling; even though, unlike the majority of psychoanalytic-psychotherapeutic theorizations, it veers dangerously, excitingly close to a terrain that is potentially transformative, we are still a long way from a psychoanalysis of the Sphinx. We are still firmly in Oedipus's domain, even though the foundations of the Freudian edifice are given a good shake up. It appears so, given Saketopoulou's view of experience as no longer something we *own*, but "something that we risk when we soften our grasp"[3] in order to secure the expected outcome. You know the drill: shreds of ephemeral life in the accountant's claws. Sample of flowing river jailed in a jar for subsequent study in the lab. The rush to equalize uncurbed instances of generosity with aesthetic/therapeutic/spiritual/material gain. The aleatory, uncertain, delicate work of analysis and therapy cramped, shrivelled, and audited to death by congregations of apparatchiks and officious busybodies at the service of conformity, the status quo, and euphoric security. Turning experience, as everything else, into another form of *hygiene* and another commodity. Libidinal double-entry book-keeping.

We all do it, of course, it would be too easy to project the lot onto the psych bureaucrats. I love you, we say for instance, but look darling, there is no way I can allow this love mess up my schedule, my project; I must keep Humpty-Dumpty propped up and dressed for business. Love is too much, and "too muchness"[4] *dis-regulates* me. I just can't do that, sweetheart. I'll be off to the library, the gym, to frantic walks around the block in the autumn drizzle. I'll grab whatever is at hand: give me mindfulness and affect-regulation. Give me exotic snorkelling in Tycoon Wharf. Give me yogic-tantric titillation and new-agey consolation on a pricey and gimmicky retreat led by Godley Didgeridoo, Grand Master of Windfart Sanctuary.

There is no other way of saying this: experience (some aesthetic and sexual experiences in particular) incites *ego-shattering*, a disruption of the ego's internal unity and a dissolution of its boundaries.[5] Saketopoulou proposes a slightly different notion: *overwhelm*, turned into a noun. Aesthetic and sexual experience operate outside the boundaries of the ego, upsetting its constitutive hubris. Overwhelm comes close to Laplanche's *detranslation*, that is, the unbinding "of the myths and ideologies through which the ego constructed itself".[6] The author likens detranslation to "pulling on a dangling thread left behind when a sweater has snagged: if one keeps going, the sweater will be reduced to mere string".[7] An apt description of analysis, from *analuein*, a term first used in the Odyssey to describe Penelope's *unravelling* the cloth she wove during the day to defer her pledge to remarry. Analysis itself as endless deferral, *entretien infini*, approaching a truth which is never unveiled, despite the hubristic endeavours of the hermeneutic tradition within which psychotherapies of all orientations are now safely entrapped.

*

Overwhelm is risky and plainly situated *outside* the terrain of affirmative consent, which is the *only* form of consent acceptable within contemporary prevailing narratives. Saketopoulou is clearly on to something. When I posted a review of her book (which this chapter builds on), I was taken aback by the spite and malice I received from trolls dressed up as moral arbiters of our profession. They insinuated that both the author and myself were inciting rape!

Saketopoulou quotes the queer writer Tim Dean who recounts an experience in a gay club when one night he decided to follow a stranger into an unlit area:

[The stranger] pushed me to my knees . . . encouraging me to work his soft cock through the mesh of his jockstrap. My mouth registered that the jockstrap was already damp. . . . When I became aware that he was gently pissing through the jock, the tasteless warm fluid flooding my lips, I spontaneously ejaculated. Both his piss and my body's response took me completely by surprise. I did not consent – and would not have consented – to being pissed on; yet I loved it. That night the man in leather cap, whose face I never saw, gave me the gift of erotic astonishment.[8]

How are we to understand this and why should we care? The author comments:

> Is his erotic astonishment, which I argue amounts to more than just physical pleasure, related to the absence of his consent? I think that it is. Of course, even intimating that a sexuality beyond consent is worth theorizing – let alone having – will raise eyebrows. Affirmative consent, we are told, is key to ethical sexual relations; it ensures that power differentials are well tended. . . . It also promises mutual sexual pleasure and a protection from trauma, not to mention legal liability. Established as the sole acceptable ethical rudder, the discourse on consent has utterly "magnetized us".[9]
>
> Today, writes the analyst Anne Dufourmantelle, "the principle of precaution has become the norm". . . . Not just the lawman but the actuary now also oversees our sexual encounters. But while the absence or violation of consent is a meaningful and important analytic for psychic and political life, affirmative consent is conceptually thin – and, to me, not very useful. In short, affirmative consent fails to deliver on its promises of mutual pleasure and safety or to adjudicate desire.

We have reached an impasse. Precaution has become the overriding concern, to the point where accountants have joined judges and lawyers in overseeing our sex life, a state of affair whose conceptual basis is affirmative consent. There is an important difference, the author maintains, between affirmative consent and what she calls *limit consent*. The former is based on Hegel's ethics of recognition and its attendant belief in "individuals with distinct centres of subjectivity who inform, negotiate, and reach agreements to minimize misunderstandings and manage expectations".[10] But, here, Saketopoulou is describing what I would call *normative consent*, the prevailing mode of consent – a travesty, in my view, of Hegel's ethics of recognition and closer to Jessica Benjamin's intersubjectivist, diluted version of Hegel, a version devoid of negation, risk, and conflict – all present in Hegel's dialectical *Anerkennung* (recognition/acknowledgement) alongside the possibility of transformation.

This bypass of Hegel – the rich potentiality found in his writings, especially in terms of master-servant dynamics that Saketopoulou relishes in her book, and their reduction to the colourless interpretations found in the intersubjectivist norm – is a serious flaw. Something similar occurs in relation to *love*, a notion the author mentions only disparagingly, when speaking of relatedness and interpersonal connection, ignoring its anarchic valence and its potential to bring about all the things the author cares about – surrender, overwhelm, the opening of new pathways, etc. Love is strangely *absent* in Saketopoulou's exploration as is understandably absent in Sade and in Pasolini's controversial version of the Marquis' *120 Days of Sodom, Salò*, a two-hour film depicting genital mutilation, psychological and physical torture, all imaginable aspects of extreme violence and torture perpetrated by a group of wealthy fascists over the bodies of nine adolescent boys and girls.

A rather naïve question comes up here: Does the fact that love has been hijacked by sentimentality and sanitized notions of nurture imply that we must ignore its tremendous transformative potential? Normative consent (what Saketopoulou calls limit consent) is of course illusory. It lures us into believing that the self and its motives can be easily grasped. But *grasping*, a notion which draws on the work of Édouard Glissant, is "neither harmless nor politically neutral".[11]

All the same, to believe that "from a psychoanalytic perspective . . . affirmative consent is revealed to be but a ruse"[12] is to inflate the scope of psychoanalysis. While it is crucial to bring to the fore Copernican, de-centred perspectives inferred but unrealized by Freud, we must also remember that these remain marginal. As with authors who utilize critiques of psychoanalysis to eventually bolster it (Adam Phillips comes to mind), Saketopoulou remains disappointingly faithful, despite her forays into uncharted waters, to the psychoanalytic matrix. She wants to bring the house down, but is protective of Freud's edifice. I am deeply ambivalent about this. Perhaps psychoanalysis (unlike, say, existential psychotherapy, whose fragile and rigid canon falls to smithereens at the first hint of critical thinking) does have greater capacity to absorb and incorporate subversions, deviations, and innovations. In reality, however, mainstream psychoanalysis and psychodynamic psychotherapy, at least in the UK, where object relations reign supreme, have nevertheless succeeded in fumigating the unconscious and biologizing human experience. Which may well be one more reason for relishing this book. Questioning normative consent is an urgent and vital task. It does not at any time entail violating professional boundaries. It does entail, however, some degree of experimentation within an alternative frame of consent – what Saketopoulou calls *limit consent*. Limit consent speaks a different language. Its starting point is that self-consciousness remains inaccessible to us. It does not recognize the subject's possessive individualism, its risible declarations of self-boundedness. It is (in a Levinasian sense) other-centred. It implies *surrender*. This is not compliance to the established role of the submissive enforced by the taxidermy of dating apps, but "surrendering to another – risking coming up against one's own and the other's opacity".[13] Does surrendering to another mean surrendering to the other's ego? I once asked the author. No, it doesn't, she replied. One surrenders to the other's (and one's own) *opacity* – a key term, borrowed from Édouard Glissant,[14] and implying, among other things, much-needed acknowledgement of our own intrinsic otherness, and of the sheer intractability of human interactions. This does not have to lead to impasse, as a hyper-rationalist approach would have it, but instead to a *poetics of relation*. Consent cannot be established by a system of determined paradigms delimiting ethical encounters and directing sexual politics. Of course, violation does exist and it is painfully real. But a different model is needed:

> Limit consent has ties to the rousing of the sexual drive and entails a nuanced negotiation of limits that belongs neither to the domain of activity nor to the sphere of passivity.[15]

Why then run the risk (by moving into the "more and more" of rising excitation, by exceeding the limit of what our body habitually accepts) of having one's own boundaries invaded? Because the more and more of experience "can produce states of overwhelm that . . . may catalyse significant psychic transformations".[16] Limit consent may also provide us with a framework for navigating the uncertainty and transformative potential of psychotherapeutic work itself.

*

We are decisively in an area of what is normally apprehended as the *perverse*, the turning about, according to late Middle English etymology, from what is right and good. Freud famously referred to sexuality as polymorphously perverse; he also ended up reframing the perverse to the area of sexual accessories, as it were. Foreplay is right and good as long as it doesn't last too long. The goal is reaching orgasm in penetrative heterosexual sex. As with his generalized theory of seduction, eventually discarded, and despite his wavering back and forth on the issue of perversion, Freud ends up bolstering the norm, a point Saketopoulou acknowledges:

> The terms "developmental theory" and "developmental stages" are, of course, psychoanalytic jargon for normalization: by telling us how things are expected to evolve, they direct the analyst's clinical attention to where intervention is needed.[17]

What would it mean to seriously entertain the notion that the polymorphous perverse is the *foundation* of sexuality rather than a picturesque adjunct? It would turn the tables of contemporary psychotherapeutic discourse. It would mean no longer demanding that the perverse explain itself. The liberal consensus on these matters is to avoid pathologization at all costs by emphasizing, for instance, that BDSM is fine, as long as enacted within the confines of an intimate normative relationship. It would appear that dominant culture (and dominant psychoanalytic/psychotherapeutic culture) is still in the grip of Kraft-Ebing's *Pathologia Sexualis*. The author shows us a way out: "masochism, sadism, exhibitionism, and voyeurism are *endemic* to the sexual rather than being the defensively sexualized debris of trauma or overstimulation".[18] It is not about kicks, nor is it about annexing the perverse within the structure of our identity so as to tame its subversiveness. Unlike more normative models, which rely on an economy of discharge of tension, what characterizes the perverse dimension, Saketopoulou argues, is continuous increase. She unconvincingly links increase to Bataille's *dépense* or expenditure which is the very opposite of increase – the shedding of the ego-self's desire for "more": relinquishment, the *lama sabachthani* that ends pleasure and ushers in impersonal desire.

*

Crudely put, the death drive is for Laplanche the undercover sex drive. Bataille reverses the equation: eros is in the end a deadly pursuit – especially when viewed from the vantage point of the ego. Saketopoulou flirts with Bataille's incandescent writing, trying to bend it to a psychoanalytic frame. But this is a tricky proposition. *I throw myself into the night dressed in white sunlight*, Bataille says unequivocally. He remains sovereignly remote to the Northern sensibilities which regaled us with psychoanalysis and psychotherapy, endeavours inevitably bent on the very opposite of expenditure, namely self-improvement. *I am not me but the desert, the night*, Bataille would insist. Nothingness, and without having known or acquired anything, dreams entering me so that I no longer know but these tears. At the heart of Bataille is the cry of *lamma sabachtani*. And only those who are open to *passibility* – the active capacity to be affected, as opposed to mere passivity – may (or may not) be gifted with a momentary, ultimately risible illumination. The freedom of the destituted subject. Call it abjection if you must.

Can Northern, protestant sensibilities, forever bent on self-improvement, understand these rich derailments of the soul? Can the Presbyterian art of psychoanalysis approach Bataille and Masoch without exploding? Or will the centripetal move of the psyche commodify excess? Air-conditioned torture gardens for the bored middle-classes. Accommodating perversion to an unchallenged chis-het neoliberal universe of commodities.

Bataille is routinely shunned or viewed as a mere provocateur, his most popular book in the UK still being the 1928 novella *Story of the Eye*.[19] Can one harness sexual vertigo into the thoroughly bourgeois frame of psychoanalysis? The outcome would be ambivalent at best: a reframing (I nearly wrote *exploding*) of the psychoanalytic foundations. A consolidation (despite the tears of eros) of the psychoanalytic frame, bent and stretched so as to bear witness to the struggles and joys of limit experiences. Historical backdrop: the elective perversions, introversions, and subversions of queer twenty-first-century New York, one generation away from Candy Darling and Marsha P. Johnson, and a long way from the moneyed bourgeois discontents in Freud's Viennese clinic a 100 years before. Incidentally, a heterosexual man writing what Saketopoulou writes (unthinkable, given the polarization of contemporary cultural-political discourse) would be summarily hanged, drawn, and quartered.

The dilemma with a tradition is whether to dissipate it, dilute it, explode it, or renew it by making it pliable to the winds of change. And when the winds are hurricanes, when we deal with vertiginously visible tectonic shifts, it is worth the gamble. Proximity to the threshold flooding the subject with the blinding light from the abyss (far more terrifying and seductive than a *dark* abyss), opening new pathways, leading to transformation: is not precisely this that the "work" is all about, transformation? This is where psychoanalysis and psychotherapy's potential lies in spite of everything. To be groundbreaking, i.e., en route to *groundlessness*. Nietzsche is the unspoken inspiration in Bataille's work (far more important than Sade). Summoning Nietzsche would imply rapture from Sade's pedantic Enlightenment ideology. It would insert levity. It would spell out in no uncertain terms that the focus of analysis is no longer the human subject but what traverses the human.

Limitations of Saketopoulou's aesthetic/ascetic sadism

Central to Saketopoulou's thesis is the stimulating but ultimately unpersuasive formulation of *exigent sadism*, a practice deemed necessary in her view, given that the ego will not consent nor "relinquish its stabilizing investments willingly" which is why "aesthetics and eroticism (perversity in particular) can be such powerful nursemaids for the psychic and political transformations that the ego's rupture can enable – and endure".[20] The author presents an extensive chronology of the varied responses to Sade's writings, registering the embracing of Sadean writings and the turn of the tide against it. A second, different perspective on Sade is promised to the reader (alongside the one that writes him off as a hyper-rationalist excrescence of Enlightenment ideas eventually finding their vent in fascism and Nazism) but not delivered. This is disappointing, given that Sade matters in sadism. Unless the aesthetic offshoots offered in the book provide us with the answers. But these are not at all convincing. The jury is out, for instance, whether Liliana Cavani's 1974 film *Il Portiere di Notte* (*The Night Porter*) is a groundbreaking work offering insights into the more intricate aspects of erotic relationships or whether it is a titillating depiction of chic decadence and an example of Nazi sexploitation whose cultural offshoots are both banal and dubious, from Madonna's *Justify my Love*, to Lady Gaga's, Siouxsie's, and Marilyn Manson's stylistic choices. The film charts the rekindling of a sadomasochistic affair between Max, an ex SS officer, and Lucia, an ex-inmate, both meeting after a decade in a Vienna hotel where the officer works as night porter and Lucia is a distinguished guest.

Similarly, the jury is out in relation to another work championed by Saketopoulou, *Slave Play*.[21] I have briefly discussed this work in a deliberately oblique fashion in Chapter 1 and will not say more here, other than pointing out, as a colleague put it to me, that it is only a matter of time until discussing *Slave Play* will become *de rigueur* in neoliberal colleges and universities, providing new staple for a host of formulaic doctoral dissertations and boring but oh so edgy PowerPoint presentations. Nothing wrong with that, right? Every transgressive work of art becomes eventually gobbled up by the neoliberal machine. As with *The Night Porter*, however, the question remains whether genuinely unsettling depictions of erotic experience can be painlessly absorbed in the wider culture without more than an element of titillation and exploitation. And whether they would eventually become as palatable to the mainstream if they had the core ingredient that makes erotic encounters rise up an octave: relinquishment. Relinquishment does not seem to attract the punters, unless it is debased into the sentimentality of redemptive tales (cue the violins). What becomes eventually co-opted in popular culture is yet another form of acquisitive cultural artefact, one that confirms the ego's idiotic forays into "experience" – the more edgy and "transgressive" the better. No one does transgression more than the assorted number of fascistic, idiotic people in power the world over at present. The question then becomes: How can we *elevate* (yes, that's right) pleasure to the level of desire, an affective force whose unknown trajectory appears to expand towards societal/political emancipation and the vast field of spiritual immanence? How can we begin to approach, in other words, the domain of *transindividuation* and move away at last from the shiny fakery of false experience?

Saketopoulou's reading of Sade, the very source for sadism, is aligned with a long line of writers who uphold the idea that he has been for too long wrongly associated with fascistic drives. Like the Surrealists and others in the first half of the twentieth century, she is keen to bring out the liberating potential in the writings of the Marquis. I imagine, perhaps wrongly, that she would agree with the venomous response Pasolini's last film *Salò*, an adaptation of Sade's *the 120 Days of Sodom*, received when it came out in 1975. Now that's an example of a work of art (which came out a year after Cavani's film and dealt with a similar subject matter) whose genuine transgressive nature will *never* be co-opted. It is easy to imagine *Slave Play* and *The Night Porter* becoming part of the mainstream imaginary. Neither of them carries the menace of Lautrèamont's *Songs of Maldoror* (or, it must be said, the aesthetic heights of a reversed sublime or the labyrinthine fecundity of any of Artaud's writings). *Slave Play* and *The Night Porter* lend themselves to titillation and sanitation. Impossible to do the same with Lautrèamont, Artaud, or with Pasolini's *Salò*.

Neither *Slave Play* nor *The Night Porter* is remotely close to the dizzy heights of avant-garde art for which I have a dedicated if wayward (and, some would say, elitist) predilection. But even avant-garde art can assist the dodgiest endeavours. There really is no pristine art, transgressive or not, within or without the scope of modernism, that is not firmly ensconced within the clutches of neoliberal ideology, and that includes both "high" and "low" art. In her recently published 1979 lectures on the Frankfurt School, Gillian Rose comes to the conclusion, after Adorno, that "the modernist position is as inherently self-defeating, and is as full of contradictions, as any popular music or art".[22]

One aspect of Blanchot's *limit experience*, an important notion apprecia-tively quoted by Saketopoulou, and to which Pasolini's last movie appeals to (Blanchot is cited throughout the film) is horror, the true transgression implied in violence, the (Dionysian) dissolution of boundaries. The other aspect is relinquishment.

Compelling, often difficult to watch, and surprisingly lyrical at the end, *Salò* equated in plain terms Sade with fascistic cruelty. Where Saketopou-lou's argument works a treat is when she contrasts sadism with its defanged incarnation, that is, the mimetic or sensible sadism found in BDSM sce-narios, wedded to the sentimentality of AT ideology. Eventually, however, her version ends up formulating a kind of *aesthetic sadism*, one that flirts with danger, comes close enough to the fire so as one can write a book, a play, or paint a picture. I'm all for it. It reminds me of Nietzsche's own self-styled methodology for his magnificently monstrous creative output. But I do find the formulation problematic. As an aesthetic example of exi-gent sadism, the author presents Jeremy O. Harris's *Slave Play*. I would invite the reader to watch *Slave Play* and *Salò* and then decide which of the two is defanged, which of the two will be banned from polite conversa-tions, and which will provide material for cool dinner talk for a whole new generation of exigent sadism-savvy psychotherapy trainees. I also remain unconvinced by the assertion that exigent sadism may foster "the other's self-sovereignty" and create a space of "immense vulnerability"[23] for those exigent sadists out there, bravely putting themselves on the line, or that exposure to similar scenarios may open up new pathways. The same could be said for *designer kidnapping*, popular among New Yorkers who pay good money to get kidnapped, bound, and gagged for hours or days so as to acquire a new experience.[24] One does not expect this trend becoming popu-lar anytime soon among Palestinians in Gaza or people who are regularly subjected to oppression and constantly exposed to war, climate disaster, and famine. Designer kidnap, participants say, is all about stepping out of one-self. How different is the thrill of the unknown experienced by rich, bored people from the opening of new pathways available to exigent sadists?

There seems to be another aspect of exigent sadism that I would call *ascetic*: the promotion of a stern, forbidding attitude towards the ego-self and its limitations, a declaration of war, the forcing of oneself on one's own ego, be it for the purpose of opening new pathways or for greater development. This stance is familiar to those among us who have pursued some kind of spiritual path. The context is of course different, but there are striking similarities: an unforgiving attitude towards the fears, anxieties, and vulnerabilities of the ego-self, a stance that suggests the presence of the super-ego at work – this time no longer in obvious garb as judge and jury, as propagandist of harsh criticisms and prohibitions, but showing up in seductive mode instead, either idealistically pursuing "enlightenment" or hungry for orgiastic *jouissance*.

I support the notion of a psychoanalysis with fangs, better equipped at addressing justice. What is unclear is how to decouple our hunger for justice from *ressentiment*, a dilemma for which one would need to bring in Nietzsche. I am far from dismissing Sade altogether. Where his writings are valuable are in their ability to say everything, bringing in and stretching free association to its ultimate consequences. Not to be confused with the contemporary fetish of authenticity, Sade's violence is above all *the violence of a speech without equivocation*. This is a far more interesting avenue to explore for those who care about the ideas of the good old Marquis, I believe. In which case one would need to leave behind, I suspect, those suburban air-conditioned middle-class little dungeons with their cute pantomimes of cruelty, submission, and surrender before joining quiz night at the pub down the road.

Traumatophilia

Saketopoulou's critique of current trauma culture is vital. What would it mean to adopt a more *welcoming* attitude to trauma? Are there alternatives to *traumatophobia*, the dominant view that imagines trauma as inert and unchanging? Can trauma be allowed to move and circulate? Could it be that trauma is decisive in the constitution of the self and potentially transformative? There is a name for this groundbreaking stance: *traumatophilia*. A necessary move, when one considers that trauma which is not "inserted into circulation does not wither and disappear: it stalls and it controls us".[25] We cannot turn away from traumata and need to recognize our being drawn to them. They can be neither healed nor cancelled, a recognition that is deeply counterintuitive in a psych world dominated by the illusion peddled by the lucrative trauma industry and its gurus, which says that trauma can be resolved. This idea has to be relinquished so that new pathways can open up. Promising to heal trauma on one level simply means rewriting the experience within the norm and the social order; it means "turning the consulting room into a Procrustean bed of normative adaptation", Saketopoulou says, adding:

> I would say that trauma is never cured and that no one has ever been delivered back to an intact, pretraumatic state, no matter how motivated they are or how good their access to care or their resources. This is a statement that many clinicians would agree with in theory. But when the rubber hits the road, that is, when we sit with patients who need help, many of us, just like many of our patients, get caught in the quicksand of imagining that psychoanalysis or therapy can restore mental health, that it can help repair and, in some way, undo wounds.[26]

This notion is prevalent in the wider culture, sustained by a *politics of injury* which claims to heal societal and political wounds while at the same time cataloguing entire communities on the basis of their wounds alone, rather than being attentive to their desires and aspirations.

Our job as psychotherapist is not to heal. We must resist the Hippocratic and societal injunction to repair; we must reject the notion that anyone can be restored to the imagined alcyon days of innocence before trauma or to a pleasant resolution towards a perfect future. The job of psychotherapy is weightier than that, namely, establishing a freer rapport between the ego and the unconscious, one implication of which is a freer relationship between self and others. We need to be ready for the unforeseen, for astonishment, and paradox. Then our life and practice become an adventure.

Notes

1 Avgi Saketopoulou, *Sexuality beyond Consent: Risk, Race, Traumatophilia.* State University of New York Press, 2023, p. 3.
2 Avgi Saketopoulou, *Sexuality beyond Consent: Risk, Race, Traumatophilia.* State University of New York Press, 2023, p. 14, emphasis added.
3 Avgi Saketopoulou, *Sexuality beyond Consent: Risk, Race, Traumatophilia.* State University of New York Press, 2023, p. 37.

4 Jessica Benjamin and Galis Atlas, 'The "Too Muchness" of Excitement: Sexuality in Light of Excess, Attachment and Affect Regulation', *International Journal of Psychoanalysis*, Vol. 96, 2015, pp. 39–63.

5 Leo Bersani and Adam Phillips, *Intimacies*. Chicago, IL: University of Chicago Press, 2008.

6 Jean Laplanche, *The Unfinished Copernican Revolution: Selected Works, 1967–1992*. New York: Unconscious in Translation, 1989, p. 198.

7 Avgi Saketopoulou, *Sexuality beyond Consent: Risk, Race, Traumatophilia*. State University of New York Press, 2023, p. 46.

8 Avgi Saketopoulou, *Sexuality beyond Consent: Risk, Race, Traumatophilia*. State University of New York Press, 2023, pp. 95–96.

9 Avgi Saketopoulou, *Sexuality beyond Consent: Risk, Race, Traumatophilia*. State University of New York Press, 2023, p. 96.

10 Avgi Saketopoulou, *Sexuality beyond Consent: Risk, Race, Traumatophilia*. State University of New York Press, 2023, p. 63.

11 Édouard Glissant, *Poetics of Relation*. Ann Arbor: University of Michigan Press, 1995.

12 Avgi Saketopoulou, *Sexuality beyond Consent: Risk, Race, Traumatophilia*. State University of New York Press, 2023, p. 63.

13 Avgi Saketopoulou, *Sexuality beyond Consent: Risk, Race, Traumatophilia*. State University of New York Press, 2023, p. 64.

14 Édouard Glissant, *Poetics of Relation*. Ann Arbor: University of Michigan Press, 1995.

15 Avgi Saketopoulou, *Sexuality beyond Consent: Risk, Race, Traumatophilia*. State University of New York Press, 2023, p. 3.

16 Avgi Saketopoulou, *Sexuality beyond Consent: Risk, Race, Traumatophilia*. State University of New York Press, 2023, p. 69.

17 Avgi Saketopoulou, *Sexuality beyond Consent: Risk, Race, Traumatophilia*. State University of New York Press, 2023, p. 33.

18 Avgi Saketopoulou, *Sexuality beyond Consent: Risk, Race, Traumatophilia*. State University of New York Press, 2023, p. 69, emphasis added.

19 Georges Bataille, *Story of the Eye*. New York: Urizen Books, 1977.

20 Avgi Saketopoulou, *Sexuality beyond Consent: Risk, Race, Traumatophilia*. State University of New York Press, 2023, p. 10; Jeremy O. Harris, *Slave Play*. Noel Coward Theatre, https://www.noelcowardtheatre.co.uk/whats-on/slave-play.

21 Avgi Saketopoulou, *Sexuality beyond Consent: Risk, Race, Traumatophilia*. State University of New York Press, 2023, p. 174.

22 Gillian Rose, *Marxist Modernism: Introductory Lectures on Frankfurt School Critical Theory*. London: Verso, 2024.
    See for instance Crissa-Jean Chapelle, 'Designer Kidnapping', *The Morning News*, https://themorningnews.org/article/designer-kidnappings. Retrieved 26 December 2024.

23 Avgi Saketopoulou, *Sexuality beyond Consent: Risk, Race, Traumatophilia*. State University of New York Press, 2023, p. 2.

24 Avgi Saketopoulou, *Sexuality beyond Consent: Risk, Race, Traumatophilia*. State University of New York Press, 2023, pp. 133.
25 Manu Bazzano, 'The Trauma Club', in *Subversion and Desire: Pathways to Transindividuation*. Abingdon, OX: Routledge, pp. 179–184.
26 Avgi Saketopoulou, *Sexuality beyond Consent: Risk, Race, Traumatophilia*. State University of New York Press, 2023, p. 133.

Chapter 7

In praise of pandemonium

Dialogue variations

A couple of years ago, I was invited to participate in a public dialogue with an esteemed colleague, and gladly accepted the invitation. The organizers suggested that I choose a topic of conversation and then prepare a relevant clinical vignette. I wrongly assumed the same request would be made to my interlocutor. The day came, and, after a brief introduction by the host, the other therapist proceeded to interview me. At first, I didn't realize what was happening, his questions being so engaging, his interest in my work seemingly so sincere. For a good 10 minutes, I went along. Then, as his questions became more searching, I began to feel that he was effectively asking me to give an account of myself and my practice. I interrupted him and asked: "Are we going to have a dialogue? Are we going to discuss the topic? Or is this some kind of cross-examination? I can talk about myself until the cows come home, but participants have paid good money to witness, and hopefully partake in a dialogue, not to hear me being interviewed."

The conversation took on a slightly different turn but never approximated the semblance of dialogue. Besides, I could no longer shake the feeling, confirmed later by some colleagues present at the event, that instead of an invite to a conversation, I had been granted an audience with the distinguished professor. Some colleagues were shocked and referred to it in no uncertain terms: it was a trap, they said, a set-up. For me, it was a missed opportunity; I had engaged with, and respectfully critiqued, my colleague's writings. I had looked forward to a fruitful meeting between equals, but right there was my mistake, to consider myself as equal. My later suggestion to both host and professor to have a slightly different format for a similar future event, with each of us presenting a short vignette and then discuss it together, was graciously dismissed.

DOI: 10.4324/9781003529095-8

Whichever interpretation one may give to the above scene, I found it to be a good example of Socratic dialogue, a popular model and trope in many sectors of psychotherapy theory and practice, and one that I am keen to discuss here. But let's proceed one step at a time.

According to Mikhail Bakhtin, a necessary feature of dialogue is *anacrisis*, a Greek term he exhumed from the New Testament and which may be described as the prompting of speech by the means of speech. In the dialogical tradition, this has been understood as setting up a series of strategies so as to bring out, elicit, "lead out" (*e-ducere* in Latin, from which "to educate" derives) the other person's speech. This is a form of maieutic, with its main exponent, Socrates, referred to as a midwife. Incidentally, the belief underlying this mode of engagement is that learning emerges not from the encounter with otherness but instead through *anamnesis*, that is, remembering a universally accepted truth that the soul deep down knows but has forgotten. As with the exchange with the professor described earlier, this scenario does not require the presence of an equal other but depends on the expert philosophical midwife whose task is to unveil the forgotten truth. Given that Socrates is "high master, of subtle, ironic anacrisis",[1] it is easy to bypass the fact that at the heart of this mode of dialogue is *coercion*. You *must* speak, and if you are disinclined to do so, the self-proclaimed bearer of truth will make you do so. Unless, that is, you simply refuse to play the dialogical game on his terms.

As Aaron Fogel points out, there is, apart from Socrates, at least one more notable model of anacrisis, overlooked by Bakhtin: Oedipus. Here, instead of Socrates's cunning tactics, we find pure coercion. Dictionaries too remind us that anacrisis often refers to "extreme physical torture".[2] It indicates "an investigation of truth in a civil law case in which the interrogation and inquiry are often accompanied by torture"[3] – at variance with the non-violent pressure to speak favoured in Bakhtin's reading. The etymology implies a preliminary (*ana*) investigation prior to the *crisis* of the trial. "Bakhtin's sublimation . . . of the term anacrisis into Socratic non-violence – Fogel comments – is curious, since he is otherwise not usually finicky about physical life, the body, or violence".[4] Bakhtin may be blocking the correlation between the pressure to talk and Oedipus, who bullies others into speaking by using both verbal cunning and intimidation. Right here we find the origins of Socratic dialogue, Fogel compellingly suggests, and it would be naïve to forget that Socrates's humour and cleverness (and the professor's in the above account) are steeped in faux denial of coercion.

One would be both naïve and complicit to forget the ever-present, shifting imbalance of power within an uncertain and indeterminable field of encounter. This perspective may sound unappealing to sensibilities steeped in the well-meaning principles of liberalism (in politics) and intersubjectivity (in psychotherapy), but it may be useful in providing a sobering antidote to the sentimentality that characterizes current thought on dialogue. For all our efforts to exude empathic attunement; for all the fluffy lingo of openness to experience displayed by various psychotherapy and counselling associations, the therapeutic space remains a contractual obligation where, as in a Conrad novel, two or more people are expected to produce words and respond to those words, and where both parties are monitored, inspected, and punished – the client for not "getting on with the program" and the therapist for making a *faux pas*. For the sake of the argument, allow me to slightly exaggerate: could it be that therapy is at heart a forced relation supervised by corporate bodies whose aims are financial gain, their own preservation, and the preservation of the status quo?

What would it mean to reaccredit dialogue, including psychotherapeutic dialogue, to its Oedipal origins? What would it mean to seriously consider a return to the consciousness of Oedipus, the first, startled inquisitor whose questioning tragically turns against himself? Could we tolerate a situation where instead of occupying the "interviewer's seat", the tables are turned, where those who elicit speech become ourselves vulnerable to danger and vengeance? Fogel's contention, following closely the work of novelist Joseph Conrad, is that we have neglected this particular dialogical mode because of our preoccupation with more ideal conceptions of dialogue. Psychotherapy in particular is stuck, I would argue, in *dialogical idealism* – from Buber to Gadamer, from Habermas to Rorty. It is mired in the fantasy of horizontal conversations between equals sanctified by the faith in *Logos*. This traditional stance – the only stance allowed it seems – is oblivious to the critique of logocentrism launched by a counter-tradition that goes from Jonathan Swift and Lewis Carroll to Derrida and Levinas. The reason why dialogical idealism is so stubbornly dominant is that it constitutes a model of social order.

Some may argue that reframing dialogue from Oedipus's perspective would be akin to framing human encounter in cut-throat terms. In which case, it may at the very least provide an antidote to the fantasy of the free encounter, out of which truth is alleged to blossom like flowers in spring. Others may argue that it would overburden an allegedly uncomplicated pedagogical dialogue. In which case, it may prove useful in highlighting the perils and pleasures of unconscious communication. The difficult balance here is between a stance that is neither detached nor soppy, one that chooses to refrain from the stale scripts of both blank canvas and unconditional regard. As it often happens (and for reasons I don't claim to understand), the ideal of unfettered conversation routinely embraced and promoted in philosophy, theology, and psychology carries less weight in the arts and the theatre. Here the classical, "tragic" view is, to some degree, still upheld. Is it too credulous of me to want psychotherapy to be an art? Is the aspiration untimely, to want a psychotherapy in a tragic key, a "dramatic" art that can welcome the classical vision? It may be convincingly objected, as I myself would have done not long ago, that the Oedipal "model" is worn out, that it no longer yields the inspiration it might have done time ago. But I confess to having an agenda here. Oedipus's essentially *secular* Logos is, I believe, a necessary passage for acquiring a glimpse of what truly matters in psychotherapeutic investigation: the encounter with the Sphinx. Perhaps all we can do is mimic Oedipus's verbal cunning in providing the answer to the potentially lethal *koan* posed by the oracle. But the investigation must at the very least recall the embodied sense of facing the Sphinx. Whether associative or analytical, linear or nonlinear, the therapeutic Logos cannot afford to forget its link to the vastness and ambivalence of the psyche, lest it turns psychical exploration into a positivist endeavour. This may be similar, incidentally, to renouncing to forget that the principles agreed upon by Athena and the Eumenides at the dawn of the *agora* mustn't allow us to forget the origins of the legal code: the Furies.

Central to our investigation is an important characteristic that is often left out of dialogical approaches, namely the *multiplicity of styles and perspectives*, with no stylistic or psychical unity. What is often overlooked is the fact that at first, Socratic dialogue was part of a differential, lighter mode of encounter and expression, in many ways similar to the memoir genre, punctuated as it was by Plato's recollections of conversations. Even though dialogism is considerably weakened from polyvalence, Socratic dialogue appeared to be genuine investigation of the truth, rather than rhetorical articulation of its possession and/or mere confutation of naïve self-assurance by those who think they know. Sadly, dialogue itself underwent a process of deterioration – towards what Bakhtin calls *monologism*, in many ways similar to the master-signifier in Lacan and to the notion of arborescence in Deleuze. Capitalism is a form of monologism insofar as it only values one thing only: profit. Our tears and laughter, our joys and sorrows, our desires-deliriums, our fear of sickness, old age, and death are mere "noise", in the information-theory sense – mere interferences in the workings of the capitalist machine. Similarly, the perspective of the nation-state is monological, with its walls, fences, checkpoints to increase border security and keep away migrants. The perspective of the police is monological, its power built on coercion and protection of privilege. A belief in the alleged purity of person-centred theory and practice – whether through insistence on "non-directivity", on a narrow understanding of congruence, or on the comforting belief in the existence of a "formative tendency" in the cosmos – is another example of monologism in action. A literal belief in a static, codifiable entity called the unconscious is yet another. Viewing a past traumatic event – in the therapy room as in the plots of movies, novels, and plays – as the "key" to understanding a person's rich tangle of struggles, dreams, and desires by reducing everything to early abuse and hypothetical biochemical modifications is another very popular example of monologism. Vicarious trauma, one of the unassailable tenets of many counselling and psychotherapy training courses, is another example of monologism.

Within the monologist view, other voices – whether in the societal or intrapsychic sphere – are not acknowledged but merely considered as objects to be either assimilated or discarded.

Alternatives to monologism – multiplicity, difference, even dialogism cleansed of its neoliberal incrustations – are not forms of postmodern assault to meaning and truth. Far from it. For Fredric Jameson (hardly a postmodernist), it is crucial that we pay attention to the multiple narratives woven within any particular culture and tradition, while trying to understand what makes one narrative more effective (if not necessarily more truthful) than others. The potential answer is *allegory*.[5] The best story is the one that is both acquainted with, and inclusive of, "other stories, other histories".[6]

In literature, we find a dazzling example of multiplicity and difference – of *polyphony* – in Dostoevsky's novels. There is, Bakhtin informs us, "profound organicism, consistency, and unity in Dostoevsky's poetics" even though his world "may appear to be chaotic".[7]

For Bakhtin, a primary example of polyphony was Dostoevsky's prose, "a plurality of independent and unmerged voices and consciousnesses, a genuine polyphony of fully valid voices".[8] He believed that truth does *not* pre-exist collective interaction (whether as a logico-analytical process or as a self-existing "entity") but emerges from encounter, in the process of collective dialogue. So far so predictable; but the implication of Bakhtin "dialogism" is that *difference and separateness cannot be transcended but are present simultaneously as an assembly of disparate meanings*.

The novelty of Dostoevsky's fiction consists in demolishing the traditional forms of the European novel – their monological, ideological, homophonic focus – by freeing up and upholding a genuine polyphony, or the multiplicity of autonomous voices, a plurality which implies and includes the freedom of people to stand beside, disagree, and rebel against their creator (the author). Not a "multitude of characters and fates" portraited within a unified world but instead the "plurality of equal consciousnesses"[9] whose unity comes together, thanks to the unfolding of a given *event* rather having to acquiesce to what Bakhtin calls a "plot-pragmatic interpretation".[10]

In upholding this position, Bakhtin is favourably critical of the Russian literary critic Leonid Grossman who, unlike Bakhtin, found the "destruction of the organic unity of material required by the conventional canon"[11] thoroughly deconstructed by Dostoevsky. Grossman's position is intriguing because it appears to support more strongly a polyphonic stance. For Grossman, Dostoevsky's later novels are akin to the *mystery play*, a form that is genuinely multilayered and polyphonic.

Mystery plays (a form of drama during the Middle Ages dealing with biblical themes) make use of the *vernacular*, a mode of expression that brings in digressions, invented/satirical sections whose targets were priests, soldiers, judges, and doctors. This has been traditionally interpreted as a deterioration of religiosity. It could also be perceived as refreshingly destabilizing and polyphonic. Polyphony destabilizes religion in the same way it destabilizes psychotherapy orientations – including psychotherapeutic approaches that, like religion, rely on a monological narrative. What would it look like, I wonder, if we were to graft a rhizome of polyphonic shoots into the sturdy trees of, say, person-centred therapy, focusing, psychoanalytic psychotherapy, and other modalities? Would vernacular, subversive, polyphonic expressions of these approaches be welcome, fostered, and promoted in therapy trainings? Or would they follow instead the fate of mystery plays: discarded and ignored by the church and by Renaissance scholars alike? My own personal experience suggests the latter. Most therapeutic trainings rely on a handful of tenets preserved in aspic.

The etymology of the word *vernacular* suggests another meaning that goes well beyond a performative act of subversion. *Verna* in Latin was the word used in the Roman household for the slave and house-servant.

By implication, the vernacular is the language used by subalterns, the language of what would nowadays be referred to as street slang, folklore, dialect – language as "collective experience, a symbol of identity, a dialect maintained by common experience".[12] Polyphonic language is then the language of those with no status, as well as those who don't *want* any status, those we call in the Zen traditions *persons of no status*. It is also the language of Black culture, of Black slang. The vernacular may at times be the language of hipsterism, but it may also be the language of sadness.[13] "As disarming as black slang [is], beneath the charm of the mode of speech lay unhappiness"[14]

There is a big difference between the conventional dialogical form, dear to mainstream culture, of relating a narrative within a monological unified worldview material and a dialogical form that is forever uncertain and unresolved. Polyphony is the very opposite of bigotry and conventional dialogism, the latter being a mode that approximates bigotry, albeit in polite garb. We see polyphony at work in Shakespeare. Reflecting on Shakespeare's work, Nietzsche wrote:

> The great poet draws *only* from his own reality – up to the point where afterward he cannot endure his work any longer. When I have looked into my *Zarathustra*, I walk up and down in my room for half an hour, unable to master an unbearable fit of sobbing. I know no more heart-rending reading than Shakespeare: what must a man have suffered to have such a need of being a buffoon! Is Hamlet *understood*? Not doubt, (but) *certainty* is what drives one insane – But one must be profound, an abyss, a philosopher to feel that way. – We are all *afraid* of truth.[15]

Both Shakespeare and Dostoevsky lived in times of enormous change, unprecedented conflicts, and crumbling social structures – a world in flux that is hard to imagine in our current neoliberal or *necro*liberal times, characterized as they are by a superficial endorsement of pluralism and difference and by the near impossibility for anything remotely resembling polyphony to emerge.

To be clear, polyphony is not mere pluralism, that catchword of woolly liberalism, least of all is polyphony that populist aberration, pluralist therapy, one of the latest products on the market, the celebration of the so-called "multiple choices" available to the patient/client-as-consumer. Polyphony, according to Bakhtin, is discovered under particular conditions. What are these conditions? In Dostoevsky, the coming together of concrete societal and historical conditions paired with the writer's bio-social uniqueness – in his particular case epilepsy as well as profound, fertile ideological contradictions. For polyphony to emerge, a "conjuncture" is needed, to borrow Stuart Hall's term,[16] an uncertain situation pregnant with transformative potential *and* the danger of *catastrophe* – a situation that, in Goldstein's terms, would be deemed pathological. A historical conjuncture cannot be manufactured, but there are at times *openings* in individual and collective history. They open up the possibility of radical transformation. Polyphony, Bakhtin implies, may be at times accessed by an organism skirting the edges of unitary consciousness. In short, *polyphony is accessed in moments of crisis and danger*, at historical junctions of upheaval and revolution, and in moments of danger and crisis in a person's existence. Danger and crisis may refer to illness, bereavement, separation. But they also relate to falling in love, gaining new insights, responding courageously to life's bidding to change the rules of the game one usually plays. Danger, Guattari would say, *reterritorializes* subjectivity; it prompts us to move within *lines of flight*, possible new connections fashioned against fixed formations, initiating both disruption and connection in an ongoing transformative process.[17]

The above scenario is wholly different from the conventional set-up of so-called "dialogue". The latter gradually morphs, in Bakhtin's account, from an already frail dialogism into the full-blown pedagogical monologism of the teacher, the ready-made incarnation of the "already-discovered, ready-made, indisputable truths", finally degenerating into *catechism* (etymologically, to "sound down", to instruct) or into the cosy, familiar "question-and-answer form of training neophytes".[18] These so-called "learning environments" do not foster thought but conformism and stale recitation of arbitrary canons. For thought to become generative, something wholly different is needed. Thought needs to be *dialogized*, a Bakhtinian term intriguingly close to *ventriloquizing* – *engastrimythía* in Greek, a speech (*loqui*) from the belly (*venter*) in Latin. This practice eventually became entertainment, but its origins are closely allied to necromancy. To dialogize is, to some extent, to ventriloquize.

Dialogue/ventriloquy emerges, in Bakhtinian terms, by weaving together *anacrisis* (*the prompting of speech by the means of speech*, a term which in ancient Greek courts described the examination of the parties involved in a lawsuit) with *syncrisis* (the comparison of several viewpoints which then move towards a measure of fairly conclusive veracity). Bakhtin makes the case for dialogizing in ways that rely on the ability of reason to find a form of synthesis. This is a decisive step forward: truth is the outcome of polyphonic dialogue, not a pre-existing object in possession of the expert. There are, however, some valid objections to this position which make the route to dialogizing and ventriloquizing a little less smooth.

A historical precedent: ventriloquists, as the etymology suggests, were necromancers – they could speak *to* the dead as well as speak *as* the dead. They were hounded by Christians in the Middle Ages, who considered their practice a form of witchcraft punishable with death – oblique acknowledgement, in its brutal bigotry, of ventriloquy's *pan-daimonic* multiplicity, a threat to the monologism of Christianity and of any religious or secular, state-sponsored, coercive belief system.

Uncomfortable as this may sound to some there is an inherently daimonic[19] or even *demonic* quality to Bakhtinian dialogism, coming to the fore in the second, 1929 edition of his study on Dostoevsky, which did not escape the attention of Dostoevskian scholar Natalia Bonètskaia, whose commentary, documented by Caryl Emerson, casts a different light on dialogism and polyphony, away from the ideology of bland pluralism and blanket relatedness popular in psychotherapy culture. There is at least one good thing about this demonic quality: its *unfinalizibility*, which in itself constitutes an antidote to dogmatism. For Bonetskaia, Bakhtin's second edition moves away from the mawkish assumptions of mutuality presiding over the original version.[20] While dialogue is present in the guise of "personality, reason, freedom, the realm of meanings, the light of consciousness and perhaps of Logos", its carnivalesque, serio-comical, even Dionysian origins, as well as its allegiance to the Menippean satire, introduce something darker, ambivalent, and complex, including what Bonetskaia calls "the night of human nature".[21] While Bakhtin may not have subscribed to this darker view of dialogue, the second edition of his book on Dostoevsky's poetics does give greater emphasis to the ambivalence inherent in dialogism. An additional, stimulating critique comes from another Dostoevskian scholar, also discussed by Emerson: Yuri Kariakin. In his view, Bakhtin misses the more embodied, affect-centred, three-dimensional scenes in Dostoevsky, focusing instead on verbal interactions. "Words come and go – comments Caryl Emerson, ventriloquizing Kariakin – taking pleasure in their own eloquence and ambiguities", and the sober, neutral distancing from "all that

polyphonic obfuscation, those thought experiments and the endless proliferation of alternatives, all those compulsive storytellers and chatterers"[22]
engender the discreet presence of the stage director, Dostoevsky himself – a
still centre, a moral voice present alongside the bewildering array of multiple perspectives. Kariakin's view is hostile to the very notion of dialogism,
but its accuracy matters less to our exploration than the recognition of the
danger of self-deception, ever-present in Dostoevsky's loquacious, ardent
characters – from the anonymous narrator of *Notes from the Underground*
to Raskolnikov to Dmitri Karamazov.

Most forms of instituted morality are founded on unequivocal, monochromatic foundations that require recurring reiteration and allegiance to
one view alone. Multiplicity of the psyche or soul is pandemonium, ushering
in not one but many demons, the bane of all monologist systems. *The heart
is hopelessly dark and deceitful*, intimates Jeremiah, a sentiment echoed
throughout Christianity and beyond. The solution? Substituting ordinary
delusion with spiritual delusion; replacing brisk, unhindered reflections
that honour and learn from the numerous affects traversing the self with
the falsely integrated voice of received wisdom; surrendering the "artistic"
drive towards self-creation for a ready-made "truth of oneself"; recoiling
from the danger of life on the brink, in favour of the safety of unlived life;
pathologizing and policing a client/patient's experimentations and explorations in the name of a misguided notion of psychological integration.

In literature as in psychotherapy, the artistic/ethical choice one might
at some point face is between monophony and polyphony, between prescribing a single unified meaning to the word, the text, the gesture and the
felt sense, or accepting instead polyvalence (poly-vailance) of meaning and
intertextuality. "Each word . . . is an intersection of other words – writes
Julia Kristeva – where at least one other word . . . can be read".[23] Not only are
there other words in a word. There is also a current of unspoken, unspeak-
able, pre-verbal expressions and inflections which would enrich the work of
psychotherapy, if one's organism were attuned to receive, in Freud's unique
image, the client/patient's transmitting unconscious. We would have to both
engage with the notion of the unconscious (rather than hurriedly dismiss
it) *and* hold it lightly, uncoupling it from monologism, allowing for a *differential*, polyvalent unconscious, acknowledging the multiplicity of views
about the unconscious present in the philosophical tradition – from Leibniz
to Schopenhauer to Nietzsche and Bergson – which Freud crystallized and
oversimplified, turning it into a monological belief.[24]

In a late, short essay, Bakhtin reminds us of the importance of philosophy as a practice that begins where science ends.[25] Nothing alive can be turned into a thing, Bakhtin reminds us. Life and meaning are forever contingent, addressed to someone, and incarnate. Incarnation – being embodied, situated "is delimitation – [and it] always means increased vulnerability".[26]

Intrapsychic or life on the brink

It is a given: *subjectivity* is the protagonist of mainstream psychotherapies, leading actor, unitary point of reference to which all experience is attributed and to which it returns. Whether the subject is seen as the personification of an existence retaining specific social and individual traits *prior* to experience, or as the terminus of a process of self-creation, its singularity, indivisibility, and individuality are taken for granted. It is a matter either of recognizing ("finding") one's own "essence", "soul", and congruent core, or of constructing these from the bewildering miasma of raw experience. They amount to the same thing. What is lacking in these two variations is what Dostoevsky's novels present us with on a regular basis. Author, protagonist, and narrator are no longer at the centre. What is central is the totality of their affects. The movement is Copernican. Something of the sort is found in the films of Greek American film-maker John Cassavetes, particularly his early work such as *Shadows* and *Faces*. Cassavetes refused the authority of the film-maker's individual vision, allowing instead the characters to come up with their own individual creation. For Cassavetes, "stylistic unity drains the humanity out of a text". He goes on to say:

> The stories of many different and potentially inarticulate people are more interesting than a contrived narrative that exists only in one articulate man's imagination.[27]

This does not mean that there is no script to begin with, or a general frame, but these are flexible, allowing actors the freedom to interpret their characters which often meant rewriting and readapting the scripts following what emerged during rehearsals. There is a striking parallel here with therapy work: *the main focus is on emergent phenomena, rather than on a pre-existing notion of what is supposed to take place.* This move is polyphonic and Dostoevskian: even the author's definition of the protagonist is merely one of the aspects of the protagonist's self-definition. Even the narrative explicitly or implicitly advocated by either the therapist or the client is merely one aspect of the experiential field. Bakhtin quotes one well-known example in this regard.

In Dostoevsky's short story "A Gentle Creature", the owner of a pawn-shop whose wife killed herself tries to make sense of it and engages in a monologue. In the introduction, Dostoevsky invites us to imagine what it would be like if a stenographer eavesdropped and noted down word by word what the protagonist said. The result would have been less polished than what the author did with the material; it would have been more chaotic and associative. This raw element he calls the "fantastic", a dimension devoid of any explanation of the character's psychology and without cathartic or salvific resolution. But what emerges in the process surprises and amazes the reader and brings vivid life into the text. Rigid psychological characterization may end up destroying the indefiniteness of human existence and experience. It often ends up glossing over our ever-present reality of living life *on the brink*, a dimension that is sadly unapproachable to psychology and only partly available to psychoanalysis and psychotherapy. As an example of clunky psychology – not dissimilar from the pop psychology of our day – Bakhtin mentions the preliminary investigation of the trial of Dmitri in the *Brothers Karamazov*:

> The investigator, the judges, the prosecutor, the defence attorney, and the expert witnesses are all incapable of even approaching the unfinalized, undetermined nucleus of Dmitri's personality. . . . For this live and burgeoning nucleus, they substitute a sort of *ready-made definiteness* "naturally" and "normally" *predetermined* in its every word and act by the "laws of psychology".[28]

Here is the crux the so-called laws of psychology determine that the protagonist – in this case Dmitri, the accused, and in our case the client/patient – is a self-existing unitary subjectivity rather than a multitude; a "he" or "she" rather than "they". Conversely, polyphony introduces us to a fully-realized indeterminacy and perpetual incompleteness which are marks of autonomy and inner freedom – not the autonomy and freedom of the allegedly transparent and universal Cartesian self but that of the insubstantial, formless self that comes into being in the performative and political domain of desire and culture. The task, the effortless effort of a psychotherapy or spiritual practice worth its salt is then letting in what Bakhtin calls "the *unclosed entirety* of life itself, of life *on the brink*".[29]

Dostoevsky loved and learnt much from Balzac's novels, equally notable for their polyphonic and genuinely dialogic nature, for the presence of voices and countervoices, talk and countertalk among characters and within the same person, interspersed with silences. These are scenarios where, especially in *The Lily in the Valley*, passion and restraint, indulgence and cynicism do their perpetual dance without denouement or resolution.[30]

In the same way as Cassavetes undermines the director's role in his films, Dostoevsky undermines the author, for in his fiction the author speaks as if the character is present and can answer back. Imagine swapping the Dostoevskian (and Cassavetian) authorial voice with the therapy supervisor in their conversation with their supervisees. It would mean speaking of clients *as if they were present in the room* – as if they could hear the conversation and were able to respond and even disagree, as if they were a second, not a third party. It would mean creating an atmosphere of true neutrality – less blank screen that genuine openness. A far cry perhaps from the tantalizing pull to pathologize, prescribe, systematize, and even indulge in a form of cosy therapy-speak whose true nature is gossip. What is at stake is the very ethos of therapeutic and supervisory practice. Having chosen a particular client, the therapist is already tied to the inner workings of the client's soul and must at least try to adhere to it. Adhering to it means not interfering with the indeterminacy, contradiction, and multiplicity of the person's consciousness, with the aim of clarifying it and bringing it to fuller expression. It means refusing to accept the popular psychological fallacy of the unitary subject and paying attention instead to the different monologues going on all the time in our mind. Bakhtin gives as example of this in Raskolnikov's first long interior monologue at the beginning of *Crime and Punishment*. It is, he says, a brilliant example, with "every word . . . double voiced . . . contain[ing] a conflict of voices", with everyone else's point of view overlapping, including his mother's voice; with the things he has seen and heard; fortuitous encounters, meaningful or meaningless events, the atmosphere of places – both the slums and the monumental section of St Petersburg, all of this "provokes him and disputes with him or confirms him in his thoughts".[31]

The above is a valid example of refuting what Bakhtin calls ideological monologism, its principles stemming from idealistic philosophy, a perspective avowing the unity of existence and the unity of consciousness – both of them fictions, both of them dominant in both psychology and psychotherapy. From the alleged unity of consciousness, it is only a short step to the unity of a *single* consciousness, and it matters very little what metaphysical cast it chooses – whether the transcendental ego, abstracted consciousness, the true self, the absolute spirit, and so on. From the point of view of what Bakhtin calls "consciousness in general" (which I interpret as *abstracted* consciousness, that is, the fantasy of a consciousness without a phenomenon to which it relates), "the plurality of consciousnesses is accidental and . . . superfluous. . . . That which is individual, that which distinguishes one consciousness from another one and from other ones, is [deemed] unessential for cognition". Bakhtin is at pains to emphasize that *truth is more likely to emerge from the event of multiple consciousnesses at play* rather than from a single and unified consciousness. Truth remains vital, but rather than a pre-existing, unveiled entity, it surfaces as a situational, co-created reality within the encounter between intra or interpsychic multiplicities. This implies a refutation of idealist philosophy, that is, of an array of metaphysical beliefs – in both western (from Plato to Berkeley) and eastern traditions (from Vedanta to Hinduism to aspects of Buddhism) – which maintains that mind, spirit, reason, and will constitute the basis for reality. An important variation of idealism (found for instance in Kant) accepts the reality of existence outside the mind but implies that all we can know of reality are representations. Both versions influence how we understand psychology and psychotherapy. No surprise there, given that both psychology and psychotherapy are derivatives of idealist thinking.

For idealist philosophy (as for, say, object relations theory), an encounter between two consciousnesses is impossible, let alone unconscious communication. The implications are momentous. This is because, in Bakhtin's words,

> [I]dealism knows only a single form of cognitive interaction between consciousnesses: [the one] who knows and possesses the truth instructs [the one] who errs and is ignorant of it, i.e., the interaction of teacher and pupil. Consequently, only a pedagogical dialogue is possible.[32]

Monologism, pervasive in mainstream thought and consequently in psychotherapy, is an ideology whose effectiveness is measured by its "common sense" appeal. It is assumed that artistic work is the product of a single consciousness and that a person's experience stems from their individual consciousness. It is assumed *that the content clients brings to therapy belongs to them rather than being something that traverses them*. Paradoxically, monologism is behind relational/dialogical approaches to therapy (endless variations on the drama of two individual consciousnesses meeting, or failing to meet) and to the collective: the spirit of a people, of a nation, even the spirit of the time, all of these are erroneously attributed to a unified consciousness.

Polyphony is above all *musical*, in the way Dostoevsky's compositions are. *Notes from the Underground* is built on the principles of *counterpoint*, of "different voices singing in different ways on the same theme".[33] This particular work, his first major one, written after Dostoevsky's prison experience and informed by his first journey to Western Europe, makes mincemeat of Chernyshevsky's "rational egoism", that is the belief that we are unified subjects acting mostly rationally. It does so by peering into the wildly associative mind which we all exhibit, a thoroughly divided self, evidenced through the narrator's edgy reflections, disconcerting complexity, and spiralling paradoxes. If when reading this text, you find yourself thinking, "that's not me", I suggest you try an experiment. Remain in silence and alone for a whole day, making sure you pay attention to thoughts, feelings, emotions, recollections, speculations going on within your mind. Then think again whether you are truly all that different, more rational, and "unified" than Dostoevsky's narrator.

Notes

1 Aaron Fogel, *Coercion to Speak: Conrad's Poetics of Dialogue*. Cambridge, MA: Harvard University Press, 1985, p. 29.
2 Aaron Fogel, *Coercion to Speak: Conrad's Poetics of Dialogue*. Cambridge, MA: Harvard University Press, 1985, p. 29.
3 Aaron Fogel, *Coercion to Speak: Conrad's Poetics of Dialogue*. Cambridge, MA: Harvard University Press, 1985, p. 263, n31.
4 Aaron Fogel, *Coercion to Speak: Conrad's Poetics of Dialogue*. Cambridge, MA: Harvard University Press, 1985, p. 263, n31.
5 Fredric Jameson, *Allegory and Ideology*. London and New York: Verso, 2019.
6 Bruce Robbins, 'Museum of Difference', *The Baffler*, No. 53, September 2020, https://thebaffler.com/salvos/museum-of-difference-robbins. Retrieved 15 October 2024.
7 Mikhail Bakhtin, *Problems of Dostoevsky's Poetics*. Munster: Ardis, 1973, pp. 6–7.

8 Mikhail Bakhtin, *Problems of Dostoevsky's Politics*. Munster: Ardis, 1973, p. 11.
9 Mikhail Bakhtin, *Problems of Dostoevsky's Politics*. Munster: Ardis, 1973, p. 4, italics in the original.
10 Mikhail Bakhtin, *Problems of Dostoevsky's Politics*. Munster: Ardis, 1973, p. 5.
11 Leonid Grossman, *Dostoevsky*. London: Allen Lane, 1974.
12 Darryl Pinckney, 'Black Talk on the Move', *New York Review of Books*, 20 July 2023, pp. 15–17, 16.
13 Clarence Major, *Juba to Jive: A Dictionary of Afro-American Slang*. New York: Viking, 1994.
14 Darryl Pinckney, 'Black Talk on the Move', *New York Review of Books*, 20 July 2023, p. 17.
15 Friedrich Nietzsche, 'Why I Am So Clever', *Ecce Homo*, pp. 702–703, §4, emphasis in the original, https://www.gutenberg.org/cache/epub/52190/pg52190-images.html. Retrieved 19 October 2024.
16 Stuart Hall, *Selected Political Writings: The Great Moving Right Show and Other Essays*. Lawrence & Wishart, 2017.
17 Félix Guattari, *Lines of Flight: For Another World of Possibilities*. London: Bloomsbury, 2015.
18 Mikhail Bakhtin, *Problems of Dostoevsky's Poetics*. Munster: Ardis, 1973, p. 90.
19 On the daimonic, see Manu Bazzano, *Nietzsche and Psychotherapy*, Abingdon, OX: Routledge, 2019.
20 Discussed in Caryl Emerson, *All the Same the Words Don't Go away*. Brookline, MA: Academic Studies Press, 2010. See also Natalia Bonetskaia, 'Bakhtin's Aesthetics as a Logic of Form', in *The Contexts of Bakhtin*, ed. David Shepherd. London: Routledge, 1988.
21 Natalia Bonetskaia, cited by Caryl Emerson, *All the Same the Words Don't Go Away*. Brookline, MA: Academic Studies Press, 2010, p. 20.
22 Caryl Emerson, 'Polyphony and the Carnivalesque: Introducing the Terms', https://www.jstor.org/stable/j.ctt21h4wh9.5. Retrieved 19 February 2023, p. 7.
23 Julia Kristeva, 'Dialogue, Novel', in *Desire in Language: A Semiotic Approach to Literature and Art*, ed. Leon S. Roudiez. New York: Columbia University Press, 1980, pp. 64–91, 66.
24 Gilles Deleuze, *Difference and Repetition*. London: Bloomsbury Academic, 2014.
25 *Towards a Methodology for the Human Sciences*, quoted by Caryl Emerson, Lecture on Mikhail Bakhtin and Human Studies, 28 October 2016, The Prokhorov Centre, https://www.sheffield.ac.uk/prokhorov-centre/news/catch-lecture-caryl-emerson-mikhail-bakhtin-and-human-studies. Retrieved 2 June 2023.
26 Caryl Emerson, 'Polyphony and the Carnivalesque: Introducing the Terms', https://www.jstor.org/stable/j.ctt21h4wh9.5. Retrieved 19 February 2023, p. 4.

27 Ray Carney, *Cassavetes on Cassavetes*. London: Faber, 2001, p. 65,
28 Mikhail Bakhtin, *Problems of Dostoevsky's Poetics*. Munster: Ardis, 1973, p. 50, emphasis added.
29 Mikhail Bakhtin, *Problems of Dostoevsky's Poetics*. Munster: Ardis, 1973, p. 51, emphasis added.
30 Honoré de Balzac, *The Lily in the Valley*, New York: New York Review Books, 2024.
31 Mikhail Bakhtin, *Problems of Dostoevsky's Poetics*. Munster: Ardis, 1973, p. 66.
32 Mikhail Bakhtin, *Problems of Dostoevsky's Poetics*. Munster: Ardis, 1973, p. 65.
33 Leonid Grossman, cited in Mikhail Bakhtin, *Problems of Dostoevsky's Poetics*. Munster: Ardis, 1973, p. 36.

Chapter 8

On necroliberalism

The implosion of the personalized submersible *Titan* in June 2023 has been described by experts in the field as a suicide mission. It may also be read as a potential turning point in the attitudes of the ruling elites. From the 1980s to the turn of the millennium, the ultra-wealthy increasingly abstained from feigning to want to save the global shipwreck they themselves instigated through so-called "de-regulation", the destruction of the welfare state, and the systematic devastation of the Earth's resources, seeking instead a swift escape from the wreckage – a stance epitomized by the millionaires and the ship's highest-ranking officials scuttling away to safety from the sinking *Titanic* in April 1912. Escaping catastrophes, enduring hardships, and coming good in the end have been the consoling narratives of many tales as well as the trope of the survival genre of TV culture, and are characterized not only by what Fredric Jameson, in his 1975 essay on Ursula K. Le Guin, called "world reduction"[1] but also by a malevolent "racialization of survival"[2] and a de-historicization of the so-called "human condition". It is also common to the dubious, universalizing representations of *Homo Sapiens*[3] and the romantic rhetoric behind groups such as *Extinction Rebellion*.

*

Elon Musk's vanity project, the creation of the aerospace company *SpaceX* in 2002, was integral to the contemporary elites' fixation with, and financing of, "existential risk studies",[4] a field characterized by a novel, sophisticated version of the old story of heroic white men saving humanity. Here, we will explore the possibility that the survivalist fantasies promoted by the ultra-wealthy and corroborated by "thinkers" on their payrolls have nearly reached a literal dead end. It will explore the hypothesis that expensive flights to Mars and submersions into the ocean depths conceal the twisted

DOI: 10.4324/9781003529095-9

dream of an atomized *Homo NeoLiberalis* and attest to the ultimate act of hubris – akin to what the poet John Donne, in his treatise *Biathanathos*, calls holding the "keys to the prison"[5] – having the power to destroy oneself, having already initiated the irreversible demise of the planet.

The biopolitics of catastrophe

Existential risk, a notion once nurtured in existential philosophy as an opportunity for radical transformation, has now transmogrified beyond recognition into *existential risk studies* (ERS), a veritable industry and academic field enthusiastically sponsored by the likes of Elon Musk, Bill Gates, Jaan Tallinn, and other multibillionaires.[6] This expanding field appears to have breezily bypassed features essential to research such as openness to diverse approaches (as opposed to inflating one's own subjective biases), the implementation of democratic methodologies, and the "separation of the study of catastrophe and extinction from the ethics of human existence and extinction".[7] ERS's growing field is animated by an apocalyptic vision closely aligned with what Frédéric Neyrat calls the *biopolitics of catastrophe*, grounded on a "perverted temporality", which ends up "block[ing] the advent of an ecopolitics that could act on the causes rather than the effects of the environmental damages that we are already suffering".[8] The biopolitics of catastrophe is also closely aligned with Foucault's biopolitics (2008),[9] Agamben's thanatopolitics (1998),[10] and Mbembe's necropolitics (2003)[11] and represents "an important ideological function for the billionaire class".[12] The type of "connoisseur" environmental conservation[13] performed by the ultra-wealthy enhances profits and adds sheen to one's social prestige. Concealed behind a sentimental love of nature lies limitless consumption, self-interested "altruism", and mounting unfairness – all strengthening the ills engendered by existing neoliberal systems. What might the reasons be for this upsurge of capitalist philanthropy and sponsorship of ecological causes? What is really at stake in the billionaires' avowed concern to offset human extinction? What is behind the politics of catastrophe and *extinctiopolitics*?

Capitalist philanthropy acts as a masked sequel to biopolitics in the sense that it misses the trees for the forest: its grand objective, eerily reminiscent of Heidegger's bypassing of embodied *existents* in favour of *existence* – an abstraction in relation to which living beings are reduced to merely instrumental functions[14] – is to save the future of the human-as-*species*.[15] This is done at the expense of real, enfleshed humans who live in the present – some of whom inhabit colonial *death-worlds* as we speak, where genocide is the order of the day. Places where "vast populations are subjected to conditions of life conferring upon them the status of living dead".[16] Places where the end of the world has already occurred and from where the apocalyptic visions broadcast by ERS may be sensibly perceived as determined by the desire to preserve *white* futures.[17] This one-sided emphasis on the future and the species at the expense of the present and individual humans chimes with what Edelman calls "the fascism of the baby's face", the subtle and not-so-subtle coercion to join the chorus of "reproductive futurism" common to both fascistic and democratic narratives. While there are considerable differences between the two, both models are inevitably geared to the reification of difference and to safeguarding "in the form of the future, the order of the same".[18]

There has been a gradual but significant turning point in the attitudes of the ruling elites, one that may be evidenced by first considering three crucial and closely linked phenomena which took place in the last 40 years: (a) *de-regulation*, closely paired with the *dismantling of the welfare state* since the 1980s; (b) the *climate change denialism* that began to rear its head at the turn of the present century; and (c) a vertiginous *increase in inequalities*.[19]

Until the 1980s, those in power arguably still had an investment in the abstract notion of leadership, however twisted and self-serving. Neoliberalism, with its reckless concoction of laissez-faire market fundamentalism and "market economy theology",[20] changed all that. It is easy to forget that neoliberalism's first measures were implemented by a mass murderer, Augusto Pinochet, and that they followed the violent overthrow of Salvador Allende's democratically elected government in Chile on September 11, 1973. It is easy to ignore that these measures were represented in the poisonous efflorescence of a stealthy "Chile Project" (integral to Washington's Cold War strategy in South America), which had begun 18 years earlier with the US Department of State instructing a set of privileged young Chilean students – the "Chicago boys" – in Chicago-style economics. Taught by Milton Freeman and Arnold Harberger, this coterie of budding intellocrats – Jorge Cauas, Sergio de Castro, Emilio Sanfuentes, Miguel Kast, Alvaro Bardón among them – all went on to become key economic advisors to Pinochet.[21] The Pinochet dictatorship gave free rein to the implementation of the first neoliberal policies so admired by Reagan, Thatcher, and subsequent believers in so-called "free' market capitalism.

In this sense, *necropolitics* – the socio-political practice that determines how some people may live and how others must die – *is coextensive with neoliberalism*. This fact is easily overlooked, given that the relevant literature of the last few decades (including psychology) has chosen to unanimously read neoliberalism as a product of the voluntary servitude of compliant profit-making subjects, neglecting various forms of violence needed to enforce and replicate neoliberal norms. Neoliberalism is a war machine powered by *demophobia* and motivated by the desire to nullify all potential opposition. This case has been convincingly made by Dardot, Laval, and others[22] and was inspired by a reinterpretation of Foucault – welcome at a time when it is fashionable to berate Foucault for the very birth of neoliberalism.[23] Above all, neoliberalism must be understood as a kind of *civil war*, as a "frequently one-sided class struggle" that has not shied away, illiberally, to take on violent forms "from the rise of Trump to the juridical coup against the *Partido dos Trabalhadores* that brought Jair Bolsonaro to power in Brazil".[24] Using the language of freedom and human rights, neoliberalist trends asserted the right of Elon Musk and Trump not to pay taxes and the right to criticize Islam and communism as fatalistic ideologies while abdicating to market fatalism.[25]

The notion that a "rational" neoliberal order would not stoop to employing violence and authoritarianism is a blatant lie. Neoliberalism should not only be understood as a political project aimed at avoiding any possibility of equality. It is also to be apprehended, despite the proliferation of institutionalized eco-politics, as the destroyer of the planet. Everybody seems to have a stake in climate politics, from Right-wing populists with their eco-national-chauvinism, to social democrats with their Green New Deal, to corporations with their handsome profits in eco-commodities: "simultaneously needing and rubbishing nature, capitalism is a cannibal that devours its own vital organs".[26]

Survival of the wealthiest

From the 1980s onwards, the elites gradually stopped claiming to lead and began instead to "shelter themselves from the world",[27] implementing a dynamic which came to be known as the "insulation equation", the aim of which was the "survival of the richest" (Rushkoff, 2022).[28] This thoroughgoing process of endogamic implosion gained momentum and became sharply defined in recent years by three events: Brexit, Trump's election, and the escalation of xenophobic reaction to migrations.

With Brexit, the UK – the very same country where the open space of the so-called free market originated – "decided on impulse to stop playing the game of globalization".[29] Vainly looking for the remnants of a faded empire, it tried to yank itself out of Europe. Similarly, with the noxious materialization of Trump, the United States, another country which had brutally inflicted on the world its own trademark globalization (the same country that once upon a time prided itself on welcoming the hungry, the poor, and the huddled masses after the genocide of its first occupants), now began to build walls and bastions. Both events were at heart animated by the terrible enthusiasm of xenophobia and the delusional need to protect nativist privilege, to glue oneself to the soil at the expense of the Earth. However, "the very notion of soil is changing",[30] and it is changing fast. The current climate catastrophe brings home the fact that there is no safety within the prison walls of a nation-state and that no planet can sustain capitalism's greed. The turning point gets closer and closer; not only did the captain lie, he also had no intention of going down with the ship.

The cliché of the *Titanic* is compelling when attempting to draw parallels with the ruling classes' shift from self-interested leadership to complete abdication of solidarity towards humans and other living beings. Knowledge of the disaster looming closer and closer has set off unbecoming acts of selfishness: seizing the few lifeboats available and telling the musicians onboard to play cheerful medleys while the ship's managing director, J. Bruce Ismay, and a handful of millionaires and their consorts rowed away to safety, as the ship's fireman Harry Senior testified.[31] At some point on the night of that Sunday 14 April 1912, the *Titanic* tilted forward, head down, with the first funnel partly under water, electric lights ablaze in every cabin, lights on all decks, and light at her mast heads. A living breathing thing, a hurt animal plunging to certain death, the sheer horror of it – *the horror, the horror,* as in Kurtz's last words in Conrad's *Heart of Darkness*[32] – the horror that perhaps only some of the more ordinary survivors could feel when witnessing hundreds of people still aboard hanging, like swarming bees – an image reminiscent of the underworld in Dante's *Inferno,* where walking by a valley he heard what sounded like bees in a summer field, as passenger Jack Thayer later recalled.[33] And when the luxury steamship finally went down, a loud cry was heard as if coming from one throat. And what about the *Titanic*'s highest-ranking official aboard, J. Bruce Ismay, the chairman and managing director of the shipping line that created and operated the

Titanic? Did he experience any *Gemeinschaftsgefühl* when he scuttled away to safety with a group of millionaires? His figure haunts our psyche in many guises – mythologized and incorporated alongside the archetypes of Ahab or Noah. He may have himself been haunted by his survival. He may have been despised by the English aristos as merely a *nouveau riche*. But after decades of neoliberalist policies, his actions speak in an unequivocal language: *only the wealthy ought to survive*.

Wicked universality

The rise of Brexit, Trump, and the xenophobic policies against migrants have taken place against the backdrop of climate disaster. The latter is at times acknowledged matter-of-factly, for instance via the mounting evidence of the effects of climate change on mental health.[34] Yet, this move often substantiates the necessity for problematic psychological tropes such as post-traumatic growth, resilience, learnt helplessness, victimology, and other aberrations – all constructs championed by *Positive Psychology*,[35] an approach whose techniques have been used by the CIA to devise its torture program in the aftermath of 9/11, to blame Asian-Americans and Black Americans for their alleged "defeatism" and "helpless cognitions", and to increase the efficiency of soldiers as killing machines.[36] As with societal issues, the psych world's talk of climate change is slanted against individuals conceived as atomized units who are castigated for the anger, dismay, and difficulty of dealing with the realities of ecological devastation and for not thinking positively enough, for not practising mindfulness or so-called "self-care" – all methods that would return us, with a spring in our step, to our bullshit jobs[37] in order to create more profit for the few. Yet, while the "profit before lives" formula is still prevalent today among the ruling elites, a further shift seems to have taken place recently.

The implosion of the submersible *Titan* in June 2023, labelled as that year's biggest procedural failure and an endeavour described by experts in the field prior to the accident as a suicide mission and an accident waiting to happen[38], may also be read as a turning point in the attitudes of the super-wealthy. Titans in Greek mythology were guilty of *hubris* – arrogance against the gods. Their actions, spurred by deliberate contempt for larger forces at play, are cautionary tales of anthropocentrism gone berserk. Stockton Rush, the millionaire founder and CEO of *OceanGate Inc.* and Xbox-controller-wielding pilot of the submersible, had one strongly held point of view regarding his undersea adventure: "I think I can do this just as safely by breaking the rules".[39] When his "nonrated, custom-made submersible predictably imploded under the pressure of millions of tons of water", he was instantly killed along with his four passengers: a British billionaire, a Pakistani billionaire and his son, and a French billionaire, Paul-Henri Nargeolet, director of underwater research at RMS Titanic Inc., the company that claims to own the ruins of the Titanic and which "had to settle its debts by auctioning off relics from the site, a practice commonly known as graverobbing".[40] Interviews with both expedition leaders and Ocean-Gate employees show how OceanGate chose to disregard serious, repeated warnings from many quarters. No psychoanalytic training is needed to recognize the presence of the death instinct at play. Otto Rank perceives the "strange paradox" of the suicide mission as connected to the psyche of someone who "seeks death in order to free himself of the intolerable thanatophobia".[41] Rank's insight could be extended to include the predominant stance of today's ruling elites: from presumed leadership to fleeing the sinking ship to exiting the world altogether through science-fiction fantasies or suicidal missions.

Ordinary hubris no longer suffices. The adrenaline rush of savouring wild spaces through frequent flying and soaring emissions is no longer enough. The effrontery of fashioning oneself as a "citizen" of the colonized world made even more unfathomable by the epistemic clichés listed in tourist brochures no longer works. It may appear at times that a change of heart has taken place among those ruling elites who dutifully recite their environmental credentials and philanthropy. Some lessons have been learnt, and some kind of universality (of the "we-humans-are-all-in-this-together" variety) has been taken on board. But is this not simply a manifestation of what Latour calls "wicked universality"?[42] The latter emerged after the collapse of globalization's faux universalism, with the mounting terror that the ground on which we stand is finally giving way. The result is an appeal to the "universal abstraction of our species identity",[43] echoed both in Harari's popular book *Sapiens* (2015) as much as in *Extinction Rebellion*'s declaration, whose rousing first sentences read:

> This is our darkest hour. Humanity finds itself embroiled in an event unprecedented in its history. One which, unless immediately addressed, will catapult us further into the destruction of all we hold dear: this nation, its peoples, our ecosystems and the future of generations to come.[44]

But who is this collective "we" that Extinction Rebellion (XR) have in mind? Minimizing the crucial role of colonialism and capitalism, XR's portrayal of humanity in its darkest hour could be seen as "the product of a culture that is registering, but not yet experiencing, the full effects of climate breakdown".[45] An attentive reading of XR's declaration uncovers a normative – white and privileged – subject. An open letter to XR by the Black, Indigenous, and People of Colour (BIPOC)-led UK grassroots collective *Wretched of the Earth* states:

> "The Truth" of the ecological crisis is that we did not get here by a sequence of small missteps, but were thrust here by powerful forces that drove the distribution of resources of the entire planet and the structure of our societies.
>
> The economic structures that dominate us were brought about by colonial projects whose sole purpose is the pursuit of domination and profit. For centuries, racism, sexism and classism have been necessary for this system to be upheld, and have shaped the conditions we find ourselves in. Another truth is that for many, the bleakness is not something of "the future". For those of us who are indigenous, working class, black, brown, queer, trans or disabled, the experience of structural violence became part of our birthright.[46]

Ben Ware makes an interesting point in relation to XR's inherent masochism, not in the meaning ascribed by Deleuze via Masoch – as a double stance which transfers the law onto the mother while implementing an ironic subversion of the law by zealous, theatrical obedience – but instead as an imploration for the father's intervention. XR effectively desires the intervention of a "new Master figure who will acknowledge the activists' 'demands' and integrate them into the law's own functioning through the creation of a 'Citizen's Assembly'".[47]

The popularity of Harari's international bestseller *Sapiens*, alongside other books that "explain it all",[48] is imputable to a general *atrophy of the noetic* – the crisis of the humanities as well as the overall shrinking of cultural transindividual/transitional spaces where, god forbid, something akin to *thinking* may emerge. Lucrative books by authors who-explain-it-all fill the thought-vacuum to perfection. Endorsed by Barack Obama, Mark Zuckerberg, and Bill Gates, *Sapiens* presents a bleak framing of a flattened-out, generic species bent on destruction and genocide as a regular, ahistorical, and universal practice – a view that ignores the specificity of racial and ethnic cleansing and that asserts a species fatalism. This form of totalizing storytelling ignores contending claims about the cultural meaning of the remote human past; it also insults the intelligence of the reader by assuming that "we" are the inheritors of a human history where "the responsibilities . . . and achievements . . . of early Homo sapiens are shared equally by all".[49]

Thinking in such generic, wide-sweeping, and decontextualized terms about species extinction and species survival narrows the focus to what "seems like first principles", regaling us with the deluded luxury of picturing ourselves outside the "determining conditions of the present".[50] This is often animated by a fanciful stripping away and radically reductive view of the future that is reminiscent of Fredric Jameson's notion in his essay on Ursula K. Le Guin, of *world reduction*, that is, "a process of ontological attenuation in which the sheer teeming multiplicity of what exists . . . is deliberately . . . weeded out through an operation of radical abstraction and simplification".[51] Science fiction's (SF's) fascination with extreme weather symbolically negates the fantasy of individual autonomy, highlighting the impossibility that one can be disentangled from their surrounding ecosystem. The relentless, intolerable winter on the planet Gethen in Le Guin's *The Left Hand of Darkness*[52] expresses this point vividly. A correlated view is presented in several SF novels that depict extreme heat – acutely relevant to climate change – wherein people are dominated by the terror of losing their neat separation from the world and become open to all sorts of illnesses and impurities.[53] There is an echo here of the popular trope present in late nineteenth- and early twentieth-century colonialist/holiday-maker/explorer literature, whose prime rational sensibility is irresistibly and temporarily lost amid the "unclean" seductions of the South and the mysterious "inscrutability" of the East.

Our world, by the way, is impermanent

There is also another side, however, to the generalized talk of species extinction, one that is potentially more attuned to the possibilities of a radical change in perspective. Its most convincing version is found in Clare Colebrook's more recent work, inspired, among others, by the work of Deleuze.[54] Unlike the commonly accepted survivalist narrative, this perspective (or set of perspectives) argues that accepting the inherently contingent and volatile nature of human life and of the impermanence of the world may be the first step in the right direction. It would shed the sense of false security in which the more privileged humans are basking. Recognizing that this world will end may perhaps "shift attention away from attempts to save the banks, save the housing market . . . save the stock market . . . save America, save the constitution, and so on".[55] It would shed the widespread delusion that capitalism is just too big to fail. It would also shed the inveterate anthropocentrism of most environmental discourses – *without* having to give in to the rather facile compulsions of posthumanism. While positively decentring the human subject in relation to other sentient beings, empiricist affirmations of the plane of immanence[56] do emphasize human difference and specificity, framing the human as "an effect of a series of institutional, planetary, geopolitical, historic, cultural, racial and linguistic forces and relations".[57] Emphasis on the difference and specificity of the human does not have to translate into a strident defence of human exceptionalism. On the contrary, it might be useful, in light of environmental catastrophe, to be rethinking the human outside the dictates of the tradition and by envisaging new forms of individuation – for instance in terms of *transindividuation*, a productive and as yet barely explored notion first formulated by Gilbert Simondon.[58] This might be useful for decoupling the *human* – a decidedly normative and often brutally exclusive notion – from the *species*. As Cole-brook explains:

> Climate change is not some unfortunate late accident . . . but is intrinsic to "the human". The human as a category is bound up with globalism, imperialism, capitalism and hyper-consumption; it is a category so large as to preclude forms of solidarity that would be possible in genuinely collective forms of existence.[59]

The keys to the prison

"Things natural to the Species, are not always so for the individual", the Renaissance English poet and Dean of St Paul Cathedral, John Donne, wrote in his posthumously published *Biathanatos* (1644), a treatise presenting an unusual defence of suicide, as well as the scandalous notion – already present in Thomas Aquinas's *Summa Theologica* – that Christ committed suicide.[60] The jury is out as to how one should consider suicide. Some will say that it is an act of individual freedom against the injunctions of coercive morality and societal pressure to work and produce. That it is up to the person to decide whether their existence has meaning and purpose enough to go on living. It could be seen as an act of defiance against the Aristotelian idea, in the *Nicomachean Ethics*, that suicide means neglecting one's obligation to the state.[61] Donne would certainly agree with this view. He defends the right to hold, as he states in *Biathanatos*, the keys to one's prison in one's own hand, affirming the right to resort to the most swift, ultimate remedy: one's own sword.

At the same time, this supposed act of individual freedom may also be read as a form of hubris, especially when juxtaposed to the implosion of the *Titan*. The ultra-wealthy and self-appointed leaders of the world nurture the delusion of holding the keys to the "prison" – an overheated planet whose countdown started a while ago. As with Hitler's suicide in Berlin's *Führerbunker*, the super-rich and tin pot dictators alike, unable by default to envision any form of transindividuation of the human subject might end up opting, unconsciously, and given their failure to act on climate change, for the swift, ultimate remedy of suicide – a choice that implicates us all.

Notes

1 Fredric Jameson, 'World Reduction in Le Guin: The Emergence of Utopian Narrative', *Science Fiction Studies*, Vol. 2, No. 3, The Science Fiction of Ursula K. Le Guin, 1975, pp. 221–230.
2 Ben Pitcher, 'The Popular Culture of Extinction and the Racialization of Survival', *New Formations*, No. 107–108, 2022, pp. 84–100.
3 Yuval Noah Harari, *Sapiens: A Brief History of Mankind.* London: Vintage, 2015.
4 Joe P. L. Davidson, 'Extinctiopolitics: Existential Risk Studies, the Extinctiopolitical Unconscious, and The Billionaires' Exodus from Earth', *New Formations*, No. 107–108, 2022, pp. 48–65.
5 John Donne, *Biathanatos: A Declaration of That Paradoxe or Thesis, That Selfe Homicide Is Not So Naturally Sinne, That It May Never Be Otherwise*, 1608, https://quod.lib.umich.edu/cgi/t/text/text-idx?c=eebo;idno=A36292.0001.001. Retrieved 7 February 2024.
6 See for instance: (a) Nick Bostrom, 'Existential Risks: Analyzing Human Extinction Scenarios and Related Hazards', *Journal of Evolution and Technology*, Vol. 9, 2002, pp. 1–30. S. Avin, B. C. Wintle, and J. Weitzdörfer, 'Classifying Global Catastrophic Risks', *Elsevier*, Vol. 102, September 2018, pp. 20–26; (b) Nick Bostrom, *Superintelligence: Paths, Dangers, Strategies.* Oxford: Oxford University Press, 2014; (c) S. Avin, B. C. Wintle, and J. Weitzdörfer, 'Classifying Global Catastrophic Risks', *Elsevier*, Vol. 102, September 2018, pp. 20–26.

7 C. Z. Cremer and L. Kemp, 'Democratising Risk: In Search of a Methodology to Study Existential Risk', 2021, https://ssrn.com/abstract=3995225. Retrieved 7 February 2017.
8 F. Neyrat, 'The Biopolitics of Catastrophe, or How to Avert the Past and Regulate the Future', *South Atlantic Quarterly*, Vol. 115, No. 2, 2016, pp. 247–265, 247.
9 Michel Foucault, *The Birth of Biopolitics*. Basingstoke, Hants: Palgrave Macmillan, 2008.
10 Giorgio Agamben, *Homo Sacer: Sovereign Power and Bare Life*. Stanford, CA: Stanford University Press, 1998.
11 Achille Mbembe, 'Necropolitics', *Public Culture*, Vol. 15, No. 1, Duke University Press, 2003, pp. 11–40.
12 Joe P. L. Davidson, 'Extinctiopolitics: Existential Risk Studies, the Extinctiopolitical Unconscious, and The Billionaires' Exodus from Earth', *New Formations*, No. 107–108, 2002, pp. 48–65, 51.
13 Justin Farrell, *Billionaire Wilderness*. Princeton, NJ: Princeton University Press, 2020.
14 Emmanuel Levinas, *Existence and Existents*. The Hague: Martinus Nijhoff, 1978.
15 Michel Foucault, *Society Must Be Defended*. London: Picador, 2003.
16 Achille Mbembe, 'Necropolitics', *Public Culture*, Vol. 15, No. 1, Duke University Press, 2003, p. 40.
17 A. Mitchell, A. Chaudhury, 'Worlding beyond "the" "End" of "the World": White Apocalyptic Visions and BIPOC Futurisms', *International Relations*, Vol. 34, No. 3, 2020, pp. 309–332.
18 Lee Edelman, *No Future: Queer Theory and the Death Drive*. Durham, NC, Duke University Press, 2004 p. 75.
19 Bruno Latour, *Down to Earth: Politics in the New Climatic Regime*, trans. Catherine Porter. Cambridge: Polity, 2007.
20 Eric Hobsbawm, *Interesting Times: A Twentieth Century Life*. London: Abacus, 2002, p. 276.
21 See Vincent Bevins, 'Make the Economy Scream: The Chicago Boys and the Tragedy of the Chilean Coup', *The Nation*, 2023, https://www.thenation.com/article/world/chicago-boys-chile-neoliberalism/. Retrieved 7 February 2023. Also: Valerie Brender, 'Economic Transformations in Chile: The Formation of the Chicago Boys', *The American Economist*, Vol. 55, No. 1, 2010, pp. 111–122; as well as: Naomi Klein, *The Shock Doctrine: The Rise of Disaster Capitalism*. London: Penguin, 2008.
22 Pierre Dardot, Christian Laval, Haud Guéguen, and Pierre Sauvêtre, *Le Choix de la Guerre Civile: Une Autre Histoire Néolibéralisme*. Lux: Montréal, 2021.
23 See for instance: Mitchell Dean and Daniel Zamora, *The Last Man Takes LSD: Foucault and the End of Revolution*. London: Verso, 2021, as well as Peter Hallward, 'Stoics and Jacobins: The Counter-Revolution in French Philosophy in the 1970s', *CRMEP Public Lectures on Philosophy, Politics and the Arts*, Thursday 30 March 2023, p. 5.

24 Alberto Toscano, 'Shifting Currents', *New Left Review*, Vol. 140/141, March/June2023,https://newleftreview.org/issues/ii140/articles/alberto-toscano-shifting-currents. Retrieved 2 April 2023.

25 Jessica Whyte, 'Neoliberal Freedom and Stoic Resignation', *LSE Online Event*, 2022, https://www.youtube.com/watch?v=wmXVdLSFzRM.

26 Nancy Fraser, 'Climates of Capital: for a Trans-Environmental Socialism', *New Left Review* 127, January/February 2021, pp. 94–127, 101.

27 Bruno Latour, *Down to Earth: Politics in the New Climatic Regime*, trans. Catherine Porter. Cambridge: Polity, 2007, p. 7.

28 Douglas Rushkoff, *Survival of the Richest: Escape Fantasies of the Tech Billionaires*. London: Scribe, 2022.

29 Bruno Latour, *Down to Earth: Politics in the New Climatic Regime*, trans. Catherine Porter. Cambridge: Polity, 2007, p. 4.

30 Bruno Latour, *Down to Earth: Politics in the New Climatic Regime*, trans. Catherine Porter. Cambridge: Polity, 2007, p. 5.

31 Frances Wilson, *How to Survive the Titanic: The Sinking of J. Bruce Ismay*. New York: Harper Perennial, 2002.

32 Joseph Conrad, *Heart of Darkness*. London: Penguin, 2007. Originally published in 1899.

33 Frances Wilson, *How to Survive the Titanic: The Sinking of J. Bruce Ismay*. New York: Harper Perennial, 2002.

34 See for instance A. Massazza, 'Explained: How Climate Change Affects Mental Health', 2023, https://wellcome.org/news/explained-how-climate-change-affects-mental-health. Retrieved 10 February 2024.

35 Martin Seligman, *Flourish: A New Understanding of Happiness and Well-Being and How to Achieve Them*. Boston, MA: Brealy, 2002.

36 See (a) Mark Neocleous, 'Resisting Resilience', *Radical Philosophy*, Vol. 178, No. 2, 2013, https://www.radicalphilosophy.com/?s=resisting+resilience. Retrieved 17 February 2024; (b) Lynne Friedli and Robert Stearn, 'Positive Affect as Coercive Strategy: Conditionality, Activation and the Role of Psychology in UK Government Workfare Programmes', *Medical Humanities*, Vol. 41, 2015, pp. 40–47, https://doi.org/10.1136/medhum-2014-010622; (c) Tamsin Shaw, 'The Psychologists Take Power', *New York Review of Books*, Vol. LXIII, No. 3, 2016, p. 39; (d) Manu Bazzano, 'Healing and Resilience', *Therapy Today*, December 2016, pp. 19–21.

37 David Graeber, *Bullshit Jobs: A Theory*. London: Allen Lane, 2018.

38 D. Taub, 'The Titan's Submersible Was An Accident Waiting to Happen', *The New Yorker*, 1 July 2023, https://www.newyorker.com/news/a-reporter-at-large/the-titan submersible-was-an-accident-waiting-to-happen.

39 Nicholas Boni, 'No Matter How Rich You Are, You Can't Own the Sea', *Jacobin*, 2023, https://jacobin.com/2023/06/titan-submersible-implosion-search-media-wealth-inequality. Retrieved 7 February 2024.

40 Nicholas Boni, 'No Matter How Rich You Are, You Can't Own the Sea', *Jacobin*, 2023, https://jacobin.com/2023/06/titan-submersible-implosion-search-media-wealth-inequality. Retrieved 7 February 2024.

41 Otto Rank, *The Double: A Psychoanalytic Study.* New York: Meridian, 1971, p. 78.
42 Bruno Latour, *Down to Earth: Politics in the New Climatic Regime*, trans. Catherine Porter. Cambridge: Polity, 2007, p. 9.
43 Ben Pitcher, 'The Popular Culture of Extinction and the Racialization of Survival', *New Formations*, No. 107–108, 2022, p. 89.
44 Extinction Rebellion, 'Declaration of Rebellion', 2018, https://extinctionrebellion.uk/declaration/. Retrieved 10 March 2024.
45 Ben Pitcher, 'The Popular Culture of Extinction and the Racialization of Survival', *New Formations*, No. 107–108, 2022, p. 90.
46 Wretched of the Earth, 'An Open Letter to Extinction Rebellion', *Red Pepper*, 3 May 2021, https://www.redpepper.org.uk/environment-climate/climate-change/open letter-to-extinction-rebellion/. Retrieved 8 February 2024.
47 Ben Ware, *On Extinction: Beginning Again at the End.* London and New York: Verso, 2024, p. 14; Stephen Shapin, 'The Superhuman Upgrade', *London Review of Books*, Vol. 39, No. 14, 13 July 2017.
48 Alison Bashford, 'Deep Genetics: Universal History and the Species', *History and Theory* Vol. 57, No. 2, 2018, p. 219.
49 Ben Pitcher, 'The Popular Culture of Extinction and the Racialization of Survival', *New Formations*, No. 107–108, 2022, p. 8.
50 Fredric Jameson, 'World Reduction in Le Guin: The Emergence of Utopian Narrative', *Science Fiction Studies*, Vol. 2, No. 3, The Science Fiction of Ursula K. Le Guin, 1975, p. 223.
51 Ursula Le Guin, *The Left Hand of Darkness.* London: Gollancz, 2018. Originally published in 1967.
52 For example J. G. Ballard, *The Drowned World.* London: Berkley Books, 1962. And Robert Silverberg, *Downward to the Earth.* London: Doubleday, 1970.
53 See (a) Claire Colebrook, *Death of the Posthuman: Essays on Extinction.* London: Open Humanities Press, 2014, and (b) Claire Colebrook, *Who Would You Kill to Save the World?* Lincoln, NE: University of Nebraska Press, 2022.
54 Nicholas Thoburn, David Bennett, Jeremy Gilbert, and Mandy Merck, 'Extinction and the Anthropocene: To End or Mend the World? A Conversation with Claire Colebrook', *New Formations*, No. 107–108, 2023, pp. 198–214.
55 Gilles Deleuze and Félix Guattari, *A Thousand Plateaus*, trans. Brian Massumi. London: Continuum, 2008. Originally published in 1980. Also: Brian Massumi, *What Animals Teach Us about Politics.* Durham, NC: Duke University Press, 2014.
56 Claire Colebrook, *Who Would You Kill to Save the World?* Lincoln, NE: University of Nebraska Press, 2022, p. 222.
57 (a) Gilbert Simondon, *Individuation in Light of Notions of Form and Information,* trans. Taylor Adkins. Minneapolis and London: University of Minnesota Press, 2020; (b) Bernard Stiegler, *Technics and Time, 3: Cinematic Time and the Question of Malaise.* Stanford, CA: Stanford University Press, 2010; (c) Manu Bazzano, *Subversion and Desire: Pathways to Transindividuation.* Abingdon, OX: Routledge, 2023.

58 Claire Colebrook, *Who Would You Kill to Save the World?* Lincoln, NE: University of Nebraska Press, 2022, p. 207.

59 John Donne, *Biathanatos: A Declaration of That Paradoxe or Thesis, That Selfe Homicide Is Not So Naturally Sinne, That It May Never Be Otherwise*, 1608, https://quod.lib.umich.edu/cgi/t/text/text-idx?c=eebo;idno=A36292.0001.001. Retrieved 7 February 2024.

60 Aristotle, *The Nicomachean Ethics*. London: Penguin, 2004.

61 Aristotle, *The Nicomachean Ethics*. London: Penguin, 2004.

Chapter 9

Dreaming of god's felt sense

Few mythical figures seem more benign than the Magi, the three Kings of nativity plays. Guided by a portent in the sky, they bring gifts to the divine child. What miracle were they hoping to find? The prevailing version, all wonder and jubilation, gives the birth as the astonishing event. In his 1914 poem *The Magi*, W.B. Yeats disagrees. He sees them as the pale unsatisfied ones who in their stiff, painted clothes expect, even desire, a catastrophe, a portent, a troubled mystery that will unfold.[1]

In this version, the Magi are disappointed by the everyday scene. Their thirst for turbulence remains unsatisfied. For a moment, they doubt what they had faintly foreseen: some other scene, elsewhere, outside the walls of Jerusalem – the turbulence of Calvary, the darkening of the sky, the earthquake at the moment of the death of an innocent young man nailed to a cross. *And behold, the veil of the temple was torn in two from top to bottom, the earth shook, the rocks broke*, the chronicler Matthew said, before adding sensationally: *the sepulchres opened, and many bodies of dead saints resurrected.*

A few moments before (this Matthew does not say), the kiss on Mary Magdalene's lips; the promise, *I will be King, and you will be Queen, and you will have power over demons*, whispered by the condemned amid insults and shouts and the bets of a crowd forever craving diversions. His jaw tightened in horror, the innocent victim shudders. The joints of his lean, desirable body explode; blood oozes from his wounds; his pale lips part to reveal a bloodied tongue and bloodied teeth.

*

I too would have once said that the Magi came from afar to honour the miracle of birth – of every birth. Now I want to say that every human birth

DOI: 10.4324/9781003529095-10

results in a new human death. That sex, reproductive or not, reveals to us that we are going nowhere. That all those future rendezvous slotted in our diaries are uncertain, and all our promises unrealistic. Reproductive sex in particular is a dead end, guiltily disjoined from pleasure in many a pious cock-and-bull story, adding emphasis to the awful insight: we are going nowhere *fast*. Turbo-teleology with a conked-out *telos*. Existence is groundless; that's what makes human sexuality possible. The death drive often overrides the desire for more life, but the desire to die is one with sexual desire. The "bad breast" of Kleinian lore is the sexual breast.

*

The Magi want to uncover a different mystery, hoping to uncover once again a cruel mystery on the barren floor. A menacing prospect. They long for another cataclysm, as if the existential cry of *lama sabachthani* ("why have you forsaken me?") uttered by Jesus, a young man on the cross (the cry that often seals the end of every human life), weren't enough. As if the inevitable demise, the ominous spell cast and spelt out in every blues song weren't enough.

Good news is no news, and the Magi are hungry for news. Not unlike those of us who doze off in the warmth of a living room to the reassuring buzz of the television showing pictures of schools and hospitals blown up by missiles or are distracted by the torrent of horrific, instantly commodified announcements on social media – dull ricochets of distant calamities, invasions, warfare – all of them diversions from the anxious gratifications of a family dinner.

"The Magi are our frozen thoughts – writes Michael Wood – our cold and continuing appetite for the disruption of human appetite".[2] Will the Magi be satisfied by a future catastrophe? Will they *ever* be satisfied? Or are they the personification of dissatisfaction itself, not dissimilar from our own very modern craving for news? If this premise is adequate, if the Magi *are* the personification of our chronic dissatisfaction, they begin to appear in a different light: from mild grandfatherly sages of Christian myth, they edge alarmingly close to the Furies of ancient Greek tragedy. They too are called "the benevolent ones" or "gracious ones" (*Eumenides*), even though their merciless pursuit of Oreste, the latest individual caught in the blood-spattered transgenerational chain coursing through the House of Atreus, is far from being gracious.

The Eumenides, the last play of Aeschylus' *Oresteia* trilogy, charts the advent of the Athenian rule of law.[3] Thanks to Athena's intervention, the Furies' ferocity and vengefulness are finally tamed, rerouted into the ways of legal justice. We are expected to think that this event signals the end of revenge and the beginning of fairness. A comforting notion, unsettled by the parallel recognition implied in Aeschylus that the law is steeped in violence, that the tutelary deities of the justice system are chthonic blood-thirsty Furies. Walter Benjamin famously wrote of *Recthsgewalt*, the violence of the law itself, in 1921. Decades later, Hannah Arendt will speak of state-owned means of violence.[4] Roland Barthes will similarly write of the violence of the law, of laws, of the police, and of the state.[5]

The Magi crave the unmanageable – the excess of violence enveloping the everyday, echoed by our own voyeurism in the face of horror, our anticipation of the coming-into-being of an endlessly deferred apocalypse played out in our hunger for news.

News can only be violent because only violence makes the news.

*

It is convenient to think of our collective craving for (bad) news as the result of the venomous hullabaloo set by the tabloids. But where does the gutter press draw from if not our own (alienated, colonized) everyday? Where does sensationalism originate if not in the nameless streets forever flowing with gossip and backbiting? In Ovid's *Metamorphoses*, Rumour (*Fama*) dwells on a rock and from myriad crevices rocks and throbs sending back the fleeting echoes of hearsay. A place without peace, without silence, plagued by a noise like rustling sea waves in the distance or the rumble just before thunder. The incessant to and fro of nasty and giddy blabbermouths, unwavering and insatiable in their piercing politeness. One or two honest news reports blended with hundred allegations and brash, idiotic bulletins. With each rebound, with every added shred of frill and hideous slander, the itching grows, and the shameless slurs. Rumour, Ovid concludes, sees it all, in heaven, sea, and land, and puts the whole world on trial.

*

When the anonymity, banality, and boredom of everyday life are transcribed and propagated, when they turn into propaganda, they are invested with an

aura of desublimated, abject drama. Everything then turns into announce-
ment, denouncement – everything turns into *image*.

There may be moments of respite from all-embracing tedium: flashes
of clarity, the Heideggerian "clearing" (*Lichtung*, both material space and
"field of consciousness"). A secular miracle perhaps, confirming our hunger for rapture, for the irruption of the extraordinary into the folds of the
ordinary. Betraying our fear of ordinariness, of inevitable boredom as pure
sign of the everyday advancing to the foreground. Besides, is not rapture
itself – mystical, secular, aesthetic, sensuous – a form of violence?

Boredom is the antidote, a meditator's true expertise. You wait and wait
for the so-called miracle, while common miracles pass you by. Here is a
Zen dialogue:

When Mu-chou was asked, "We dress and eat every day; how do we tran-
scend the everyday, having to put on clothes and eat food?"
Mu-chou answered, "We dress; we eat".
"I don't understand", said the monk.
"If you don't understand, put on your clothes and eat your food".[6]

*

The street is also the *outside*, a domain, alongside "nature", seldom if ever
apprehended, sovereignly indifferent to human subjectivity. Even the greatest of French phenomenologists Merleau-Ponty, writing about Cézanne,
ends up saying *le paysage se pense en moi*, "the landscape thinks itself in
me" – a luminous statement which nevertheless replicates the sentimentality of an undisputed subjectivity high on sightseeing. It makes no difference whether the object in question is a landscape or the experiential
domain of therapy. What could the alternative be to "the landscape thinks
itself in me"? One suggestion, heard from an art critic once: "the landscape
un-thinks me in *it*".

A scoop of water taken from the river to a lab for study is no longer
rivering. Artists at times come close to sensing the outside's breathtaking
verve. Themselves rivering, they step-and-not-step not-even-once into the
river. Nietzsche startles us with the meandering curve of his thought. Open
any of his books at random, Gilles Deleuze tells us in a tender tribute to the
nomadic philosopher. You will find that thought does not spring from or is
reduced to an atomized consciousness. You will also find the philosophical

tradition (existential phenomenology included) nonchalantly pulverized. Before Nietzsche, philosophers had never started thinking from the outside, even when discussing politics, even when referring to a walk in the fresh air.

I dream of fresh air spilling into the clinic, of the morning light flooding the room. I dream of a gust of wind, the rustle of two white pigeons on the windowsill one December afternoon. This is not the abstract world of phenomenologists – not even the concrete otherness of the other across the room. I dream of God's own felt sense on this everyday day.

Notes

1 W. B. Yeats, *The Magi.* The Poetry Foundation, 2014, https://www.poetryfoundation. org/poetrymagazine/poems/12892/the-magi. Retrieved 10 October 2023.
2 Michael Wood, 'Yeats, Violence', *London Review of Books*, Vol. 30, No. 16, 14 August 2008, https://www.lrb.co.uk/the-paper/v30/n16/michael-wood/yeats-and-violence. Retrieved 24 October 2023.
3 Aeschylus, *The Oresteia (Agamemnon, The Libation Bearers, The Eumenides)*, ed. W. Stanford, trans. Robert Fagles. London: Penguin Classics, 1977.
4 Hannah Arendt, *On Violence*. San Diego, CA: Harcourt Brase Javanovich, 1970.
5 Roland Barthes, *Camera Lucida: Reflections on Photography*. New York: Hill and Wang, 1981.
6 Alan Watts, 'Zen and the Art of the Controlled Accident', https://www.organism. earth/library/document/zen-controlled-accident. Retrieved 17 November 2024.

Chapter 10

Legitimate strangeness

For Lucian

Tuesday 25 June, 2024. Early morning, a sunny, hot day in London. On my way to work, I think of Michel Foucault, who died 40 years ago on this day at the age of 58 from AIDS-related complications. I think of the many ways in which this *maître-penseur* helped shape my own ideas. Of heady days on campus in the late 1970s, inspired by his hands-on activism alongside Genet and Sartre. I think of his masterly *Madness and Civilization*, exploding and expanding the naïve and scholastic Marxism of my youth. Then in the early 2000s, stumbling upon his published lectures at the *Collège de France* on "Care of the Self" added much-needed depth to the crushing platitudes I had been subjected to during the course of my therapy training.

In late July 1978, Foucault had a near-death experience. Hit by a cab while crossing rue de Vaugirard in Paris, he was thrown into the air. He landed on the car's bonnet, splinters of glass in his head and face. He thought he would die and was overcome by a pleasurable sense of acceptance. Five years later, he told a Canadian interviewer:

> Once I was struck by a car in the street. I was walking. And for maybe two seconds I had the impression that I was dying and it was really a very, very intense pleasure. The weather was wonderful. It was seven o'clock during the summer. The sun was descending. The sky was very wonderful and blue and so on. It was, it still is now, one of my best memories [laughter].[1]

Anti-philosopher

Like Walter Benjamin before him, Foucault didn't like to be called a philosopher. Too narrow a term for the depth and breadth of his exhaustive,

DOI: 10.4324/9781003529095-11

impassionate enquiry which drew from, and expanded on, psychology, history, existential phenomenology, sociology, ancient Greek thought, Zen Buddhism, medicine, psychiatry, traditional philosophy, and more. And yet, he was a true philosopher in Nietzsche's sense: one who can unsettle us; one who does not reinforce the conformity and dull-wittedness of the status quo. As an activist, he then employed his impressive array of inter-disciplinary knowledge in support of marginalized communities who, then as now, are at the receiving end of the hatreds and prejudices of bourgeois society.

In the late 1940s, Foucault attended Merleau-Ponty's lectures at the *École Normale Supérieure*, and, like some of his fellow travellers (Sartre, de Beauvoir, Derrida, Levinas, Deleuze, Guattari, Kristeva, Lacan, Cixous, Irigaray, Althusser), found himself at the heart of that extraordinary flourishing of thought rarely seen in human history, comparable in grandeur and imaginative power to the flowering of philosophy in Ancient Greece. In the British Isles, that extraordinary burst of innovative thought is superciliously called "continental philosophy" (as opposed to what? "Insular" philosophy?).

The joys of self-policing

Both in *Madness and Civilization*[2] and in *Birth of the Clinic*,[3] Foucault expressed the still-relevant view on one of the constitutive aspects of modern society. Unlike forced segregation on a mass scale (the "Great Confinement" of the Classical Age), power is no longer exercised solely through overt violence but via agencies of control and the diffuse presence of the medical gaze. By the 1970s, his position will shift somewhat, even though concerns about modes of surveillance and control will remain central.

Following a hunger strike among detainees, in the early 1970s Foucault helped set up GIP (Group for Information on Prisons), an experience which informed his 1975 book *Discipline and Punish*,[4] a history of the rise of the prison system as we know it. In that book, with his distinctive genius for the striking image, Foucault condensed the historical shift from coercive dominance to more cunning modes of control through the image of the Panopticon ("all-seeing-eye"), the structural device proposed by Jeremy Bentham at the end of the eighteenth century. As many readers will know, this was a device consisting of a central high watchtower within a circle of prison cells. From the tower, a guard can see every cell and inmate, but they can't see into the tower. Prisoners don't know whether or not they are being observed. As a result, they begin to police their own behaviour out of fear. The Panopticon illustrates effectively how power is exercised in the modern society. No physical violence is needed, Foucault commented, but a clever use of geometry and architecture. Modern forms of social administration – centralized, pervasive, bureaucratized – exert coercion on ordinary citizens much more effectively than blatant violence. As a result, the modern citizen becomes duly disciplined, atomized, and self-policing. Every decade construes its own form of self-policing, aligned with contemporary forms of cultural pressure. *McMindfulness* is a good example of self-policing on a wide scale.[5] Apportioning the blame entirely on the atomized individual for failures that are structural and social, *McMindfulness* is duly sanitized and decontextualized of its existential and spiritual links to the Dharma (where mindfulness, or *sati* in the language of the Buddha, is apprehended instead as mindfulness-of-impermanence, i.e., awareness of the transient nature of existence). Neoliberal psychotherapy is another example of an efficient system of self-policing, including the brand of conventional existential therapy in the UK. Both methodologies cheerfully lend us a hand in policing ourselves so we can go back to our reserved seat in the traffic jam, our bullshit jobs, our narcotized existence, our euphoric security where no transformation can ever happen.

Despite their avowed championing of "diversity", modern societies carry out punishment within a system of surveillance and correction which centres on the foibles of the particular case and on the psychology of the person. This is because *intention*, instead of transgression, is now the main principle of culpability. While in feudal societies power was exercised randomly, in the modern world it circulates through highly developed channels, invading individuals' bodies, gestures, and all their daily activities. Foucault realized this long before algorithms, social media, and smartphones became ubiquitous in our lives.

Then came, as Sohrab Ahmari writes, Foucault's lecture of March 14, 1979, essential in understanding the first part of the twenty-first century, a time in history dominated by biotechnology and the return of eugenics, a time when every person is understood as human capital, an "entrepreneur" of themselves, an era when human relations, including marriage, are seen as economic investments geared towards the co-production of future human capital.[6] Prophetic? You bet. But also paving the way for the work of political thinkers such as Wendy Brown who argue for reiterating the primacy of politics over economics against the neoliberal ideology of market domination.

Cultivate your legitimate strangeness

How does one respond to this sorry state of affairs? By cultivating *care of self*. In Foucault's hands, care of self, inspired by the *epimeleia heautou* of ancient Greek thought, whose meaning is *exercise of bodymind*, is as far removed from current anodyne notions of "self-care" as one can imagine. Less about bubble baths and more about *acting* in the world. It is an existential stance that goes beyond the ideology of trauma repair and the politics of injury. It is, in Foucault's own words, "the formation of the self through techniques of living, not of repression through prohibition and law" and, as such, intimately linked to the task of embracing our finitude as a necessary stepping stone to contributing to social and political life.

As a heterodox historian, Foucault was interested in the things history does not register: the seemingly marginal, what gets lost in the folds of mainstream events. For instance the interaction between the young girl or boy discovering masturbation and their Victorian governess who forbids it. Those who hold power and knowledge – be they educators, judges, priests, doctors, psychotherapists – are bound to classify people according to moralizing guidelines which always champion normativity. Inspired by one of his teachers, Georges Canguilhem, author of the seminal book *The Normal and the Pathological*,[7] Foucault launched a scathing indictment of the complex machinery of social control, deconstructing the false claims of what constitutes normality and abnormality, unmasking the attendant punishment and persecution of those who belong to racial minorities, who cultivate different sexual practices, who are disabled or "mad", of just about anyone who doesn't fit with the *normotic majority*. René Char, a poet whose work Foucault knew and loved, wrote of *companions* in pathos, *who barely murmur*. He incites them to go with their lamp spent and return the jewels. A new mystery sings in your bones, he says, *cultivate your legitimate strangeness*.

The strangeness in question is precisely the focus of the thoroughly documented histories that Foucault explored in his unique way and gifted to the world. Strangeness is not necessarily marginal. It could be said, especially if one is attached to the notion of "Being", that strangeness is ontological, that it is the very fabric of existence. In his *Existence and Existents*, Levinas argued that the strangeness of existence constitutes its very reality; that an investigation into the nature of Being itself cannot but acknowledge its inherent strangeness.[8]

With relations to ethics (and by implication to psychotherapy), it is far more crucial for Foucault to explore and understand the relationship we have with ourselves than to blindly obey moral rules. For instance one may want to practise sexual abstinence not as a result of prohibitions but as a personal choice, as a way to cultivate an aesthetics of existence. Rethinking ethics means rethinking the subject – how we think of the self, which is where therapy comes in. What Foucault tells us – via the Greeks, via Nietzsche – is that there is no such thing as a true self. Instead, the self must be created. One way of understanding this in relation to therapy is to think of the true self by imagining our lives freed from the clutches of the super-ego's harsh and dull propaganda. Not easy, considering how deeply implicated we are in the construction of power. Not only does power constitute the subject, Foucault is saying, we play an active role too in its creation. We can also rebel, however, and shape ourselves creatively, explore new ways of being, finding new pleasures, new experiences, new modes of living and thinking.

Surprisingly for a French thinker and activist normally associated with poststructuralism, the starting point for refashioning the self comes from Buddhism and, in particular, the notion of *śūnyatā*, a term normally translated as "emptiness". In the Dharma, and specifically Zen, Foucault found a credible alternative to the trappings of both Christianity and Western Humanism. The point he makes following his visit to Japan is also helpful for the contemporary spiritual practitioner caught in a wild-goose-chase for "enlightenment". What matters to Foucault is that Zen practice *attenuates* the individual, making space for greater fluidity and fostering one's ability to think and act in new ways outside the usual loops of mental habits. Viewed in this way, Zen practice can be seen as a political act, as immanent reflection on the role of relations of power in the making of our subjectivity, and as a stepping stone towards creating new ways of being and being with others. A long way from the Christian notion of *metanoia* or conversion with its attendant guilt and *mea culpas*. It is also strangely similar, in my view, to Montaigne's motivation for self-reflection: less a way of beating oneself up and more a process of exploration born out of curiosity.

Notes

1 Cited in David Macey, 'The Use of Pleasure: Foucault on Sexual Practice', https://www.versobooks.com/en-gb/blogs/news/4284-the-use-of-pleasures-foucault-on-sexual-practice?srsltid=AfmBOoowKk99QJ9_bRhNEXalB7fu0ZwT4u_tnAdUCCVzvwzpPsrrf7sl. Retrieved 28 December 2024.
2 Michel Foucault, *Madness and Civilization.* London: Vintage, 1988. Originally published in 1961.
3 Michel Foucault, *The Birth of the Clinic.* London: Vintage, 1994. Originally published in 1963.
4 Michel Foucault, *Discipline and Punish.* London: Penguin, 1991. Originally published in 1975.
5 Ronald Purser, *McMindfullness: How Mindfulness Became the New Capitalist Spirituality.* London: Repeater, 2019.
6 Sohrab Ahmari, 'The Bleak Genius of Michel Foucault', https://www.compactmag.com/article/the-bleak-genius-of-michel-foucault/. Retrieved 2 June 2023.
7 Georges Canguilhem, *On the Normal and the Pathological.* Princeton, NJ: Springer, 1978.
8 Emmanuele Levinas, *Existence and Existents.* Pittsburgh, PA: Duquesne University Press.

Chapter 11

Against integration

Introduction

Where do we go for counsel? Faced with a crisis, doubt, or loss of direction, the usual first step is to find external resources – a guide, a trusted friend. Unlike a guide or a well-meaning friend, a good-enough therapist may assist a person in finding their own voice, or *voices*, whether through a stance of open neutrality (often caricatured as the psychoanalyst's blank screen) or the discovery of a felt sense/internal locus of evaluation (often satirized as an example of humanistic/client-centred naivety). Regardless of the theoretical orientation and the applied methodology, both stances nevertheless appear to strive to honour and support the client/patient's self-determination.

However, this first important step towards self-determination (or more accurately *individualization*) is never painless. To become individualized, that is, to leave behind the groupthink of one's own nation, parish, and tribe, invariably requires courage and resolve. A radical example is given by Kierkegaard in *Fear and Trembling*. The case of Abraham who decides to follow God's injunction to kill his beloved son Isaac represents a swift exit from the mores of the tribe and a stark example of the teleological suspension of the ethical. For Kierkegaard, the biblical story illustrates the disturbing side of individualization – standing alone by stepping out of the cosy domain of belonging. For that reason, Kierkegaard was reprimanded in the past (e.g. by Levinas[1] as well as Buber)[2] and is being reprimanded today (e.g. by Spinelli),[3] for emphasizing the initial part of the story – the harrowing decision, the moment of madness which cast Abraham out of *Sittlichkeit* – instead of the happy ending, with God's last-minute intervention.

Individualization is a crucial step in therapy, all the more difficult in a cultural/political climate which tends to discount it in favour of integration.

DOI: 10.4324/9781003529095-12

No nation-state is keen for refugees to individualize; they are forced instead to integrate and adopt the cultural frame of the hosts.[4] As a result, the cultural life of a nation becomes monochromatic. "Many migrant individuals and families are under pressure to integrate – Sara Ahmed writes – where integration is a key term for what they now call in the United Kingdom 'good race relations'".[5]

Similarly in the therapy world: the manifold life of the psyche is suppressed in the name of psychical integration.

No doer behind the deed

One of the many side effects of the death of God declared by Nietzsche 140 years ago was a necessary reformulation of the notion of the "self". Not only does it turn out to be removed from the solid entity we wish the self to be; not only does it reveal itself to be made up, at close inspection, of a complex cluster of affects.[6] It cannot even claim to be the *locus* where affects assemble. All the same, and at least for pragmatic reasons, being able to construct (rather than find) an internal locus of evaluation appears to be an important step in the process of individualization – away from tribal conformism and the cosy clutches of orthodoxy. *As long as*, that is, we do not confuse individualization with *individuation* or with what the philosopher of science Gilbert Simondon calls *transindividuation*.

An internal locus of evaluation is allegedly the "place" from which we make a judgement, a decision, an assessment. This notion relies on the belief that there is a thing (a place or *locus*) distinct from affects – from instincts, drives, feelings, emotions, thoughts, from all the comings and goings within our so-called "interiority". My contention is that *there is no such place*. There is no locus. What we call, after Carl Rogers, an internal locus of evaluation is yet another affect or, more precisely, a necessarily transient function – in turn governed by a particular cluster of affects which (depending on our circumstances, experiences, past decisions/evaluations) becomes dominant at a given time. This applies also to another notion closely linked to the internal locus of evaluation, namely, the organismic valuing process, a fluid, constant development through which experiences are said to be accurately symbolized, evaluated, and directed towards optimal enhancement of the organism.[7]

There seems to be no direct discussion of integration in person-centred/client-centred and experiential psychotherapy literature. A quick search only brings up the topic of integration in relation to "integrative" therapy, namely, how to combine client-centred theory and practice with other modalities and orientations. But I suspect that the desired outcomes of key aspects of the approach come very close to the notion of integration, defined as the process or action of making whole, from the Latin *integer* and *integrare*. Psychodynamic practitioners will predictably argue that the very aim of psychotherapy is to integrate split-off parts of ourselves. Even though other orientations, including humanistic and client-centred may use a different language, they tend to essentially agree with the above assertion.

The idea of unity, of making whole, is central to integration. There are two main reasons why I dispute it.

(a) The first reason is *philosophical*. To integrate is to make whole – often associated with an idea of "one" as well as "unity". Unity is a notion we ascribe and even impose onto the world.

The *intellect* has the tendency to interpret the chaos of the world and reduce it to unity – an oversimplified operation which attempts to compress the vividness, intensity, and sheer uncomfortableness of the world into a manageable dimension. This manoeuvre is, strictly speaking, nihilistic; it assigns unity to a bewilderingly plural world out of our denigration of the world and our inability to sustain its power. The manoeuvre is understandable: it yields results; it makes our existence habitable; it consoles us, even though a good deal of life's richness and intensity is lost in the process.

The *body*, however, translates experience not in terms of unity but in terms of multiplicity. The body is more directly linked to the world because the border between the two is so porous as to be virtually non-existent. I am deliberately adopting the Cartesian rift here partly because one of the ways in which integration is commonly understood is as the integration of mind and body. What I *am* saying, however, is that the body is *the great reason*, "a revolving door between the wonderful chaos of the world and the sweeping simplifications of the intellect",[8] and if the shorthand holism that speaks of bodymind as one is to be of any use, it certainly cannot bypass the inherent multiplicity of the body.

(b) The second reason is inspired by *mathematics*. In mathematics, integration is the reverse of differentiation. In psychology, integration is the reverse of difference. In striving to make whole the so-called "split-off parts of ourselves", we fail to honour not only difference in ourselves – the difference which we intrinsically *are* – but also difference of, and within, others. Within the tradition, difference is solely understood in relation to the same. The tradition has coerced difference; it has downgraded it in such a way that we are mostly able to conceive it exclusively from the point of view of the self rather than in its own terms.

From monad to nomad

A few considerations present themselves. For instance: What would it mean in therapy to refrain from ascribing unity to experience? Could it mean to truly follow the route of the organismic valuing process without ascribing a notion of *unity* to the organism? Could it mean that the organism is itself multiple, as well as, at some level, unfathomable? If we entertain this hypothesis, then the second step after individualization – becoming an "individual" above and beyond the injunctions of one's group – would be becoming a *dividual*, to embrace our inherent multiplicity. This is a movement from monad to nomad, from subjectivity to multiplicity. The therapist's task then becomes different: to assist the journey from monad to nomad or at the very least to hold this perspective when working with the client/patient's issues. This may be uncomfortable for the practitioner for several reasons, chief among them the difficulty or unwillingness to fully acknowledge the existence of autonomous aspects in one's own psyche. It is far cosier to take on a stance of specialized detachment when working with a client. This is understandable – up to a point. It gives us a sense of control and power; it protects us from becoming affected by the other in ways which may disorient us. A more or less "integrated" therapist who more or less consciously assists their clients in achieving a greater level of "integration".

Except that neither the therapist nor the client needs integration. In my view, integration gets in the way of therapy work; it is repressive: it tries to re-absorb something which we imagine has been "split off", so that the self becomes a "manager" of organismic experiencing.

How would it look in therapy if a practitioner were to refrain from applying the notion of integration and support instead *nomadic experiencing*? Here are two sketches taken from clinical practice.

Alice: Turning a crisis into work in progress

Instead of trying to anchor Alice's erotic confusion with a false sense of stability while appeasing my own discomfort in relation to her strong attachment to me, I begin to accept "erotic confusion" as an emergent phenomenon, an independent "character" in her experience – essential in opening the door to unknown areas of experience for both the client and the therapist. The client experienced the emergent phenomenon in question as a crisis, an instance of danger which may distract her from her goals. Her desire for greater connection, intensity, and shared vulnerability continued to haunt her after some extra-marital liaisons. At the same time, she experienced this desire as unsafe and destabilizing.

Dangerous and uncertain it may be, but a crisis also represents an atypical moment of departure from the enclosure of our alienated existence; the psychotherapist's ethico-political task is to make sure that therapy acts as the point departure from that enclosure, not as its keeper. The question is: "Are we to build [through the creation of] a psychic space a certain mastery?" Or would we be better off pursuing a different course of action, namely, to pursue, propel, progress lines of flight? Merely attempting to stitch together the old psychic patchwork of identifications and projections that rests on the reassuringly dull and claustrophobic bedrock of family sagas recycled *ad infinitum* by a narcotic pseudo-culture: this would be the task for a psychic constabulary, not for a psychotherapist. Under the guise of crisis, a different way of being may be struggling to emerge. In this domain of *undecidability*, the therapist's/analyst's task is to help others speak, write, and mould an uncertain language through *free association* – a lost art in our barren psychic landscape. For there are no words (yet) for the cluster of emergent phenomena we often call a crisis. The eccentric, polyvalent nature of this new discourse is a breakthrough, a threshold outside the old mummy-daddy scenarios, something that cannot be achieved via that tired existential trope, "meaning", nor through the tired trope of symbolization and the rather naïve idea that by "accurately symbolizing clients' problematic experiences", one allows the latter to be "assimilated and transformed into personal resources".[9]

It is not a matter of filling a client's "crisis" – their sense of emptiness – with meaning, but to generate a discourse where their "emptiness" and "out-of-placeness" become essential elements, indispensable "characters" of a work in progress. What is at stake is turning the crisis into a *work in progress*.

Beyond the fear of "vicarious trauma"

Instead of lowering my empathic attunement and protecting myself as a therapist by creating greater distance with clients presenting traumatic experiences, I endeavour to welcome the affective impact of their suffering. This means rejecting the popular notion of *vicarious trauma* and trusting the inherent intelligence of feelings and emotions, as well as our own ability to navigate difficult terrain. This sort of issue comes to the fore particularly when working in supervision, a domain that has become, in our over-regulated profession, more akin to management and to the stiffening of free exploration and relational fluidity.

In her enlightening discussion of vicarious trauma and supervision, Zoe Krupka writes:

> Underlying the idea of something being vicarious is the belief that there is a rightful owner, or recipient of a particular experiential happening. This "owner" is meant to be a kind of ground zero of a traumatic event, and others around them, the witnesses, those who hear their story, read or transcribe the event, are meant to be spaced out in concentric and ever widening circles which are ideally less and less impacted by what has happened. . . . The concept of vicarious trauma . . . cements the idea that some trauma of painful reckoning is surrogate or derivate experiencing and needs to be challenged through various means, including compassion, reducing empathic connection and sometimes more physiologically distancing and buffering strategies.[10]

In both cases, the idea is, in other words, to work not as the police but as psychotherapists, not as "fixers" but as fellow explorers, embracing a joyous and risky dimension of play and experimentation.

When I use the term "police", I am not merely refereeing to the professionalized police forces but to the multifarious ways in which the state patrols society in the name of "security".

Euphoric security

There are many ways to understand integration, and one which I am keen to emphasize is related to the work of a major cultural critic of the last century, whose work has been often applied – some might say engineered – in the service of dialogical therapy and, indirectly, of the current notion of integration. I'm referring to Mikhail Bakhtin. If one applies Bakhtin's notion of *monologism*, integration could be understood as a monological process. What is monologism? On a societal (and political) level, it refers to a view according to which "one transcendental perspective or consciousness integrates the entire field", assimilating within it all the "signifying practices, ideologies, values and desires"[11] that it perceives as meaningful, while discarding those which are not attuned to this transcendent perspective. The latter are not acknowledged as different forms of consciousness in their own right but reduced to the condition of objects. In my view, this understanding can be extended to the intrapsychic level: the "truth" of a presiding consciousness regards all other psychical aspects (other "voices" so to speak) as split-off "parts", as objects with no autonomous value which have to be marshalled ("integrated") in the service of what Husserl would call the transcendental ego[12] and Rogers would call a "fully functioning self". It is only through the latter that the external world is ordered, structured, and acquires constructive meaning, according to this thoroughly Kantian view – one which still dominates psychology and (most of) psychotherapy.

One of the harmful effects of monologism is to demarcate the world in terms of what it deems acceptable, workable, quantitatively measurable – often expressed in a language that mimics qualitative discourse. It cannot be *truly* qualitative, however, because the presiding consciousness has seized all other affects and, in the process, denied the qualitative and differential values of most psychical life. As a result of this repressive methodology, both client and therapist may experience some comfort. The upheavals of the heart harboured in the soul's recesses are held back; they do not disturb the therapy hour with unwanted disruptions. As a result, the chance of psychical transformation evaporates and, with it, the likelihood of anything new emerging. All a comfortable therapist can do is make the client comfortable too, assisting a process of superficial, "positive" change. This mode of doing therapy – the dominant mode at present – is inscribed within a closed system. It is one dimensional,[13] a form of tautology providing *euphoric security*[14] and the docile pleasures of confirming an insubstantial "truth" which requires no effort from either the practitioner or the patient/client. It presents itself as genuine dialogue but is nothing of the sort. There can be no dialogue when the voices of difference both on an intrapsychic and interpsychic level are muted and/or pathologized. This form of therapy ceases to be a vehicle for change and becomes a close ally of other closed systems.

Trauma talk

The notion of integration is at the forefront in the burgeoning field of trauma, an ever-flourishing industry with its own gurus and set of dogmas.[15] Often relying on a mélange of oversimplified versions of Attachment Theory, object relations theory, addiction literature, and the like, the trauma industry's tendency is to focus excessively on the wounding, often bypassing the inherent ability of a person to restore the recollection of vitality and desire before the wounding. There have been considerable repercussions in the culture at large through the widespread phenomenon of "trauma talk".[16] More recently, the field has been overshadowed by the questionable notion of post-traumatic growth, originally put forward by Martin Seligman's positive psychology movement, successfully implemented in the CIA's torture programs,[17] and subsequently adopted by psychiatry and, bafflingly, by humanistic and person-centred practitioners.

Moreover, the notion of trauma integration is counterproductive: it *insulates* further an already self-bound subject, encouraging pathologization, and inhibiting of lines of flight which may result in transformation. Clearly, two opposing perspectives are a play here: on the one hand, preservation of an arguably narrow hold of what constitutes personhood and, on the other, exploration of difference to the point where personhood itself is called into question.

Against holism

Over the last decade or so, as I became increasingly disillusioned with the person-centred approach (PCA), I held tightly to one notion, which, in my understanding, allowed for a modicum of weightiness which may help differentiate the PCA from the many practices and methodologies flooding the global neoliberal market and dancing to its tune. This notion was formulated by the neurologist Kurt Goldstein's in 1934: the *organism*. To utilize even Goldstein's most elementary ideas in relation to what is now passively termed "mental health" would already entail a subtle but important shift in perspective, namely, ceasing from hankering back to an ideal homeostasis and instead, in Goldstein's words, understanding "being well [as being] capable of ordered behaviour which may prevail in spite of the impossibility of certain performances which were formally possible".

"The new state of health – Goldstein writes – is not the same as the old one. . . . Recovery is a newly achieved state of ordered functioning . . . a new individual norm".[18] The practitioner's aim is not to facilitate a return to a state of abstract well-being. Recovery implies instead navigating a necessary period of chaos until a new organization can be created.

There is much to appreciate in Goldstein's work. Emphasis on the body, the attempt to find a third way between a localizationist and holistic neurology which may include both perspectives, the implicit bridging of aspects of science and the humanities in ways that are virtually unthinkable today. Most captivating of all is the outlining of two instances in the study of the organism. In the first instance, if we observe an organism in the abstract, captured in a frozen moment in time, it will appear to us as entirely rooted in its world, as a prototype or "like a statue in its mould". If, in the second instance, we notice "a grave discrepancy" between the organism and the world, we will be faced with what Goldstein calls a "strange organism, . . . a distorted semblance of the prototype".[19]

The first moment he calls "Being-in-order" or "in adequate stimulus evaluation". The second moment he calls "Being-in-disorder" or "in inadequate stimulus evaluation" or in "catastrophe". In Goldstein's view, "if the organism is 'to be'", it needs to move from moments of catastrophe to states of more ordered behaviour. Catastrophic moments – shocks or moment of instability – cannot be avoided. If the organism is to survive, it finds a way to come to terms with them and overcome them. The startling conclusion Goldstein draws in this instance is:

> If it is true that these catastrophes are the expansion of a clash of the individuality of the organism with the "otherness" of the world, then the organism must proceed from catastrophe to catastrophe.[20]

The phrase is uncannily similar to Marina Tsvetaeva's meditation on what she calls catastrophic development, a perspective entirely devoid of idealistic notions of harmony.[21]

Allow me to underline Goldstein's astonishing statement: *the organism must proceed from catastrophe to catastrophe*. To think otherwise, it would imply that there is no discrepancy, contradiction, or friction between the individual organism and the world. It would also mean that there would be no learning in any real sense.

At this critical point in the investigation, almost as if himself startled by its trajectory, Goldstein takes a reassuring and disappointing step back. This is somewhat similar to what happened with Freud with his abandonment of the theory of general seduction and with Rogers with the inflating of the actualizing tendency into the formative tendency: a move away from an uncomfortable terrain in the former and a move towards comfortable and woolly metaphysics in the latter.

In Goldstein's case, the richly dialectical to and fro he had described between crisis and balance, chaos and order is *not*, he writes, "intrinsic Being, rather only the transition to its true realization".[22] The backdrop to this is that Goldstein, influenced by Kant and Husserl, clings tooth and nail to the notion of a person's "essence". His notion of "intrinsic Being" is Kantian and Husserlian through and through, and emphasizes the organism, "as Being enduring in time or, if we may say so, in eternal time".[23]

I confess to my disappointment in learning that the attentive investigation of the organism by this remarkable scientist ends up giving way to notions borrowed from idealistic philosophy. To be fair, submission to the latter is not without (a stimulating) struggle. At times, multiplicity and the creative agon present in the organism appear to take over. "The higher the organization – he writes – the more differentiated and the more individual the creature, the greater is the inner imperfection, together with the relative perfection".[24] Alongside "pronounced individuality" and "relative perfection", we find in the human organism, he goes on to say, "forces adverse to both",[25] forces which can bring the organism's own destruction.

The solution to this ever-present danger is *holism* – a thoroughly feeble solution. All the same, and against what proponents of organismic psychology might say (including myself, up until six years ago), Goldstein is cautious in presenting the organism as a whole. What do we mean by "whole"? he asks. Is holism sufficient? It is not, for even though "general rules of holistic and organismic processes [are] appropriate, [its] procedure [is] always exposed to a certain scepticism".[26] Knowledge is achievable not by looking at the whole but only through what he calls the "anatomizing method".[27] After which we must consider carefully whether our observation requires of us that we observe the organism as a whole, and, if so, how we come to that notion. Goldstein is far from being a proponent of a facile, comfortable holism. I suspect he would be at odds with some of its current manifestations. I also think there might be something more to Goldstein's contrasting of the anatomizing method with the vision of the whole than a simple to and fro between foxes and hedgehogs as suggested by Archilochus and popularized by Isaiah Berlin (namely, the fox knows many particular things, while the hedgehog knows one big thing; hedgehogs have a single extensive idea that they apply to everything, while foxes think up a new idea for every situation).

Where it gets more problematic is when Goldstein discusses, rather abruptly, the *drives* or, as he calls them, "the so-called drives" asking "towards what are the drives driving?". He understands them as a way for the organism to discharge tension and as a "pathological phenomenon" inasmuch the very tendency to release tension is, in his view, "an expression of a defective organism, of disease".[28] It is the only way a sick organism can, imperfectly, actualize itself. What I find appealing in Goldstein's argument here is that the drive for self-preservation is in his view pathological because only a sick organism would want to preserve itself instead of exploring outside the narrow confines of habitual experience. "The tendency to maintain the existent state for sick people is a sign of . . . decay of life".[29]

Goldstein has no patience with the theory of the drives and claims the existence of only *one* drive in the human organism: the drive for self-actualization. It is because of the existence of various conditions under which the organism operates, he argues, that various actions come to the fore and appear to be directed towards different goals. This view presupposes the existence of an essence, an overarching unitary "whole" presiding our various activities. This is at least what happens according to Goldstein in what he calls a "normal organism" living in a "normal, adequate environment".[30] It is only when these conditions are not provided, he argues, that the organism appears to be momentarily ruled by a particular tendency. These conditions are then described as situations of danger, crisis, instability, etc., prompting abnormal behaviours disconnected from normality, whatever normality may be. Drives, he argues, "can never comprehend normal behaviour". Interestingly, Goldstein sees drives as "abstractions from the natural behaviour of the organism", as "special reactions in special situations".[31] Once posited, one must then introduce another agency, a "higher agency" that elects what course of action to take in the struggle of different drives. While this perspective may indeed describe some psychodynamic theorizations, much confusion may have been spared if Goldstein, well versed in philosophy, had read Nietzsche properly. For there is no need for another agency, whether higher or lower. That agency would simply be another drive. It is by positing self-actualization as the goal of the organism that an abstraction is introduced into the picture – a higher, ordering principle. The latter will then snowball into the entire cosmos via the preposterous notion of the formative tendency.

Integration – or the illusion of it – is very useful to the apportioning of blame under the moralistic guise of responsibility within our societies of control.

> Forces of repression – Deleuze writes – always need a Self that can be assigned, they need determinate individuals on which to exercise their power. When we become the least bit fluid, when we slip away from the assignable Self, when there is no longer any person on whom God can exercise his power or by whom He can be replaced, the police lose it.[32]

Integration – or the illusion of it – is no longer a valid proposition and it still holds back to a positivist reading of psychology. What recent developments have shown – I'm thinking for instance of affect theory – is how psychical life is made up of discontinuities rather than integration and mutual adaptation. Goldstein's mistake (and consequently Rogers') was to see discontinuities as abnormal and pathological. Instead, discontinuities between perception, cognition, emotion, and action are the rule, not the exception.

*

Notes

1 E. Levinas, 'Review of Leon Chestov's Kierkegaard and the Existential Philosophy', *Revue des Etudes Juives*, Vol. 101, No. 1–2, 1937, pp. 139–141, trans. James McLachlan, http://www.angelfire.com/nb/shestov/sk/Levinas.html.
2 Martin Buber 'On the Suspension of the Ethical', in *Eclipse of God: Studies in the Relation Between Religion and Philosophy*. Amherst, NY: Humanity Books, 1952, pp. 115–120.
3 Ernesto Spinelli, 'Kierkegaard's Dangerous Folly', *Existential Analysis*, Vol. 28, 2 July 2017, pp. 288–300.
4 I have developed this idea in my book *Spectre of the Stranger: Towards a Phenomenology of Hospitality*. Eastbourne: Sussex Academic Press, 2012.
5 Sarah Ahmed, 'Happy Objects', in *The Affect Theory Reader*, ed. Melissa Gregg and Gregory J. Seigworth. Durham: Duke University Press, 2020, pp. 29–51, 47.
6 For a detailed discussion of this topic, see Manu Bazzano, *Nietzsche and Psychotherapy*, Routledge, 2019.

7 C. R. Rogers, 'A Theory of Therapy, Personality, and Interpersonal Relationships, as Developed in the Client-centered Framework', in *Psychology: A Study of Science*, ed. S. Koch. New York: McGraw Hill, 1959, pp. 184–256.
8 Manu Bazzano, *Nietzsche and Psychotherapy*, Abingdon, OX: Routledge, 2019, p. 106.
9 Willliam B. Styles, 'Finding the Right Words: Symbolizing Experience in Practice and Theory', *Person-centred and Experiential Psychotherapies*, Vol. 16, No. 1, 2017, pp. 1–13.
10 Zoe Krupka, 'Challenging Snoopervision', in *Re-Visioning Person-Centred Therapy*, ed. Manu Bazzano. Abingdon, OX: Routledge, 2018, pp. 265–276, 270.
11 Andrew Robinson, 'Bakhtin: Dialogism, Polyphony, and Heteroglossia', *Ceasefire,* 29 July 2011, https://ceasefiremagazine.co.uk/in-theory-bakhtin-1/. Retrieved 28 February 2023.
12 Edmund Husserl, *The Paris Lectures*, trans. Peter Koestenbaum. The Hague: Martinus Nijhoff, 1967.
13 Herbert Marcuse, *One-Dimensional Man: Studies in the Ideology of Advanced Industrial Society*. Abingdon, OX: Routledge, 2002.
14 Roland Barthes, *The Pleasure of the Text*. New York: Farrar, Straus & Giroux Inc, 1975.
15 See Manu Bazzano, 'The Trauma Club', in Manu Bazzano, *Subversion and Desire: Pathways to Transindividuation*. Abingdon, OX and New York: Routledge, 2023, pp. 179–184.
16 Colin Wright, 'Lacan on Trauma and Causality: A Psychoanalytic Critique of Post-Traumatic Stress/Growth', *Journal of Medical Humanities*, Vol. 42, 2021, pp. 235–244.
17 Tamsin Shaw, 'Invisible Manipulators of Your Mind', *New York Review of Books*, Vol. LXIV, No. 7, 2017, pp. 62–65.
18 Kurt Goldstein, quoted by Oliver Sack in his Introduction to Goldstein's *The Organism: A Holistic Approach to the Biology Derived from Pathological Data in Man*. New York: Zone Books, 1995. Originally published in 1934, pp. 7–14, p. 11.
19 Marina Tsvetaeva. *Art in the Light of Conscience*, trans. Angela Livingstone. Cambridge, MA: Harvard University Press, 1992, p. 148.
20 Kurt Goldstein, *The Organism: A Holistic Approach to the Biology Derived from Pathological Data in Man*. New York: Zone Books, 1995. Originally published in 1934, p. 388.
21 Kurt Goldstein, *The Organism: A Holistic Approach to the Biology Derived from Pathological Data in Man*. New York: Zone Books, 1995. Originally published in 1934, p. 387.
22 Kurt Goldstein, *The Organism: A Holistic Approach to the Biology Derived from Pathological Data in Man*. New York: Zone Books, 1995. Originally published in 1934, p. 387.

23 Kurt Goldstein, *The Organism: A Holistic Approach to the Biology Derived from Pathological Data in Man*. New York: Zone Books, 1995. Originally published in 1934, p. 391

24 Kurt Goldstein, *The Organism: A Holistic Approach to the Biology Derived from Pathological Data in Man*. New York: Zone Books, 1995. Originally published in 1934, pp. 387–388.

25 Kurt Goldstein, *The Organism: A Holistic Approach to the Biology Derived from Pathological Data in Man*. New York: Zone Books, 1995. Originally published in 1934, p. 391.

26 Kurt Goldstein, *The Organism: A Holistic Approach to the Biology Derived from Pathological Data in Man*. New York: Zone Books, 1995. Originally published in 1934, p. 66.

27 Kurt Goldstein, *The Organism: A Holistic Approach to the Biology Derived from Pathological Data in Man*. New York: Zone Books, 1995. Originally published in 1934, p. 67.

28 Kurt Goldstein, *The Organism: A Holistic Approach to the Biology Derived from Pathological Data in Man*. New York: Zone Books, 1995. Originally published in 1934, p. 161.

29 Kurt Goldstein, *The Organism: A Holistic Approach to the Biology Derived from Pathological Data in Man*. New York: Zone Books, 1995. Originally published in 1934, p. 162.

30 Kurt Goldstein, *The Organism: A Holistic Approach to the Biology Derived from Pathological Data in Man*. New York: Zone Books, 1995. Originally published in 1934, p. 166.

31 Kurt Goldstein, *The Organism: A Holistic Approach to the Biology Derived from Pathological Data in Man*. New York: Zone Books, 1995. Originally published in 1934, pp. 166–167.

32 Gilles Deleuze, *Desert Islands and Other Texts: 1953–1974*. Los Angeles, CA: Semiotext(e), p. 138.

Chapter 12

The unbearable nearness of utopia

With thanks to Aneesh Manangath

Jane doesn't like J.K. Rowling. *Harry Potter* is a gripping story, but there is one major flaw, she says. Despite the protagonist's appeal as an orphan who discovers magic powers and so forth, his fate is predetermined. In *my* story, my client continues, the main character, a girl, is not fated from birth to do "great things". Instead, she stumbles on it by chance. It is an accident that makes her realize who she is. Doesn't something of the sort happen in Greek tragedies? I ask. That moment of recognition, effected by circumstances, makes the person aware of themselves for the first time. The deed precedes the doer, or something like that. Yes, Jane says enthusiastically. Didn't Borges say that of Judas? He realizes who he truly is only on receiving his 30 pieces of silver in exchange for delivering Jesus to his killers.

*

Something akin to the fixity of predestination surfaces elsewhere in J.K. Rowling, namely in her defence of gender essentialism and the attendant transphobia. As with another gender-critical feminist, the academic Kathleen Stock – who believes that a trans man is not a man, a trans woman is not a woman – Rowling was exposed to unacceptable online bullying, a mode of address that is now sadly the order of the day and in which the "anti-gender ideology" movement is also deeply implicated.

Many will have noticed, even within the relatively cocooned world of therapy, the rise of an intense debate around issues concerning gender. But is it a *debate*? The latter would involve some degree of reasoned, articulate discourse paired with a willingness to properly hear,

DOI: 10.4324/9781003529095-13

understand, and critique the other side of the argument. This is far from what is happening at present in the so-called "culture wars". A reasoned, articulate argument is precisely what Judith Butler's book *Who is Afraid of Gender?* offers.[1] It also presents us with an impassioned, compassionate appeal towards greater solidarity among those who find themselves scattered and weakened by internecine wars rather than united in the common struggle towards greater inclusion and emancipation. Judith Butler is a major contemporary philosopher who inherited and significantly expanded on various schools of thought including Critical Theory, existential phenomenology, feminism, queer theory, and psychoanalysis. Their commentaries on key thinkers such as Hegel, De Beauvoir, Sartre, Fanon, Merleau-Ponty, Freud, Laplanche, Arendt, Agamben, and Foucault advance and challenge the received wisdom and common understanding of key cultural, political, and philosophical currents of our time. It may be a strange thing to say about a thinker at times associated with poststructuralism, but I feel that by taking over from where Fanon left off, Butler challenges further the myopic tribalist essentialism now in vogue and ends up making, perhaps unwittingly, a compelling case for a *universalist* political ethic that evades the mystifications of earlier manifestations. Or it could be said, more simply, that the only acceptable version of universalism would need to be based on the experience of those whose lives are thought to be expendable and even ungrievable.[2] This is, admittedly, a *utopian* notion of universalism, one that would certainly carry more weight than the discredited universalism of imperialist and majoritarian stances. Similarly, taking over from where De Beauvoir left off (*one is not born a woman, but rather becomes a woman*),[3] Butler questions exclusionary gender essentialism, inviting us to consider *becoming* for what it is, namely a process without end. If one *becomes* a man or a woman, does becoming come to a sudden halt? Besides, if one really attributes value to the oft-quoted existentialist refrain *existence precedes essence*, reverting back to biologism (as many anti-gender ideologists do) is a backward step.

Butler's work is invaluable to psychoanalysts and existential and humanistic therapists willing to tackle complex contemporary issues invariably emerging in clinical work. It is invaluable to practitioners open to develop (rather than merely replicate) the insights of our various traditions. For over 35 years they have consistently focused, through a series of ground-breaking books, on the issue of gender.[4] They return on it now with *Who is Afraid of Gender?* – a multilayered book – at once informative, philosophically astute, investigative as well as surprisingly uplifting.

*

The spark for writing the book came from wanting to understand what motivated a series of ugly episodes the author was subjected to. Arriving in São Paulo airport with their partner Wendy Brown in 2017, and scheduled to speak at a conference on the threats to democracy around the world, they were threatened with physical harm. A young man with a backpack threw himself between them and the attacker, taking on his body the blows meant for them. Brazilian members of the Catholic movement called *Tradition, Family, and Property* had staged a protest against Butler, burning an effigy of the author and claiming that their philosophy endorsed immorality and even paedophilia.

In the spirit of debate, the book invites us to examine closely the arguments and actions that continue to prompt from many quarters a concerted attack against gender difference. Why is it that *gender*, a term considered harmless until not long ago, is now associated with a cluster of evils, with spoken and unspoken fears, hatreds, prejudices, and violence? Several chapters in the book survey the global "anti-gender ideology" movement. Not a pretty picture. It shows the many facets of a tidal wave of venom unleashed against LGBTIQA+. Sexism, homophobia, and hatred of difference have of course been around from time immemorial. But the phenomenon under scrutiny here is something new. Attacks on gender diversity are now coming fast and furious not only from the usual suspects (the Vatican, religious fundamentalists, the global far-Right) but also from ostensibly progressive quarters such as UK feminists. Regardless of the disparities within its ranks, there now exists a veritable army of the righteous mobilized around what is euphemistically described as "gender debate" about "gender ideology". But is the object of their hatred an *ideology* as such? The word "ideology" gets bandied about a lot, usually disparagingly, but what is it? Butler takes a look at the work of Karl Mannheim who in 1929, four years before Hitler became chancellor, published a seminal book in Germany, *Ideology and Utopia*.[5] His work contemplated whether "fascism could be understood as an ideology" arising from capitalism and attempted to study the "unconscious origins of mental fictions that deny the actual nature of society".[6] Mannheim (a Hungarian scholar who was associated with Lukacs, later with Polanyi, and who was influenced by Kierkegaard and Dostoevsky) makes an interesting distinction between *ideologies* and *utopia*. Ideologies safeguard the existing social order or seek to revert back to a past social order. Utopias, on the other hand, excite a set of potentials so as to engender a collective imaginary of transformation. Butler comments:

> Fascism was an ideology because it sought to reestablish nationalism and racist hierarchies, drawing on older social orders to detain and forcibly subjugate, attack, kill, and expel communists, Jews, the Roma, the physically challenged, gay and lesbian people, and the ill.[7]

Mannheim claimed that fascists assaulted what they saw as dangerous and that the danger in question invariably came from ideas of *transformation*.

*

Understanding that an ideology is driven by mental fabrications distorting one's experience of social reality is an important first step, but it does not shed light on the violence of its manifestations. If it did, all one would need to do is to show the flaws and contradictions of the ideological stance. Another factor comes into play here, specifically in relation to the anti-gender ideology movement: *existential terror*, the sense of threat of one's own identity, out of which *phantasmatic projections* and reactive formations are assembled and directed towards a culprit whose semblance shifts in the course of history: Black and brown people, Jews, women, communists, the Roma, the poor, the homeless, migrants, gays, lesbians, transgender people, the ill, and just about anyone whose way of living and loving does not conform to the norm. Stating one's opinions and beliefs is one thing. Killing oppressed minorities, curbing their human rights, their health provisions, denying in every possible way their very existence is quite another.

*

The horrors of the past are much closer to us than we like to imagine.[8]

What are the so-called gender wars *really* about? The very word "gender" evokes phantasmatic reactions, Butler argues. They activate fears and anxieties which at heart may have to do with economic and ecological insecurities. War on "gender ideology" has now become a focus for political mobilization on the Right. It associates gender with a range of social threats, including possible harm done to children in its name. Other fears include being robbed of one's identity; becoming confused about the unassailable truths of selective forms of biology and science; becoming victim of what are perceived as bogus, arbitrary identitarian claims; as well as being subjugated to an "ideology" that refuses the "natural" demarcation between men and women. For some anti-gender agitators, gender is a form of fakery. It is also construed as danger to the natural heteronormative family and, alongside migrancy, seen as heralding the destruction of national identity. These highly contradictory statements share one aspect: gender is seen by the Right as a destructive power that must be stopped. What made this situation possible? And why the increase in attacks (whether by threat, murder, or legal disenfranchisement) on vulnerable communities such as trans people? Would it be right to label these attacks and the ideology behind the attacks as *fascist*? The temptation to do so is great, given that authoritarian regimes and movements from Hungary to Italy to Brazil to Russia and the United States have implicitly or explicitly courted fascist rhetoric and implemented policies that silence the judiciary, curtail democratic debate, and erode freedoms. The vehemence of the passions aroused by the phantasm of gender could be labelled fascist in a variety of ways. For instance by appealing to narrow notions of national identity that risks being "contaminated" by external bodies. Migrancy and gender were central topics at the 11th meeting in Budapest in 2017 of the WCF (World Congress of Families), an American Christian organization accused of being a hate group with links to the Kremlin.[9] In his address, Hungarian Prime Minister Viktor Orbán spoke of the importance to increase the defence of the Southern borders of the European Union and not let in anyone who incites even the slightest suspicion of wanting to assault families and children. He went on to bemoan the fact that marriage and birthrates are declining and that so-called "illegal immigration" weakens the natural family, which he sees as the basis of the nation. He concluded that natural reproduction would foster the European cause. "The natural family – Butler comments – is thus a national norm . . . [it] reproduces the nation along national lines. . . . What is natural is not any kind of heterosexuality but only the kind that reproduces the nation".[10] For Orbán, self-styled saviour of white, supremacist, heterosexual Europe, the solution is twofold: *natural reproduction* and *anti-migrant policy*. The first is opposed to miscegenation and is closely linked to eugenics and aggressive heteronormativity.

The second is opposed to the danger of "race mixing" – what Heidegger, another eulogist of ethnic national purity, liked to call *mish-mash* – which would obliterate the solidity of the nation.[11]

Contemporary authoritarians promise "freedom" from the moral responsibilities promoted by an alleged leftist super-ego and its dutiful call to caring for the planet, paying taxes, cultivating decent civic solidarity. *Me ne frego* ("I don't give a damn") was after all a popular motto among Mussolini's thugs. "The posture and practice of impunity and shamelessness" found in "Trump, Bolsonaro, Orbán, Meloni, and Erdoğan" – Butler writes – are "distinctly different" from those of twentieth-century fascists. Nevertheless "contemporary fascist trends [that] engage in death-dealing and rights-stripping in the name of defending the family, the state, and other patriarchal institutions . . . support ever-strengthening forms of authoritarianism".[12]

A vital expression of both old and new fascist rhetoric clusters around fears and obsessions around the body and sexuality. It tends to manifest via anxious and futile attempts to shield one's own encased identity from the inherent porousness of embodied existence. It is driven by the fear of being contaminated by difference, a fear partly assuaged sadistically, by inflicting damage on bodies whose very existence threatens one's own brittle sense of self. One of the collective (conscious and unconscious) fantasies of contemporary fascist narratives is that fear of annihilation will abate once we have managed to incarcerate and eliminate gender difference and migrancy.

Late fascism doesn't look like its old version. It promises and even seems to deliver "freedom".[13] Those in power (and those whose interests it represents) seem to be having a field day. Think of white supremacists in the United States, of high-caste Hindus in India, of the petit bourgeoisie just about everywhere, and of all those who benefit from the relaxation of environmental and civic rules upheld by liberalism. Late fascism promises a "freedom" with no holds barred. It slackens the moral airs and graces of liberalism, bringing out and giving free rein to greed, anger, and unbridled stupidity. The one principle of liberalism it leaves untouched, however, is *property*. Property remains sacrosanct for liberals and fascists alike. Not just the property of the castle, kids, and home variety; not only property ratified and sanctified by god and fatherland but also, crucially, that property, acquired by sex assignment at birth and confirmed by the interpellations of policemen and doctors, of what constitutes my identity as a man or a woman. Would it be acceptable to apprehend current anti-gender ideology as fascist? For Butler, the answer is *yes*. Anti-gender ideology is a neofascist excrescence. In the name of religion, family, and the nation, fascist passions are fuelled and disseminated – passions which result in supporting autocratic regimes and antidemocratic policies. Anti-gender ideologists rationalize their war against what they consider as destructive by creating destruction in turn. Sound psychosocial knowledge teaches us that this is a process of *inversion* and *externalization*:

> When the anti-gender movement says that gender will strip you of your sexed identity, they are trying to strip a group of people of their identity. [This] should be read as a confession: it is rights-stripping that they are advocating. They warn against "recruiting" by gay and lesbian teachers or books, but they are recruiting the public into a phantasmatic scene in which they are the ones who are being stripped of a sexed identity by progressive laws.[14]

A Nietzschean/Deleuzian *axiological* reading of these passions will appraise them as *reactive* –forces that turn against the experimental quest for greater actualization[15] while perversely shrinking the range of experience. This deliberate, fearful shrinking of experience is a definition of pathology.[16] Fascist passions are pathological in that they perform the double act of endogamic reduction and projective identification onto those deemed undesirable.

*

The presence, especially in the UK, of feminists against gender greatly confuses the topic investigated here. If for instance transphobia were the sole province of a variegated but consistent conservative front (Pentecostal churches in Africa, the Catholic Church, the Russian Orthodox Church, the US Evangelical Right, some Muslim states, Orthodox Jews, and a host of reactionary secular groups), things would be relatively straightforward. The struggle for gender difference would be an integral component of progressive, intersectional struggle of the Left for human rights and freedoms against the characteristic assemblage of bigots and authoritarians. The current picture, however, is much more complex. It is puzzling and painful to realize how feminists readily quote and authenticate Right-wing distortions of gender studies. All the same, it would be valuable to understand why feminists, particularly in the UK, are happy to do so despite the obvious and important differences. For Butler, the difference between the two camps revolves around questions "of who can count as a woman or a man, but also on what they call the 'matter' of sex, a term that always brings up the matter of the body and the issues that the body presents".[17]

On the materiality of the body, gender-critical feminists surprisingly and uncritically rely on pure and simple, outmoded *positivism*, contending that those who champion the idea of "gender" deny the material reality of sex. This argument relies on biological differences and more or less explicitly on what is considered the distinctiveness of women, namely their reproductive capacity, an argument which ends up venerating reproduction as the essential instance of sex, a point of contention put to bed long ago by feminists (or so we thought). Regardless of the conservative worship of women as mothers (also found in Attachment Theory) not all women can become pregnant. The latter are no lesser women than those who did become pregnant. Some trans men and non-binary people may also be able to become pregnant, and for that reason it would only be sensible to revise our agendas, expand our lexicons, and open our minds and hearts to accept the situation we find ourselves in. When one considers the sheer breadth of "capacities, desires, and gender identities", it is absurd "to identify a *specific biological capacity as defining gender, which should never serve as the exclusive fundamental criterion by which gender is determined*".[18]

This is one of the many valuable lessons we learnt from feminism: women are not defined by motherhood. Some feminists, Butler goes on to say, see sex difference as foundational and will make the point that it is crucial to rely on it so as to protect reproductive rights. This argument founds patriarchal domination in women's reproductive systems. But the opposite is true, the author responds, for it is the "patriarchal social organization of reproduction that leads to the conclusion that states should decide whether or no abortion is appropriate",[19] rejecting the sovereignty of those who are pregnant to choose how best to live their lives. There are grounds here for solidarity between feminist, trans, and non-binary struggles, if one is able to link reproductive freedom to the freedom of gender self-determination. It is a sad state of affairs when that potential and necessary solidarity is undermined by some feminists' support of state's intervention in limiting the freedoms of those seeking reassignment. Time and again, this book admirably calls for the formation of new alliances based on focused opposition to the state interference on people's embodied existence.

*

The British author Shon Faye writes:

> What it means to be a woman or a man (or neither) is not a fixed and stable entity, but a complex constellation of biological, political, economic, and cultural factors, which may shift over time. In contrast to this complexity, British anti-trans feminism . . . has tended to market itself as a common-sense approach that breezily waves nuance away.[20]

It has been often claimed that the "gender theory" is anti-science, but that claim ignores the crucial work of science scholars such as Anne Fausto-Sterling and others,[21] for whom biology is at all times intermingling with social and ecological forces. It is reductive to think of biology without taking these into consideration: the biological necessitates the social to be stimulated, and the social necessitates the biological to be put into effect.

*

The appeal to solidarity goes a long way and includes opposition to the violence of the prison system. The trans-exclusionary academic Kathleen Stock[22] concentrates on a few episodes of trans women transferred to women's prisons and committing sexual violence and ignores the fact that in the UK, trans prisoners are routinely subjected to violence – one person every month[23] – alongside migrants and people of colour. Stock imagines that sex segregation will afford greater protection for all women. But what about trans women? Is the violence they are subjected to of no consequence?

The hallucinatory rhetoric of anti-gender ideologists assumes, more or less consciously, that anyone who has or had a penis is a potential rapist. Butler writes:

> Rape is an act of social and sexual domination arising from social relations that establish masculine domination and access to women's bodies without consent as a right and a privilege. The reason for this domination is not biological; the body, rather, is suffused by the operative relations of power at work.[24]

As with other instances of anti-gender rhetoric, the scene conjured up is phantasmatic, as if in a dream: the penis is the cause of rape, and without a penis, rape will not happen. It would be helpful to consider, Butler argues, other kind of objects and body parts used to violate other people's bodies. If one sees trans women as abusive because, deep down, they are men and all men are seen as abusive, we must ask, the author goes on to say, whether this perspective is grounded on "a romantic idea that women are only victims and never abusers, even though children of abusive mothers know how untrue this can be, as do survivors of lesbian intimate and domestic violence".[25] If one imagines rape as the wild biological urgency of an organ, then one has thoroughly misread the social element of rape culture. The penis, Butler continues, "is phantasmatically invested with social power under some conditions and becomes the site of fearful fantasy under others".[26]

Trans women – with or without a penis – constitute one of the most vulnerable groups. They do not identify with traditional masculinity. They suffer on their body masculine violence and abuse. How profoundly sad and thoughtless to fail to understand the straightforward alliance between trans people and feminists. Not acknowledging trans women as women because one fears that they are men, that is potential rapists, is to allow a "traumatic scenario loose on one's description of reality".[27] It is to project onto a particular group one's own unchecked fears. It is to fail to understand the complexities of social reality. Butler develops this point further:

> If I become convinced that a trans person carries or represent my personal trauma, then I have accomplished a projection and displacement that makes it even more difficult to tell my story, as well as theirs. Trans people now represent the violence of what has happened to me, even though they were not there, and someone else, who is strangely nameless, and notably a cis male, certainly was. Are feminists not inflicting a form of psychic violence on trans people by projecting in this way, associating them with rape when they are themselves struggling to get free of myriad forms of social violence as well?[28]

Is feminist politics a politics of alliance? If it is, trans-exclusionary feminists would not only defend women but also counter all forms of coercions, insisting that Black and brown women live at the crossroads of combined form of subjugations. They would equally assert that women suffer from

poverty and prejudice; that their being in the world has been framed in relation to geopolitics, sub-standard conditions of work and health care, and
vulnerability to varying degrees of violence. Attacking "gender" as some
feminists do ends up weakening an alliance to a broader leftist politics,
which is part and parcel of feminism itself. A long invaluable tradition of
socialist and Black feminism in the UK is being irresponsibly eroded by
anti-gender feminists in exchange for exclusive focus on the single issue
of sex.

Why does sex matter so much now? And what are the politics behind this
deeply divisive stance born and bred in conservative Britain? In other parts
of the world, strong coalitions spring up incorporating feminist, trans, and
LGBTQIA+ groups against extractivism, racism, and class inequality. One
great example is *Ni Una Menos* (NUM) in South America, a transnational
movement that was sparked in Argentina in response to the brutal murder
of 14-year-old Chiara Páez at the hands of her then-16-year-old boyfriend
who beat her to death for wanting to keep the baby in her womb. In the UK,
on the other hand, gender studies programmes are shut down on a regular
basis. A series of myopic British governments certainly bears responsibility
for this sorry state of affairs. On top of that, gender-critical feminists dispute trans identity, in particular the assertions of trans women. They argue
that sex is real whereas gender is a construction, in the sense that it is fake
and unnatural. For Butler, they fail to understand what social construction
is. For some, the social construction of gender means that we are simply the
product of conditioning and conventions. For others, construction is itself
fake, obstructing the living reality of the body. Both perspectives are incor-
rect: they do not take into account an important phenomenon observed by
Laplanche, a key influence in Butler's understanding of psychoanalysis and
a key thinker in my own formulation of *Affect Therapy*.[29] This important
aspect is the enigmatic message unconsciously implanted into the infant
by parents and caregivers – a message that carries an assemblage of desires
implicated within, without, and around societal norms and conditionings.
In that sense, no one comes into the world in a pristine state that is separate from the norms that lie in wait for us. We are not simply "formed",
nor are we simply and unconditionally "self-forming". Which is another
way of saying that we live in *historical* time; that historical time lives
in us in a gendered form and its layers of connotations. It could be said
that anti-gender ideologists want to interrupt this unpredictable aliveness,

historical complexity, and its attendant ambiguity. The Vatican spells it out in no uncertain terms: admitting to the aliveness and ambiguity of self-determination is a sin, for one takes over a power that solely belongs to God. Similarly, gender-exclusionary feminists substitute God in favour of a reductive, positivist understanding of the body which then proceeds to advocate the stripping of elementary rights of self-definition for trans women and men, the stripping of the rights of sex workers to organize and receive health care. The issue at stake is that TERFs (trans-exclusionary radical feminists) demand proprietary rights to categories of gender. But gender categories "are not property, and they cannot be owned". Gender categories precede and exceed our individual lives.[30]

*

In her seminal book *Gender and the Politics of History*, Joan W. Scott wrote:

> "Man" and "woman" are at once empty and overflowing categories. Empty because they have no ultimate, transcendental meaning. Overflowing because even when they appear to be fixed, they still contain within them alternative, denied, or suppressed definitions.[31]

To deny trans people their rights to self-determination is *deadening*: it obliterates their experience. It is also *paternalistic*: it claims to know the lived experience of trans people better than they do themselves. It is both sad and frustrating that such positions are found among psychotherapists in the UK. But, then again, British psychotherapy arguably latched itself onto the most conservative versions of psychoanalysis and existential/humanistic psychology. Think of the undisputed hegemony of Attachment Theory, of the uncritical acceptance of Heidegger among existential therapists, and of the whitewash of the shadow in person-centred therapy.

For Butler, gender-critical feminists' "critique" is not real critique. There is more to critique than opposition and desire to abolish something. Critiquing masculinism implies that existence and society do not have to conform to masculinist norms. Critiquing the gender binary implies asking questions as to why gender is constructed in the way it is. It is also, in a moving turn of phrase, "a way of imagining living otherwise".[32]

*

What is sorely missing from current gender "debate" is a *genealogy* of dimorphic idealism of gender and the gender binary, which, when undertaken, traces it back to the extensive and cruel history of colonial power and slavery.[33] It is crucial that we look closely at dimorphic idealism – what the far-Right and trans-exclusionary feminists superficially see as "natural"– and begin to understand how gender has historically been violently enforced. Discussion of gender cannot be uncoupled from colonial legacies and their still-existing frameworks and histories of racism, immigration, and diaspora.[34]

The colonial history of gender dimorphism illustrates how colonial powers enforce gender normative frames on brown and Black bodies, naturalizing and fetishizing white heteronormative modalities. The Vatican and the far-Right like to concoct the idea that "gender" is an imposition from white metropolitan elites, but the histories of colonialism tell a different story. The assumptions is that "natural" biological dimorphism was the norm before "deviant" ideas were "imported". On this particular point, the limits and prejudices of structuralism are evident, presuming as they do the universality of patriarchal rules – a notion that is also present in Lacanian ideas of the name-of-the-father and reflected in mainstream anthropology from Levi-Strauss onwards.

*

The feminist philosopher Catherine Clune-Taylor writes:

> Within biology, male and female sex is determined solely on the basis of gamete size – those members of a species who produce the smaller gametes ("sperm") are identified as male, whereas those who produce larger gametes ("eggs") are the females.[35]

Interaction is the model that can best account for the multiplicity of processes operating in the making of sex. One of these modes of interaction is between "nature" and "culture". We have supinely accepted the liberal ideology sold to us by some social scientists during the last century, Donna Haraway writes, allowing "the theory of the body politic to be split in such a way that natural knowledge is reincorporated covertly into techniques of social control instead of being transformed into sciences of liberation".[36]

A useful work in understanding the connection between dimorphic ideal-ism and colonial power is Riley Snorton's *Black on Both Sides: A Racial History of Trans Identity*,[37] detailing a history of gynaecological interven-tions on Black women during and after slavery. They were routinely denied anaesthesia and regarded as flesh to be used by medics for their experi-ment. This research reveals that in the United States, the history of gen-der, and in particular trans identity, is implicated in slavery and brutality. Snorton draws on Hortense Spillers' seminal article "Mama's Baby, Papa's Maybe",[38] highlighting in particular her notion of *ungendered flesh* in order to depict the deep-rooted derealization of Black bodies in relation to the white normative frame and its entanglement with slavery.

There are many other convincing examples from different cultures, including South America and Africa, which counter in their beliefs and tra-ditions the gender binary. Luminaries such as Maria Lugones, Oyèrónké Oyewùmì, Zethu Matebeni, and others have done much to add much-needed clarification on issues that are often plagued by ignorance and prejudice. A disturbing picture emerges from the research carried out by these schol-ars, documenting the fact that the colonial assault on local cultures has been historically carried out through and alongside the imposition and regulari-zation of colonial gender binary frames.

*

Who is Afraid of Gender? presents a thoroughgoing and necessary *ideology critique* (as it used to be called in Critical Theory and Hegelian studies on the Left) of the anti-gender movement, unmasking its prejudices and reac-tionary agendas. At the same time, Butler acknowledges that mere critique is not enough. Continuing a case made with their previous book *The Force of Non-Violence*,[39] where they wrote of the need to create counter-fantasies, they similarly call for a *shared imaginary* to counter the phantasmatic projection of the Vatican, the far-Right, and trans-exclusionary feminists, helpful in creating new alliances and free assemblages of people. They draw on the quiet yet powerful force of active positive desire and on Han-nah Arendt's forgotten plea for public happiness. The struggle for gender self-determination is more than mere identitarianism. It embodies a call for complex relationality; it is one with environmental and anti-racist struggles. It can draw greater force and momentum by establishing solidarity with indigenous epistemology.

Ideology can be countered by pragmatic utopia. This book inspires us to move in that direction. An empathic and rigorously utopian stream of thought that were to capitalize on counter-traditional thought and alert us to *the unbearable nearness of utopia*[40] would be a welcome change from the politics of division and defensiveness, of internecine wars, of passivity and pessimism that has plagued progressive thought and praxis for such a long time.

*

My client Jane is keen to develop her story along different lines, away from what she sees as Harry Potter's deterministic, fate-oriented narrative. Maybe, I suggest, there is a difference between fate and destiny. While fate is predetermined, destiny is destination, journeying, and it calls for particular choices. Maybe that's what your story emphasizes at some level. She is silent for a while. Sounds interesting, she says finally. I'll think about it, thanks.

Notes

1 Judith Butler, *Who Is Afraid of Gender?* London: Allen Lane, 2024.
2 Judith Butler, *Frames of War: When Is Life Grievable?* London: Verso, 2009.
3 Simone de Beauvoir, *The Second Sex*. London: Vintage, 1997.
4 See for instance: *Gender Trouble: Feminism and the Subversion of Identity*. New York: Routledge; *Bodies That Matter: On the Discursive Limits of "Sex"*. New York: Routledge, 1993; *The Psychic Life of Power: Theories in Subjection*. New York: Routledge, 1997; *Undoing Gender*. New York: Routledge, 2004.
5 Karl Mannheim, *Ideology and Utopia: An Introduction to the Sociology of Knowledge*. Eastford, CT: Martino Publishing, 2015.
6 Kurt Goldstein, *The Organism: A Holistic Approach to the Biology Derived from Pathological Data in Man*. New York: Zone Books, 1995. Originally published in 1934, p. 24.
7 Kurt Goldstein, *The Organism: A Holistic Approach to the Biology Derived from Pathological Data in Man*. New York: Zone Books, 1995. Originally published in 1934, p. 25.
8 Paul Gilroy, 'The 2019 Holberg Lecture: Never Again: Refusing Race and Salvaging the Human', *Holbergprisen*, 11 November 2019, https://holbergprisen.no/en/news/holberg-prize/2019-holberg-lecture-laureate-paul-gilroy. Retrieved 9 June 2024.
9 Robert Tait, 'Hungary's Prime Minister Welcomes US "Anti-LGBT Hate Group"', *The Guardian*, 26 May 2017, https://www.theguardian.com/

world/2017/may/26/hungary-lgbt-world-congress-families-viktor-orban. Retrieved 6 June 2024.

10 Judith Butler, *Who Is Afraid of Gender?* London: Allen Lane, 2024, p. 51.

11 Martin Heidegger, *Überlengungen: Schwartze Hefte*, VIII. Frankfurt: Klostermann, 2014, p. 224.

12 Judith Butler, *Who Is Afraid of Gender?* London: Allen Lane, 2024, p. 263.

13 Alberto Toscano, *Late Fascism: Race, Capitalism, and the Politics of Crisis.* London: Verso, 2023.

14 Judith Butler, *Who Is Afraid of Gender?* London: Allen Lane, 2024, p. 251.

15 Manu Bazzano, *Nietzsche and Psychotherapy.* Abingdon OX: Routledge, 2019.

16 Kurt Goldstein, *The Organism.* With a foreword by Oliver Sachs. New York: Zone Books, 2010.

17 Judith Butler, *Who Is Afraid of Gender?* London: Allen Lane, 2024, p. 13.

18 Judith Butler, *Who Is Afraid of Gender?* London: Allen Lane, 2024, p. 172, emphasis in the original.

19 Judith Butler, *Who Is Afraid of Gender?* London: Allen Lane, 2024, p. 173.

20 Shon Faye, *The Transgender Issue: Trans Justice for All.* London: Verso, 2022, p. 239.

21 Anne Fausto-Sterling, *Sexing the Body: Gender Politics and the Construction of Sexuality.* New York: Basic Books, 2000.

22 Kathleen Stock, *Material Girls: Why Reality Matters for Feminism.* London: Fleet, 2021.

23 V. Parson, 'Ministry of Justice Dispels Bigoted Myths around Trans Prisoners and Sexual Assault with Cold, Hard, and Indisputable Facts', *Pink News*, 21 May 2020, https://www.thepinknews.com/2020/05/21/trans-prisoners-victims-sexual-assault-more-than-perpetrators-ministry-of-justice-liz-truss/. Retrieved 12 June 2024.

24 Judith Butler, *Who Is Afraid of Gender?* London: Allen Lane, 2024, p. 157.

25 Judith Butler, *Who Is Afraid of Gender?* London: Allen Lane, 2024, p. 159.

26 Judith Butler, *Who Is Afraid of Gender?* London: Allen Lane, 2024, p. 160.

27 Judith Butler, *Who Is Afraid of Gender?* London: Allen Lane, 2024, p. 160.

28 Judith Butler, *Who Is Afraid of Gender?* London: Allen Lane, 2024, p. 167.

29 Manu Bazzano, *Affect Therapy*, unpublished manuscript.

30 Judith Butler, *Who Is Afraid of Gender?* London: Allen Lane, 2024, p. 137.

31 Joan W. Scott, *Gender and the Politics of History.* New York: Columbia University Press, 1988, p. 43.

32 Judith Butler, *Who Is Afraid of Gender?* London: Allen Lane, 2024, p. 141.

33 Lisa Lowe, *The Intimacies of Four Continents.* Durham, NC: Duke University Press. 2015.

34 See for instance: (a) O. Oyewumi, 'Conceptualizing Gender: The Eurocentric Foundations of Feminist Concepts and the Challenge of African Epistemology', *JENdA: A Journal of Culture and African Women Studies*, Vol. 2, No. 1, 2002. pp. 1–9; (b) C. De Magalhaes Gomes, 'Genero como categoria de analise

decolonial', *Civitas*, Porto Alegre, 2018, pp. 65–82; (c) G. Thomas, *The Sexual Demon of Colonial Power: Pan-African Embodiment and Erotic Scheme of Empire*. Bloomington, IN: Indiana University Press.

35 Catherine Clune-Taylor, 'Is Sex Socially Constructed?', *The Routledge Handbook of Feminist Philosophy of Science*, ed. S. Crasnow and K. Inteman. London: Routledge, 2015, p. 190.

36 Donna Haraway, *Simians, Cyborgs, and Women: The Reinvention of Nature*. New York: Routledge, 1991, p. 13.

37 C. Riley Snorton, *Black on Both Sides: A Racial History of Trans Identity*. Minneapolis: University of Minnesota Press, 2017.

38 Hortense Spillers, 'Mama's Baby, Papa's Maybe: An American Grammar Book', *Diacritics*, Vol. 17, No. 2, 1987, pp. 64–87.

39 Judith Butler, *The Force of Non-violence*. London: Verso, 2020.

40 Jonathan Greenaway, *A Primer of Utopian Philosophy: An Introduction to the Work of Ernst Bloch*. London: Zer0 Books, 2024.

Chapter 13

Bringing the plague

For Iana Trichkova

Introduction

Despite the doubts and misgivings towards psychoanalysis acquired in the course of my root training as a humanistic/existential psychotherapist, I have over the last decade found refreshing ambivalences at the heart of it. As a result, I began to regard psychoanalysis as a set of theories and practices that straddle both modernist and poststructuralist narratives ending up problematizing its penchant for generic universalism. Parallel to this discovery, I have also found that when phenomenological and heuristic styles of research are held lightly and critically, and no longer constricted by subjectivism and a philosophy of consciousness, they can be more effective in navigating the intricacies of human experience and open the exploration to postqualitative investigation.

Conquest and adventure

A clear-cut distinction is often assumed between modernism and postmodernism, each of them represented as standing for something specific: reliance on grand narratives in the case of modernism; perspectivism, or even "relativism", in the case of postmodernism. This assumption, however, may betray an inherently modernist narrative.[1] While we are busy diagnosing the end of ideology and the dawn of an age of difference, we may unwittingly affirm ideology in its most powerful guise – hidden, pervasive, heralding the triumph of pluralism-as-consumer-choice, of perspectivism as anything-goes-philosophy, and affirming, via a generic postmodernist

DOI: 10.4324/9781003529095-14

stance, the ideology of "the market" of neoliberalism and of what has been recently called *vectoralism*.[2]

The above reflections came up when reading Onel Brook's paper *Looking like a Foreigner*, where we are invited to understand postmodernism as "a name for an attempt to escape from and think about . . . assumptions and convictions", or as an effort "to come to terms with the "limits and limitations" of modernism" as a manner of staying with "doubts, uncertainties and anxieties".[3] This invitation to think critically and deconstruct the universalizing axioms inherent in psychoanalysis is attuned to the critique found in Critical Theory but perhaps without the caveat found in the latter: critique of reason does not have to entail obeisance to Heideggerianism nor to the concealed irrationality common to now canonical "postmodern" stances. Critical Theory invites us to question not reason per se but *rationalization*. For Adorno and Horkheimer, what often passes for reason is not the clearing of clouds heralded by the *Aufklärung*/Enlightenment, nor the maturity of thought praised by Kant, but its opposite: *degeneration* of reason, which is in my view what a generic postmodern stance has substantiated and promoted.

But what *is* postmodernism? Can its troubled, many-sided, and sedimented histories since Lyotard's book in the 1970s be condensed in one formula?[4] Is the postmodern really contiguous with the preoccupations highlighted by Sophocles "through to Kierkegaard, Nietzsche and Wittgenstein"?[5] And what is the connection, if any, between postmodernism and deconstruction or postmodernism and poststructuralism? Brooks' paper presents telling and convincing illustrations from clinical practice and everyday experience; it mounts an engaging critique of the universalizing tendencies in psychoanalysis, seen as part and parcel of a generalized modernist project which assumes western culture's epistemological superiority against the alleged credulity of cultures arrogantly perceived as subaltern and even accursed. I will leave aside the argument that modernism in art, literature, and culture has given birth to a tidal wave of experimentation, innovation, and daring of the kind our profoundly acquiescent age cannot even dream of.

Brooks alerts us to the alarming levels of conformity and compliance present in psychoanalytic training (and, I would add, in most psychotherapy trainings). One cannot simply dismiss Freud's claim, in a letter to Wilhelm Fliess, of "not being a man of science, not an observer, not an experimenter, not a thinker [but] by temperament, nothing but a conquistador".[6] Freud's claim must be accurately read and understood. The term "conquistador" rings alarm bells, insinuating blatant similarity, allegiance, and complicity with the criminal pillaging perpetrated by Spanish and Portuguese plunderers and mercenaries who exploited human and natural resources between the sixteenth and the eighteenth centuries. It would be good, however, not to forget the very next thing Freud writes in his letter. He says, "I am by temperament nothing but a conquistador – an *adventurer*, if you want it translated".[7] Freud is conquistador *and* adventurer, colonizer *and* dissenter, bringing forth a perspective/praxis that is both conventional *and* subversive, both loyal to, and discontented with, civilization.

One way to understand the dichotomy between conquest and adventure is intrapsychic. Take for instance Freud's gnomic dictum *where it was, there I shall be*. With the majority of psychodynamic therapists now taken up with the delusional task, in our times of "hypertrophied consciousness",[8] of striving to make the unconscious conscious, the dictum may be read as the attempt by an essentially reactive, *symptomatic* faculty, consciousness (for consciousness is but a symptom), to conquer the multiplicity of *psyche* and the complexity of difference and of becoming. A reading that were to take poststructuralism and deconstruction to heart may edit Freud's motto to *where it was, there others shall be*, a notion that is inspired by the remarkable work of Laplanche.[9]

"*I* shall be" has set off the entire psychotherapy enterprise on the wrong foot, establishing the primacy of the self, leading us to believe that the unknown can be known, that the enigma of psychical life can be translated, and that what is other can be reduced to the same. Despite their nominal protestations, all therapeutic approaches followed suit, via appeals to "evidence-based" claims, the wild-goose chase for "authenticity", as well as the fashionable delusions of integration and regulation. "*Others* shall be" may help us, on the other hand, reveal the essential *heteronomy* present at the heart of autonomy,[10] the profound impact of concrete others in our life, whether present or absent, alive or dead.

Brooks' critique of Freud may not be new but is nevertheless urgent; it applies to psychotherapy as a whole and its various gurus on whose persisting ascendancy current therapy trainings are based. Freud emerges in Brooks' paper as the advocate of a methodology of conquest upholding a monological view of his creation, with obvious and questionable blind spots in relation to race, culture, class, and gender – views which then predictably fossilized through tedious internecine and sectarian wars among the various psychoanalytic parishes. The other aspect, of psychoanalytic modes of experimentation and adventure,[11] is equally present in Freud and must be taken into account.

One immediate association to Freud as an adventurer relates to what Lacan heard *viva voce* from Jung:

> Thus Freud's words to Jung – I have it from Jung's own mouth – when, on an invitation from Clark University, they arrived in New York harbour and caught their first glimpse of the famous statue illuminating the universe, "They don't realize we're bringing them the plague," are attributed to him as confirmation of a hubris whose antiphrasis and gloom do not extinguish their troubled brightness. To catch their author in its trap, Nemesis had only to take him at his word. We could be justified in fearing that Nemesis has added a first-class return ticket.[12]

They don't realize we're bringing them the plague are not the words of someone carrying the tables of the law to the superstitious but of one instilling the Schopenhauerian worm of perplexity and pessimism in a societal fabric built on bland positivity and positivism (the "American dream"). The statement chimes with the first generalized reception of psychoanalysis in the United States. Jacqueline Rose reminds us of the story of the American woman who, during a lecture by Ernest Jones on dreams, objected that Jones could speak only for Austrians; in her case, as with her fellow Americans, all dreams were positive and altruistic.[13]

They don't realize we're bringing them the plague are the words of a *European*, of someone schooled in European high culture and highly sceptical of the commercialism and superficiality of the American way of life. It is true, as Brooks writes, that Europe has "plundered, massacred, enslaved and dominated the foreign others it has encountered".[14] It is also true, if one is to believe with Adorno[15] and Said,[16] that at the heart of European high culture, there was (is) that *transcendental homelessness* that became painfully tangible through the horrors of the twentieth century. One could argue that the very notion of "Europe" is specious: not only does Europe have deep roots in the East and the Middle East,[17] but also the flowering of European culture is itself the product of exiles, rather than the uncomplicated manifestation of a European identity. In Freud's case, the rabid anti-Semitic prejudice he was subjected to, in France and elsewhere, also reminds us of the way in which his creation was inextricably associated with otherness and the attendant fear of contamination.

There is one crucial aspect (half-concealed and barely articulated in Freud; conspicuously absent from current psychotherapeutic discourse) that would make psychoanalysis immediately relevant to any project aspiring to be post-existential. This is Freud's brief, tentative admission of the *primacy of the other* present in his discarded theory of seduction and in his (attempted yet unrealized) Copernican revolution. *Primacy of the other* runs parallel in poststructuralism and deconstruction in their *decentring of the self.* There is no serious move away in psychotherapy from grand "modernist" narratives without instituting these two crucial aspects: (a) primacy of the other and (b) decentring of the self. Without these, all talk of "post-existential", critical-analytic psychotherapies is ineffectual and potentially lenient to the platitudes of a vacuous "pluralistic" approach to psychotherapy. Equally, without paying due attention to the primacy of the other and the decentring of the self, there can be no significant shift away from the modernist, biology-driven pieties of Attachment Theory (a universalized grand narrative if there ever was one, supinely accepted by *all* psychotherapies).

It may be necessary to add a third aspect alongside primacy of the other and decentring of the self, namely, an emphasis on the *ontology of actuality*, a notion that is alive in Critical Theory, and one that Foucault[18] rightly saw as a necessary antidote to the inherent trappings of that philosophy of consciousness within whose precincts existential phenomenological therapies continue to stumble.[19] By focusing on the deed rather than the doer, on history rather than an imaginary fall from being, on situational, progressive action rather than abstract ontological principles, we may perhaps avoid bolstering the same old *cogito*. History, actuality, and even contingency appear to be absent from conventional existential phenomenological therapy, an approach that did not pay heed to Hegel, in whose writings the ontology of actuality figures prominently:

> An individual cannot know what he is until he has made himself a reality through action. However, this seems to imply that he cannot determine the end of his action until he has carried it out; but at the same time, since he is a conscious individual, he must have the action in front of him beforehand as entirely his own, i.e. as an end.[20]

Good players and bad players

Winnicott valued *play* as an activity that is not dissimilar from *being*. He regarded play, in Jared Russell's felicitous turn of phrase, as "a type of doing that being is".[21] This view implies an expansive notion of "wellbeing" that exceeds the miserly view, currently in vogue, of mental health as mere avoidance of illness. The latter is a *reactive* notion – the stance of a *bad player*. What makes a bad player? A calculating stance; playing in order to win; arbitrarily assigning purpose, unity, and meaning to the unfathomability of existence; pervasive fear of becoming and its inherent innocence, imbued, that is, with "the truth of multiplicity".[22] What makes a *good player*? Disposing of notions of loss and gain when throwing the dice; actively accepting the limitations of our Promethean will to control, measure, and quantify everything under the sun. Can phenomenologists be good players? Yes, if they no longer see phenomenology as mere prelude and propaedeutic to the study of abstractions such as "Being" but are capable of actively partaking in the play of multiplicity. A phenomenologist can be a good player if he/she is able to appreciate *phenomena* as semblance/ emergence rather than "mere" appearance, without assuming the existence of *noumena*, essences, or "the things themselves". This, however, would require a momentous shift; it would involve abandoning notions of purpose, evolution, and *telos*; it would involve replacing the revered old pair of probability/finality with the Dionysian pairs of chance/necessity and chance/destiny.

It would also involve, holding (very) lightly the structuralist view of language common to Saussure and early Lacan and move the investigation further, spurred by that openness to difference already present in Merleau-Ponty who understood language less as a sum of signs and more as an orderly way to single out each sign from another, thus weaving a *multi*verse, never bypassing the importance of subjective difference in the name of universality. This essential move into difference is hindered when we frame phenomenological research within a positivist model. Must the researcher's need to respond to the inevitable uncertainty of the encounter with others be narrowed down to positivist narratives? The general trend in psychotherapy trainings appears to confirm this. Perhaps a shred of hope in a psych landscape dominated by obsessive measurement disorder[23] may exist: *postqualitative research* is a case in point. Despite being tentative and sporadic, these attempts significantly gesture towards new creative possibilities. The notion of language as gesture cuts through the solipsism of self-reflection; it presents us with a language able to retrieve those voices that rationalization cannot hear, making possible a "remembrance of nature within the subject".[24] From its initial babbling and its onomatopoeic beginnings, language *sings the world*, expressing an emotional essence that resonates in the human *weatherscape*.[25] Having made the most of Merleau-Ponty's work and the notion of language-as-gesture, the next stage of an exploration of language which were to embrace poststructuralism involves absorbing Artaud's (and Deleuze and Guattari's) notion of the *body without organs*, which describes a world of intensities-in-motion, a primal order of language that is already there before the infant can begin to grasp words and sentences, the perception of a voice endowed with the dimensions of language but not its meanings. It also provokes phenomenologists (habitually confined by the intrinsic limitation of their ideology to an aseptic notion of experience as a contemplative, irremediably Kantian connection with the world) to the tragic and potentially emancipatory meaning of experience as liberation from a body-subject subjected to interpellation[26] and the surveillance and cataloguing of medicine and biology.[27] It is this more overtly political aspect of experience – politics of the gesture as much as politics of experience – that may provide the researcher with a glimpse of a more objective *Stimmung* outside the Cartesian cocoon within which existential phenomenology remains trapped. This, rather than appeals to "the body", a term which cannot itself "escape the reproach of reification".[28]

A beach beneath the street?

It is hard to resist the romantic notion that imagines the beach beneath the street, "experience" as raw, immaculate, full of richly entwined complexities which elude us because we have been so fatally obstructed by synthetic methods and theories. It is even harder when the theories/methods in question are gimmicky, put in place in order to subtly coerce researchers into complying with the various transactions that keep that commercial enterprise going that we grandly call "university".

All the same, the notion that by practising phenomenology we are less likely to become bogged down in the constrictions of conventional research methods must be resisted. The view of phenomenology as a method and a theory which apparently escapes abstract meanings in favour of a more direct, sensuous link to experience is at best naïve. If anything, "bracketing" – the original *epoché* of Pyrrhonism – makes us painfully aware of our inevitable biases and (equally inevitable) estrangement from supposedly raw and immaculate sensuous meaning. This error is inbuilt in the apparatus assembled by Husserl's followers, old and new, with its unwavering Cartesian itch towards the "things themselves", setting back phenomenology to Kantian psychology. It would be incongruous for any self-styled "post-phenomenologist" to advocate the undoing of all layers of knowledge and metaphysics in order to arrive at the final unveiling of a natural substratum. From Nietzsche we have learnt that there is no natural substratum; that the "naked' body is not the ultimate ground; we have learnt that there is no "ground", ultimate or otherwise. What we can hope for is to weave a garment that better fits, rather than constrain and distort, the contours of the human body.

How to give up the essentialist notion of the subject? The subjective sphere is itself an oversimplification, an essentially repressive banalization of *affect* and of pre-subjective subjectivities.[29] I see this as a failing that is constitutive of Husserlian phenomenology. It is certainly a *creative* failing, strategically valuable in shielding the "absolute *solitude* of the *existent* in its *existence*"[30] from the onslaught of data and those mechanical generalities that are now the staple of neoliberal therapy training and research. But it is a failing all the same, for it hampers the enquiry through an *a priori* form of sensibility and *private logic*, Adler would say, that is inimical to common sense, a.k.a. shared wisdom.

Subjectivism breeds objectivism; how to steer clear of this epistemological trap? One way out is offered by Gilbert Simondon who in *L'individuation psychique et collective* writes:

> If knowledge rediscovers the lines that allow for interpreting the world according to stable laws, it is not because there exist in the subject a priori forms of sensibility, whose coherence with brute facts coming from the world would be inexplicable; it is because being as subject and being as object arise from the same primitive reality, and the thought that now appears to institute an inexplicable relation between object and subject in fact prolongs this initial individuation; the *conditions of possibility* of knowledge are in fact the *causes of existence* of the individuated being.[31]

The task of "post-phenomenology" is to go beyond hermeneutics, a science championed by Husserl and glorified by Heidegger, and one that entirely relies on givens, "on a *prior pre-comprehension* or proto-comprehension",[32] or on notions such as *habitus* and the abidingly *arché* of the Ego.

Forswearing science

The task in (Merleau-Pontian) phenomenology is not to abandon science but momentarily *forswearing* it by comparing it with other facets of human experience of which science is but one aspect. One potential way out of an almost inevitable and sterile opposition between "science" and "heuristic" experience is offered by *neuro-phenomenology*, a method championed by Chilean scientist Francisco Varela. A key method consists in combining *first-person report* with *third-person description*.

The process sparks a dynamic feedback which takes the enquiry beyond both mere subjectivity and the objectivism of hard science. The above is not only compatible with both Moustakas's formidable template[33] and Sela-Smith's update and critique of the former;[34] it also offers one possible way out of a defensive subjectivist position.

At the same time, for some of us, the time has come to exit not only the stifling dwelling of quantitative research but also the formulaic vagaries of qualitative research whose touchy-feely lingo barely hides what truly runs the show: *algorithms*, *impact factor*, tribal waving of shibboleths ("I'm being truly person-centred, I have mentioned the word 'empathy' ten times"), and so forth. A five-year stint as an editor of a humanistic psychotherapy journal has cured me of any illusion on that front. What to do? One interesting field of investigation is currently offered by postqualitative research.[35] Still in its infancy and despite possible misgivings (e.g. excessive reliance on the tenets of posthumanism), the latter offers a prospective way out of the stiffness of quantitative research and the indulgent preciousness of qualitative research. Among others, its strong points are, as I see it: (a) deconstruction and critical re-evaluation of the subject/researcher to include the nonhuman in the field of an awareness not bound by a philosophy of consciousness and (b) due attention paid to ongoing decolonial conversations and to the findings of poststructuralism.

Think again

Reading Iana Trichkova's paper "What Gets in the Way of Working with Clients Who Have Been Sexually Abused?"[36] stopped me in my tracks. Not only because of the disturbing and painful content directly evoking a range of feelings within me. Not only because of the crystal-clear clarity, competence, and attention to detail with which the article is written. The paper is also a great example of the effectiveness of heuristic inquiry when done properly. The latter point prompts me to rethink my own stance around research. My eagerness to abandon qualitative research methods has justifiably fed on years of reading and assessing formulaic, box-ticking exercises that pay lip-service to "experience", "felt-sense", "empathic attunement" while promoting a conformist agenda that in its convenient and at times cynical adoption of humane/humanistic lingo is as far removed from the tragic joys and tribulations often at the heart of the subject being explored. What gets in the way of working with clients who suffered sexual abuse? Well, virtually everything, from feeling overwhelmed to experiencing "anger, repulsion, and hatred, fear and helplessness, confusion, puzzlement, even shock and horror, grief and sadness, anxiety, guilt and shame".[37] What responses are unhelpful? Most of the usual ones: from questioning the content to voyeuristic interest, to the usual array of (nevertheless useful) counter-transferential responses. All but *one* response are a long way from being even adequate. The heart of Trichkova paper is the letter to their client.

This is what presents us with an incredible mixture of disarming honesty, profound insight/hindsight, appropriate personal disclosure, and thorough self-reflection. It shows directly – rather than merely telling – what heuristic research can accomplish. In questioning the researcher's own responses and the author's general sense of self, it also presents me with a fitting reminder that alongside the critique of heuristic and phenomenological styles of research I have expressed throughout this piece, there is room for discovering anew their inherent and implicit value.

Notes

1 Fredric Jameson, *Allegory and Ideology*. London and New York: Verso, 2019.
2 McKenzie Wark, *Capital Is Dead: Is This Something Worse?* London and New York: Verso, 2019.
3 Onel Brooks, 'Looking Like a Foreigner: Foreignness, Conformity and Compliance in Psychoanalysis', *European Journal of Psychotherapy and Counselling*, June 2020, pp. 1–21, https://www.researchgate.net/publication/341942924_Looking_like_a_foreigner_Foreignness_conformity_and_compliance_in_psychoanalysis. Retrieved 20 September 2023.

4 Jean-Francois Lyotard, *The Postmodern Condition: A Report on Knowledge*. Manchester University Press, 1984. Originally published in 1954.

5 Onel Brooks, 'Looking Like a Foreigner: Foreignness, Conformity and Compliance in Psychoanalysis', *European Journal of Psychotherapy and Counselling*, June 2020. https://www.tandfonline.com/doi/abs/10.1080/13642537.2020.1766530, retrieved 4 February 2023.

6 Onel Brooks, 'Looking Like a Foreigner: Foreignness, Conformity and Compliance in Psychoanalysis', *European Journal of Psychotherapy and Counselling*, June 2020.

7 S. Winter, *Freud and the Institution of Psychoanalytic Knowledge*. Stanford, CA: Stanford University Press, 1999, p. 341n, emphasis added.

8 Christopher Bollas, *The Freudian Moment*. London: Karnac, 2007, p. 81.

9 See for instance Jean Laplanche's following titles: (a) *New Foundations for Psychoanalysis*. London: Blackwell, 1989; (b) *Essays on Otherness*. London: Routledge 1999, as well as the succinct essay 'Psychoanalysis as Anti-hermeneutics', *Radical Philosophy*, Vol. 79, September/October 1998, pp. 7–12.

10 Manu Bazzano, 'Where It Was, Others Shall Be: Desire, Otherness, and the Alien Inside', in *Society of Existential Analysis Seminar*. London: Birkbeck College, 8 February 2020.

11 This point has been made by practitioners influenced by Nietzsche, for instance Jared Russell, *Nietzsche and the Clinic: Psychoanalysis, Philosophy, Metaphysics*. London: Karnac, 2017 and Manu Bazzano, *Nietzsche and Psychotherapy*, Abingdon, OX: Routledge, 2019.

12 Jacques Lacan, *Écrits: A Selection*. New York: Norton, 1977, p. 116.

13 Jacqueline Rose, *Proust among the Nations: From Dreyfus to the Middle East*. Chicago, IL: Chicago University Press, 2011.

14 Onel Brooks, 'Looking Like a Foreigner: Foreignness, Conformity and Compliance in Psychoanalysis', *European Journal of Psychotherapy and Counselling*, June 2020.

15 Theodor Adorno, *Minima Moralia: Reflections on Damaged Life* London: Verso, 2005. Originally published in 1951.

16 Edward Said, *Reflections on Exile and Other Literary and Cultural Essays*. London: Granta, 2012.

17 Edward Said, *Reflections on Exile and Other Literary and Cultural Essays*. London: Granta, 2012.

18 Michel Foucault, 'Structuralism and Post-structuralism: An Interview with Michel Foucault', *Telos*, Vol. 55, 1983, p. 200.

19 Peter Dews, 'Adorno, Post-Structuralism and the Critique of Identity', *New Left Review*, Vol. I, No. 157, 1986, pp. 28–44.

20 G. W. F. Hegel, *Phenomenology of Spirit*. New York: Oxford University Press, 1977, p. 240.

21 Jared Russell, *Nietzsche and the Clinic: Psychoanalysis, Philosophy, Metaphysics*. London: Karnac, 2017, p. 105.

22 Gilles Deleuze, *Nietzsche and Philosophy*. London: Continuum, 2006, p. 21.
23 Manu Bazzano, 'The Skin Is Faster Than the Word', *Existential Analysis*, Vol. 31, No. 1, 2020, pp. 53–64.
24 Theodor Adorno and Max Horkheimer, *Dialectic of Enlightenment: Philosophical Fragments*. Stanford, CA: Stanford University Press, 2003, p. 32. Originally published in 1944.
25 See for instance Daniel Stern, *The Interpersonal World of the Infant*. New York: Basic Books, 1985m and by the same author *Diary of a Baby: What Your Child Sees, Feels, and Experiences*. New York: Basic Books, 1992.
26 Louis Althusser, *For Marx*. London: Verso, 2005.
27 Michel Foucault, *The Birth of Biopolitics: Lectures at the Collège de France, 1978–1979*. Basingstoke, Hants: Palgrave Macmillan, 2008.
28 Fredric Jameson, *The Antinomies of Realism*. London and New York: Verso, 2013, p. 31.
29 Muriel Combes, *Gilbert Simondon and the Philosophy of the Transindividual*. Boston, MA: M.I.T., 2013.
30 Jacques Derrida, *Writing and Difference*. London: Routledge, 2005, p. 110. Originally published in 1967, emphasis added.
31 Muriel Combes, *Gilbert Simondon and the Philosophy of the Transindividual*. Boston, MA: M.I.T., 2013, pp. 7–8, emphasis in the original.
32 Jean Laplanche, 'Psychoanalysis as Anti-hermeneutics', *Radical Philosophy*, Vol. 79, September/October 1998, p. 7, emphasis added.
33 Clark Moustakas, *Heuristic Research: Design, Methodology and Application*. Newbury Park, California: Sage, 1990.
34 Sandy Sela-Smith, 'Heuristic Research: A Review and Critique of Moustakas's Method', *Journal of Humanistic Psychology*, Vol. 4293, 2002, pp. 53–88.
35 Lesley Le Grange, 'What Is Postqualitative Research?', *South African Journal of Higher Education*, Vol. 32, No. 5, 2018, pp. 1–14.
36 Iana Trichkova, 'What Gets in the Way of Working with Clients Who Have Been Sexually Abused? Heuristic Inquiry', in *Critical Existential-Analytic Psychotherapy*, ed. Del Lowenthal. Abingdon, OX: Routledge, 2021, https://www.taylorfrancis.com/chapters/edit/10.4324/9781003140276-7/gets-way-working-clients-sexually-abused-heuristic-inquiry-iana-trichkova-del-loewenthl-betty-bertrand-catherine-altson. Retrieved 21 October 2021.
37 Iana Trichkova, 'What Gets in the Way of Working with Clients Who Have Been Sexually Abused? Heuristic Inquiry', in *Critical Existential-Analytic Psychotherapy*, ed. Del Lowenthal. Abingdon, OX: Routledge, 2021, https://www.taylorfrancis.com/chapters/edit/10.4324/9781003140276-7/gets-way-working-clients-sexually-abused-heuristic-inquiry-iana-trichkova-del-loewenthl-betty-bertrand-catherine-altson. Retrieved 21 October 2021.

Chapter 14

Someone else, someone good

For Colin "Stoner" Bentley (1949–2014)

Forbidding, forbidden

Sitting zazen in the early hours of Monday October 28, 2013, before work, Sarita comes in to tell me that Lou Reed has died. The news pierces my heart. I continue to sit, so as to feel my heart break in slow motion. A broken heart is an open heart, and the wind still howls. Roaring gusts all night and stormy weather off New York too. *The tornados come, up the coast they run/hurricanes rip the sky forever* – the song "Cremation", written for his friend and mentor Doc Pomus. *Though the weathers change, the sea remains the same. The coal black sea waits forever.* They'll play that song at your funeral, an interviewer once said. No, Lou replied, when I'm dead, they'll play "Walk on the Wild Side", and he was right.

Everything kept changing in the wayward pilgrimage that is my life – friends, lovers, cities, beliefs, passions, the language I spoke, the clothes I wore – except my love for Uncle Lou and his work. Changes in his life weirdly shaped some of my own winding turns on this ailing planet. A love for the forbidden and the forbidding – be it sensual, chemical experimentation, or keen interest in the avant-garde and the fringes in art, music, and writing. Wanting to bridge the torn halves – the remote with the everyday, complexity to simplicity, maximum expression with minimum amount of chords. *You can't beat two guitars, drums, and bass.* The various bands I played in, best of all *Daedalo* with Colin Stoner and Tri Hadi, inspired by Uncle Lou and the Velvets. We hit it off for a few years, Colin and I, and the starting point was our boundless love for Lou. Colin was the real thing, an exquisite musician who lifted my songs onto another realm. Colin who had

DOI: 10.4324/9781003529095-15

his baby daughter asleep in his velvet guitar cases during his early concerts with the Doctors of Madness.

The love of drugs and the love of literature. The gender-bending days. The eyeliner and mascara I used to wear and that so annoyed my blokeish pals. Lou's love of trans – the celebration of Holly Woodlawn, Jackie Curtis, and Candy Darling in "Walk on the Wild Side", a song originally meant for a musical based on the novel by Nelson Algren, Simone de Beauvoir's Chicago lover, of the same name. Uncle Lou's relationship of four years with the transsexual male Rachel in the seventies. *And you, you really are a queen, oh such a queen. You know, I'd give the whole thing up for you.* That woke me up as a young man to a sense of solidarity for an oppressed minority in the light of the rabid transphobia around us and within us – that very same transphobia given space to strut at an existential conference in London only a few years ago.

Second year at Uni feeling lonely, I found solace listening to Lou sadly serenading *She's my best friend /she understands me when I'm feeling down,* except that moving to university meant saying goodbye to both hometown and sweetheart. The campus loves were so transient we barely remembered each other's name after hazy squeezes between a philosophy lecture and a smoky barricade. Or that time in Spain, travelling alone after the break-up, humming for days that line from the *Berlin* song, *you're right and I'm wrong, you know I'm gonna miss you now that you've gone one sweet day.* Doesn't every break-up repeat and compound the first?

Hallucinated mediocrity

For several reasons, J. Edgar Hoover, long-dead law-enforcing administrator, founder, and director of the FBI for 37 years, exerts a covert yet pervasive influence today. He was the Avatar of Conformity, eliciting that peculiar Ecstasy of Obedience, within his tightly run little regiment of bigots, a "style" which is nowadays all the rage, albeit in jeans-and-T-shirt casual attire. He came up with a card-index system tracking every political dissident in the United States – pacifists, socialists, union leaders, anarchists, "deviant" writers, and artists – all diligently compiled by organization and location. J. Edgar Hoover adored his mum, was horrible to his dad because he suffered from depression, and couldn't stand granddad because he was mentally unwell. He was intolerant of anyone who was imperfect, flawed, human. His innovative indexing system was a smart and feeble attempt to master life's complexities. Assembling and subduing data as he did so well may of course come in handy if one were to, for instance, pursue a doctorate in psychotherapy. Shrinking the complexity of existence to a desiccated collection of data; submitting oneself to the same arbitrary research criteria to which tutors, supervisors, essay-markers, and Viva panellists also sheepishly succumb in exchange for a buck; conforming to a cluster of recycled platitudes congested inside an arbitrary "canon" – all of this would be useful indeed. Forget "existence before essence". Electing J. Edgar Hoover as your inspiration will help your career, and match to a fault the *data before existence* formula now all the rage.

It may be disturbing, however, to learn that cataloguing, statistics, and collection of data are at their origins intertwined with racial classification and eugenics. Nineteenth-century pioneers of statistic and social science Ronald Fisher and Francis Galton were eugenicists and "racial optimizers". Besides, what is produced by the statistical, "objective" rendering of "types" is a merging of the abstracted average – what Hyto Steyerl strikingly calls *hallucinated mediocrity*. A good term, I believe, for what is being currently casseroled in the lucrative, exploitative trade of many psychotherapy training and research combos.

There is another reason why J. Edgar Hoover is oddly the unsung hero of our violent and tangled times, namely, his stance in life, summarized by biographer Curt Gentry in the formula *avoiding the appearance of misconduct is more important than avoiding misconduct.*

Uncle Lou epitomized the opposite stance, one that I've naïvely fostered (until recently): *cultivating the appearance of misconduct is more important than avoiding misconduct.* To appear as a wild card has its appeal. It's kind of groovy, but you'd be surprised at the amount of bile it will bring upon you if you were to try it on. All sort of nasty nonsense will be hurled at your frail human frame by those who project their longing for freedom and "wildness". The constipated beigeness of their existence will have found a hook, a voodoo doll, an effigy to burn. Beware. It will make you sick. Literally.

In Uncle Lou's case, "wildness" took, among other shapes, the Baudelairean, *maudit* glorification of heroin and speed. I was lucky; only had a touch-and-run approach to the stuff, but have known some who died of it and others who got cured but couldn't bear to listen to his songs. Riffing on the brilliant, edgy secretions of Poe, Burroughs, Van Gogh, Sacher-Masoch, Hunter S. Thompson. *I wish that I was born a thousand years ago . . . that I'd sail the darkened seas on a great big clipper ship going from this land here to that on a sailor's suit and cap.* Playing with fire. Coming close to the flame, getting smudged, retaining the whiff of hellish sulphur all your life. My modest tap-dance between good and evil, aged 21, playing truant during a *Lam Rim* course at a Tibetan monastery in Tuscany and fleeing to a Lou Reed's concert in a stadium in Florence, next day hitchhiking to Naples to watch Lou again go through the old tunes next to his soul-searching *Growing up in Public* set, and then inject speed on stage. Gave his partner Betty a black eye and got a black eye in return. Dumped friends at the drop of a hat, interrupted a gig to shout at his manager "Where is my fucking money?". In years to come, bad appearance became more and more trendy as well as bankable – pricey torn jeans, hair expensively dishevelled, the cultivated doom of crooner Nick Cave, dispenser of new-agey homilies, court poet to King Charles' Coronation; or the punk haute couture of hyped-up celebrities Vivienne Westwood and Malcolm McLaren.

To find my soul, I've got to lose it first, and slowly walk my way up to a temporary salvation. Then yes, *the road of excess leads to the palace of wisdom*, but take good care, excess could make you stupid and the palace in question may turn out to be a ruin after all. For some, this means embracing ancient models and symbols. *A diamond crucifix in his ear is used to ward off the fear that he has left his soul in someone's rented car.*

There is a difference between good and goody-two-shoes. A good person is able to do wrong but chooses to do right instead. Or, having recognized their wrongs, they're then able to rectify them. Not easy. It takes courage to do wrong and even more courage to recognize it and rectify it. In contrast, a goody-two-shoes doesn't have the courage to do wrong, indulging instead on a "virtue" whose root is fear, whose identity is victimhood, and its payout social respectability.

Mentoring the impossible

Uncle Lou had formidable mentors. Delmore Schwartz, his creative writing teacher at Syracuse University, author of the masterpiece *In Dreams Begin Responsibilities*. Delmore was Leopold Bloom to Lou's Stephen Dedalus, in a playful re-enactment of James Joyce's *Ulysses*, themselves re-enactments of Odysseus and Telemachus, themselves reenactments of ancient multiple characters back in the mist of time.

The dream of intelligence, wanting to infuse a 3-min pop song with the same brainpower and impact of a Shakespearean play or a Joycean novel.

Another mentor was Andy Warhol, their difficult friendship and appreciation of Warhol's art documented in *Songs for Drella*, a tribute of Reed and John Cale to Warhol, whose nickname Drella was a compound of Dracula and Cinderella, a description not entirely out of place perhaps with aspects of Reed's personality.

Another mentor was the great songwriter Doc Pomus (*Save the last dance for me*) who died of cancer and to whom the album *Magic and Loss* is partly dedicated. *Radiation kills both good and bad, it cannot differentiate. To heal you they must kill you, the sword of Damocles hangs above your head.*

Mentorship is a funny thing. Reed generously mentored others, including Anthony, now Anonhi (of Anonhi and the Johnsons) a *nom de plume* whose Hindi etymology may hint at the impossible, the unlikely event. In Anonhi's performances with Lou, the current of deep affection between them moves me deeply: Socratic mentorship of love; cellular transmission of craft, knowledge, and crazy wisdom, unthinkable today to contemporary sensibilities over-sensitized by the ideological manoeuvrings of a trauma industry which has quickly morphed from valid response to trauma to traumatization of the entire psychic landscape.

Despite his sophism and sophistication, Socrates was ignorant of the transference. He fatally discounted the hate hiding in its folds. He would fare no better today in an atmosphere of persecutory victimhood – seemingly, the only permissible form of agency, in the same way as the only permitted politics are the politics of injury, categorizing individuals and communities solely on their suffering rather than their aspirations and humanity. In the cultural climate we inhabit, what may be transmitted through mentorship, teaching, and therapy are merely a bunch of withered data paired to a handful of platitudes. This is why I found it helpful (even though it's not everyone's cup of tea) to summon at times Uncle Lou's spirit of defiance and artistry. "Be yourself" is a cliché; practising it requires courage. It takes courage to make (personal, professional, artistic) choices which are neither popular nor profitable. Uncle Lou did it three times. After the relative success of *Transformer*, he came out with *Berlin*, the chronicle of a couple's descent into addiction and abuse.

That time in Oregon doing a "past lives" session; in the induced reverie becoming an Eastern European single mother taking her own life and after that experience vowing to never again listen to Uncle Lou's album *Berlin*, a masterpiece of melancholia, despair, and existential angst. Needless to say, I returned time and time again to that magnificent album.

Lou's second bold, deeply unpopular decision was *Metal Machine Music*, a double album of avant-garde noise and guitars feedback. Then his final release, *Lulu*, recorded with the band Metallica, an album even Yours Truly finds hard to listen to, with lyrics based on Frank Wedekind's late-nineteenth-century play *Earth Spirit* and its sequel *Pandora's Box*. A parting shot, a "rage against the dying of the light" thing that eventually found its way to my heart, the last track in particular, *Junior Dad*, providing musical backdrop to the last part of my Butoh performance *The Angel of History*. *Would you come to me if I was half drowning? Would you kiss me on the lips?*

All three ventures were commercial disasters – now gradually hailed as milestones.

Passing through fire

The arc of Reed's life is that of a man transformed by love. A tender core had always been there, of course, concealed behind those rough edges. I've often noticed, in individual and group work with men, the presence of this tender heart under the tough exterior. I have also noticed, in men and women alike, the presence of a hard interior under a soft exterior, but that's another story.

His existential trajectory reached the peak of human and artistic flourishing. He passed through fire, as the last song in *Magic and Loss* says. *Surviving your own war. Passing through fire, through "I'm better than you all". Finding that the fire is passion and that there is a light ahead, not a wall.* In her song "Sliver of Ice", Anonhi describes her last conversation with Lou: a carer had placed a shard of ice on his tongue one day, and it was such a sweet and unbelievable feeling that it caused him to weep with gratitude.

In her tribute to her companion of 21 years, the artist Laurie Anderson spoke of the wonder and joy of their relationship: singing, fighting, making unlikely friends, loving and protecting each other. She mentioned Lou's illness, which had become terminal, and how he fought to stay alive until the last hour when he suddenly accepted it. She got him out of the hospital, and even though he felt very weak, insisted on going out into the morning light. She describes his last moment:

I have never seen an expression as full of wonder as Lou's as he died. His hands were doing the water-flowing 21-form of tai chi. His eyes were wide open. I was holding in my arms the person I loved the most in the world, and talking to him as he died. His heart stopped. He wasn't afraid. I had gotten to walk with him to the end of the world. Life – so beautiful, painful and dazzling – does not get better than that. And death? I believe that the purpose of death is the release of love. At the moment, I have only the greatest happiness and I am so proud of the way he lived and died, of his incredible power and grace.[1]

Note

1 Laurie Anderson, 'Farewell to Lou Reed', *Rolling Stone*, 6 November 2013, https://www.rollingstone.com/music/music-news/laurie-andersons-farewell-to-lou-reed-a-rolling-stone-exclusive-243792/. Retrieved 10 September 2023.

Figure 15.1 Manu performing "Angel of History".
Photo courtesy: Jake Pitcher

Chapter 15

Wayward angel

For Subhaga

Last October, I was invited to my hometown of Lamezia, Calabria, to do a *Butoh* performance and a one-day workshop at *Tip Teatro*, in the old part of town. I hadn't been there for 40 years, and stepping out of the plane late at night, my first impression was that I had landed in Greece. Layers of history peeled off to unveil an ancestral place unharmed by distance. My hometown, one and the same with Greece, home of new beloved friends through other homecomings. The theme for the performance was Walter Benjamin's IX Thesis of History, known as the "Angel of History" and inspired by Paul Klee's painting *Angelus Novus*. Wide-eyed, his mouth open, his wings spread, the angel seems to walk back from something he is gazing at intently. The angel is staring at the past, Benjamin writes. When contemplating the past, we normally see a sequence of events. But the angel sees catastrophe, the piling up of ruins upon ruins flung at his feet. The angel wants to stay, wake the dead, redeem what has been shattered. This is impossible. A storm raging from Heaven is keeping his wings open, and the angel is propelled backwards towards the future. The name of this storm, Benjamin says, is *progress*.

For Benjamin, progress is intimately linked to catastrophe. That things remain as they are, that is the real catastrophe. Hell is not something waiting for us in the future but this life as it is. There are echoes on Nietzsche's eternal recurrence here. Another presence hangs over this perspective: the nineteenth-century revolutionary thinker and activist Auguste Blanqui, who was briefly elected president of the Paris Commune, the revolutionary government that took power in Paris from 18 March to 28 May 1871 and who was the author of numerous texts including *Instructions for Taking Up Arms*, a manual for urban guerrilla warfare, and a lesser known and experimental book, *The Eternity of the Stars*.

DOI: 10.4324/9781003529095-16

Klee's painting and Benjamin's interpretation continue to affect me in different ways, each time opening a different layer. Benjamin is speaking of collective catastrophe and redemption, intimately linked to one another. He speaks of the dangerous naivety of our human notion of progress, a rosy idea that forgets the collective losses of history. One would need to constantly, wilfully avert one's gaze so as not to realize the very real collective suffering of the past and present. My first impression was that catastrophe and redemption are also irredeemably intertwined on an individual level, and circumstances confirmed this insight. The (personal) story behind the story is that my first performance of the "Angel of History" scheduled for May 2022 in central London and organized by the Society for Existential Analysis had to be cancelled because of illness. I won't go in details here, but the notion that catastrophe and redemption go hand in hand – or better still, that redemption requires catastrophe – became suddenly real for me.

To restage the event in my hometown became an act of defiance and healing. Health can be measured in several ways, including the willingness to contribute and create against all odds.

In the dead of night I open my eyes wide and find ancient and new towns engulfed, silence and stillness all around, tall shadows everywhere. A disembodied voice sings a tune for a commercial; I slowly realize it is simulating orgasm. I am chained to a rock; a Brighton seagull chews my organs. I alone can hear Ann Quin's distant cries as she drowns off the old pier and from the promenade cafes echoes of God's Country *by the Lambrini Girls. I'm falling forever until I can fall no more and this is what flying is, this is how angels are made, from falling and breathing stardust and celestial debris.*

I meet Subhaga at the airport. We embrace with all the tenderness of half a century of friendship. Friend, comrade, confidante, fellow writer, dreamer, conspirer, our love for one another shuffling through decades. Subhaga who rekindled my mother tongue, half-forgotten through my wayward pilgrimage to India, Germany, California, and England. I meet Dario, the theatre manager. A sticker on the back of his van says, "bomb on board". You'd get instantly arrested in London if you drive around with that, I tell him. We drive through the silent outskirts of a place I no longer recognize. I am exhausted as we sit in the little mansard, and we fill ourselves with sweet talk, cracking walnuts shells with early autumn itself coming to eat from our hands like a feral child. Alone, later, I glance at the night of my childhood, all changed, *nothing lasts forever*, no inclination for nostalgia, for what pain there is (*algia*) is not for a home (*nostos*); this is the all-too familiar longing, paired to the feeling of sweet shipwreck in the vast sea of life. The starry night another firmament above the noise of southern mopeds and cars echoing in the small hours as I fall asleep and dream of losing my shoes. It's a big deal to me, but a young woman with lustrous black hair smiles and shrugs, perhaps as if to say *you lost everything, why make a fuss about your shoes*. Later that morning, it rains and rains in the old part of town. Dilapidated houses, overgrowing reeds, faded icons of the Virgin. We are practically inside an Andrei Tarkovsky film: rain, verses of his father's poetry, and the impossible retrieval of what once was, holding a quivering candle wading through a deep pool of water. We head to the theatre to look at technicalities, and I decide to have a candle at the end of the performance with the place shrouded in darkness. Over lunch, Dario tells me of when he was a young boy and saw my band *Ganesh* play on stage and winning the local competition. I was married at 24 to a wife of 21 and how truly beautiful you both were, Dario said, and I thought, if only I knew it then, that we had everything, if only we had known.

Benjamin and his lover Asja Lācis – the Latvian theatre director and actor who worked with the Bolshevik theatre and later with Brecht – meandered through the streets of Naples. They noticed how porous stone and architecture were, how construction and action intertwined in stairways, porticos, and courtyards. They caught Naples's spirit, its verve and passion for improvisation, buildings as a popular stage, splintered into countless, synchronized animated theatres. Everything here, Benjamin reflected later, wants to become the theatre of the new, it shuns certainty and conclusion.

I nursed, absorbed, and digested these and other images, from the Angel to Benjamin's own life, allowing them to gradually inhabit my body. Fast clouds over Paris as evening shadows are falling. Benjamin walking the Parisian streets alone, thinking of another *flâneur*, Charles Baudelaire who in the poem *À une Passante* gave birth to the very modern feeling of love at last sight. Each cornerstone sprayed sparks, from every gate darted a flame.

To his dear friend Gershom Scholem, the German-Israeli historian who like himself was interested in Jewish mysticism, Benjamin wrote on August 6, 1921 from San Antonio, Ibiza, speaking of the Angelus having taken flight. Don't be alarmed, he says, the angel is here in the graceful shapes of Miss Burchardt from Halberstadt. We are sitting in a café, the angel and I, surrounded by diplomats, and she is slurping with gusto the divine ambrosia of the gods selected especially by me. In a subsequent letter, he urges Scholem to send him a poem on Klee's *Angelus Novus* that he knows Scholem has written. Here it is, replies Scholem a week later, *my wings are ready for flight, I would love to turn back but if I would I'd be lost forever*. I love the poem, Benjamin says, sorry for my late reply. I have been very ill, and congratulations by the way Gershom on your new title of Professor.

I move slowly to these words in the semidarkness of the theatre. On the screen a black and white clip of Paris to the sound of a haunted piano.

Your manuscript on the *flâneur* and on modern times has disappointed me Walter, Adorno writes on November 10, 1938. Too many motifs left undeveloped. In Königstein, you once told me that your writing edges close to madness without giving in to it, do you remember? You refuse interpretation and even mediation in favour of immediacy. You seem to disdain discipline, but yours is a dangerous game; you let history and magic sway together. You are such a romantic Walter; you want to call things by their name, but your descriptions turn into the disquieting depiction of pure facticity. You are stuck, in other words, between magic and positivism – you are *bewitched*. But you have it in you, Walter, to break your own spell, by making use of your own agile theory and power of speculative thought! My wife Gretel says tongue-in-cheek that you enjoy living in the musty recesses of your Parisian arcades and are forgetting about your work. Let us in, Walter, Gretel says, allow us access to your holy shrine.

No Teddy, Benjamin replies, what you call disquieting depiction of facticity is the pure philological method, allowing things to assemble and find their own form – the *forma fluens* of medieval doctrine but this time with no demiurge. Matter is gifted with its own intrinsic movement and intelligence, you see Teddy? Write soon!

The angel, Benjamin says, is everything I have left behind. People, but above all things, infused with ghostly presences. That is where the angel resides.

My slow walking in the semidarkness of the venue becomes strained. I no longer walk on my soles but on the edges of my feet, and as I stumble, I begin to undress; shedding, moulting, leaving exposed another layer of my own ghostly presence traversed by those I have loved and lost. *Thought of you as everything I had but couldn't keep. Linger on your pale blue eyes.*

In September 1940, Walter Benjamin and a group of Jewish refugees made the hike over the Pyrenees from Banyuls-sur-Mer in France to

Portbou, Spain. He was trying to flee Nazi-infested Europe. Normally, this would take up to ten hours maximum, but it took him two days. His guide was Lisa Fittko, a resistance fighter who nicknamed him "old Benjamin" despite the fact that he was only 48. He suffered from a heart condition, and Fittko later remarked on his unfailing courtesy and kindness in all his interactions with her. He carried a heavy black suitcase. It must be saved at any cost, he told Fittko. It contains a manuscript that is more important than myself.

Benjamin planned the hike carefully. He would walk for ten minutes, then rest for one minute. It was by no means an easy hike; rough mountain terrain, with long stretches where the hiker has to clamber over rocks without a discernible path and often on the edge of a cliff.

I walk on eggshells, on nails, on glass, the music hints at crumbling earth. The audience becomes one animal body of variegated hues and intensities. The music turns vampiric, the wounded earth reclaims its dead, the maimed, and the stillborn.

In a dream, Benjamin writes, I see a desolate land and recognize it as Weimar market. There are excavations all around. I too am rummaging in the sand.

Walking by Chalk Farm tube station most afternoons on my way home from work, I notice the slow but inexorable collapse of a huge building being demolished, another chunk of London wiped out to make place for something new.

Fittko carried a map sketched by hand, and when the small group got to a clearing next to a huge rock, she resolved to turn back to Banyuls. Worn-out and discouraged, Benjamin refused to do so. He spent the late September night with no blanket or provisions in a dangerous place – a rough mountain region with wild bulls roaming around and smugglers.

The rest is history, in the Benjaminian sense, as inescapable movement towards catastrophe with a faint hope for redemption. The end of his life reflects the melancholy view he had of history itself. When his body was found in a hotel room in a small village in the Pyrenees, the diagnosis declared cerebral apoplexy. He had taken a large dose of morphine – all planned beforehand if things did not go well. Franco's fascist government had cancelled all transit visas. The Spanish police told the small group of refugees that they would be transported back to France. Fearing the possibility of being taken to an extermination camp, Benjamin took an overdose of 15 morphine tablets. His precious manuscript was never found.

I don't see a way out, his hand-written note read. I have no other choice. My life comes to a halt in a small village where nobody knows me. Please pass my thoughts to my friend Adorno, he wrote, tell him the situation I found myself in.

I take off the grey-black suit I rarely wear. I fall on the ground half-naked as in the black and white photo my parents took of me as an infant chuckling with delight at the world. Lying on my back with arms and legs stretched out I sing a line from an old Italian song of longing, of lost love, a song of memory turned into dream. I sing of Pier Paolo Pasolini and Ninetto Davoli's dream, him running after Pier Paolo just taking off in his car: "Take me with you!". It was the journey of life.

The angelic dimension should not fool us. "Your dance was terrifying – a person in the London audience said later – it evoked past horrors". A very apt response. Alongside benediction and melancholy, the angel's gaze in Klee's painting contains horror. The desire to redeem a shattered past blooms out of the stone-cold irreversibility of the horrors and genocides that continue to pile up as we speak. Can a stone bloom? A poem by Paul Celan dedicated to his lover, the writer Ingeborg Bauchman, suggests that it can. It is high time for the stones to bloom. Contemporary philosophers of materiality would concur, for there is no such thing as the inanimate. Gillian Rose must have thought something similar when aged 16, she decided to change her surname from that of her harsh biological father Leslie Stone to that of her stepfather, the kind, humorous Irishman Irving Rose.

It has been suggested that not unlike Benjamin's work, *Butoh* also emerges from wreckage and ruins: Hiroshima and Nagasaki (Kristina Burvill-Ridler, personal communication, 2024). Movement starts from this ground zero as if the dancer has been struck by lightning.

As a homage to the great Butoh dancer Ko Murobushi (whom I had the great fortune to train with briefly in the late 1990s), I prowl on all four at the sound of Vincenzo Bellini's *Casta Diva*, and throw a handful of flowers at the audience from my clenched teeth.

In Benjamin's writings, history is unable to make the sort of bland, preposterous claims of conventional historiography as if to illustrate how things really were back then. Walter Benjamin is no ex Oxbridge don, Ivy League Professor doing a cosy gig at the BBC. Being able to truly articulate the past is rare; it implies a now of knowability (*das Jetzt der Erkennbarkeit*): an opening, an understanding that may emerge when the conjuncture we live in presents us with vivid parallels with a particular historical period which was until now unintelligible. A simplistic example would be the analogy between the shift in ancient Rome from the republic to imperial power and the current political situation in the United States. In both cases, one side of the elite fights another faction of the very same elite in the name of "the people" – with catastrophic results. The now of knowability is most useful in alerting us to the possibility of revolution – of radical change every time a window unexpectedly opens up in the course of history. This is partly what is meant by Benjamin's messianism, a decidedly secular view that values *now-time*, a non-measurable account for a specific temporal constellation that short-circuits past and present and suspends the linear flow of time. Benjamin does not present us with so-called "progress", in many ways a delusional idea which entirely depends on linear time. He is interested instead in redemption. The angel wants to repair what has been broken.

There have been, as it were, *four* Benjamins, if one looks at the main interpretations of his work following his death. Fragmentation is not necessarily a bad thing, as Habermas would have it. It becomes a problem only for those who crave the illusion of unity and systematicity. Gillian Rose examined these four views in her early introductory lectures to the Frankfurt School.[1] All of these interpretations stemmed from Benjamin's own friends. One of them has been positively misleading, Hannah Arendt's, who befriended Benjamin in Paris and helped the publication of *Illuminations*. Hers, Rose tells us, is an "existential" Benjamin, his subtle insights relegated with an ahistorical view of the "human condition" which is both abstract and worryingly bordering on Heideggerianism. Then there was the Brechtian interpretation, aligned with Benjamin's interest in anti-illusionist art. Another view, championed by the Frankfurt School and in particular by Adorno, reads Benjamin in a Hegelian/Marxist key. Finally, his friend Scholem echoed and amplified Benjamin's interest in Jewish messianism and religious thought in general.

During the Butoh performances in Italy, Greece, and London, I pivoted on these last two as I found the cross-fertilization between the secular, dialectical materialist and religious redemptive narratives most rewarding and also inspiring for our own troubled times. Did Benjamin really fail, as some commentators believed, in integrating his compelling version of non-dogmatic, modernist Marxism with his equally compelling version of religious messianism? He did. Perhaps success is an overrated idea, trapped within the clutches of our prevalent narratives of gain and acquisition born out of the society of the spectacle. When the situationists initially formulated this notion, it was done as an attempt to grapple with the disembodied nature of human interactions, eaten up and colonized by capitalism. What could not be known in the late 1960 was that the spectacle would become the only game in town, and that our anxiety of being out of touch would mean that we would be 24/7 in touch with our smartphone screen. We have succeeded at being in touch, but it doesn't feel that great, does it?

Perhaps failure is a far more inspiring idea, not only for artists, philosophers, and psychoanalysts but also for revolutionaries. The alleged failure of the Paris Commune was taken up by the October revolution, and this in turn was taken up by May '68 and in turn taken up by Occupy, Black Lives Matter, and so on. The value of failure was obvious to Benjamin when he wrote about Kafka. The unique beauty of Kafka consists, he said, in the purity and fervour of his failure.

In a political landscape dominated by successful and dangerous buffoons, let us fail once more, with feeling. Let us pull the emergency brake on the mad runaway train that is destroying the planet and the existence of those whose life are deemed expendable. Benjamin had a name for the emergency brake: revolution.

Note

1 Gillian Rose, *Marxist Modernism: Introductory Lectures on Frankfurt School Critical Theory*. London: Verso, 2024.

References

Theodor Adorno, *Hegel: Three Studies*, trans. S. W. Nicholsen. Cambridge, MA: MIT Press, 1993.

Theodor Adorno, *Minima Moralia: Reflections on Damaged Life*. London: Verso, 2005. Originally published in 1951.

Theodor Adorno and Max Horkheimer, *Dialectic of Enlightenment: Philosophical Fragments*. Stanford, CA: Stanford University Press, 2003, p. 32. Originally published in 1944.

Aeschylus, *The Oresteia (Agamemnon, The Libation Bearers, The Eumenides)*, ed. W. Stanford, trans. Robert Fagles. London: Penguin Classics, 1977.

Giorgio Agamben, *Homo Sacer: Sovereign Power and Bare Life*. Stanford, CA: Stanford University Press, 1998.

Brenda J. Allen, *Difference Matters: Communicating Social Identity*. Long Grove, IL: Waveland Press, 2023.

Louis Althusser, *For Marx*. London: Verso, 2005.

Laurie Anderson, 'Farewell to Lou Reed', *Rolling Stone*, November 6, 2013.

Anonhi and the Johnsons, 'Scapegoat', in *My Back Was the Bridge for You to Cross*. Music album. Bloomington, IN: Secretly Canadia, 2023.

Hannah Arendt, *On Violence*. San Diego, CA: Harcourt Brase Javanovich, 1970.

Aristotle, *Nichomachean Ethics*, trans. David Ross, Oxford, MA: Oxford World's Classics, 2009.

Mikhail Bakhtin, *Problems of Dostoevsky's Poetics*. Munster: Ardis, 1973, pp. 6–7.

Etienne Balibar, *Reading Capital*. London: Verso, 1985.

Etienne Balibar, *Equaliberty: Political Essays*, trans. James Ingram. Durham: Duke University Press, 2014.

Etienne Balibar, *Spinoza, the Transindividual*, trans. Mark G. E. Kelly. Edinburgh University Press, 2020.

Honoré de Balzac, *The Lily in the Valley*. New York: New York Review Books, 2024.

Roland Barthes, *The Pleasure of the Text*. New York: Farrar, Straus & Giroux Inc, 1975.

Roland Barthes, *Camera Lucida: Reflections on Photography*. New York: Hill and Wang, 1981.

Alison Bashford, 'Deep Genetics: Universal History and the Species', *History and Theory*, Vol. 57, No. 2, 2018.

Georges Bataille, *Story of the Eye*. New York: Urizen Books, 1977.

Georges Bataille, *Inner Experience*. Albany, NY: State University of New York Press, 1988.

Manu Bazzano, *Spectre of the Stranger: Towards a Phenomenology of Hospitality*. Eastbourne: Sussex Academic Press, 2012.

Manu Bazzano, ed., *Re-Visioning Person-Centred Therapy*. Abingdon, OX: Routledge, 2018, pp. 265–276.

Manu Bazzano, *Nietzsche and Psychotherapy*. Abingdon, OX: Routledge, 2019.

Manu Bazzano, 'Sons of our Fathers', *Therapy Today*, Vol. 20, No. 9, November 2019.

Manu Bazzano, ed., *Re-visioning Existential Therapy: Counter-Traditional Perspectives*. Abingdon, OX: Routledge, 2020.

Manu Bazzano, 'Making Love to Your Data', *Therapy Today*, March 2021.

Manu Bazzano, *Subversion and Desire: Pathways to Transindividuation*. Abingdon, OX: Routledge, 2023.

Simone de Beauvoir, *The Second Sex*. London: Vintage, 1997.

Jessica Benjamin and Galis Atlas, 'The "Too Muchness" of Excitement: Sexuality in Light of Excess, Attachment and Affect Regulation', *International Journal of Psychoanalysis*, No. 96, 2015.

Walter Benjamin, *The Arcades Project*, trans. H. Eiland and K. McLaughlin. Cambridge, MA: The Belknap Press, 1999.

Walter Benjamin, 'Capitalism as Religion', in *Selected Writings, Vol 1: 1913–1926*. Cambridge, MA: Harvard University Press, 2004.

Walter Benjamin, *Selected Writings*, Vol. 4, ed. Howard Eiland and Michael W. Jennings. Cambridge and London: Belknap Press, 2006.

Leo Bersani and Adam Phillips, *Intimacies*. Chicago, IL: University of Chicago Press, 2008.

Arne De Boever, Alex Murray, Jon Roffe, and Ashley Woodward, eds., *Gilbert Simondon: Being and Technology*. Edinburgh University Press, 2012.

Christopher Bollas, *The Freudian Moment*. London: Karnac, 2007.

Onel Brooks, 'Looking like a Foreigner: Foreignness, Conformity and Compliance in Psychoanalysis', *European Journal of Psychotherapy and Counselling*, June 2020, pp. 1–21.

Clare Bucknell, 'His Own Dark Mind', *London Review of Books*, Vol. 45, No. 23, November 2023.

Judith Butler, *Bodies That Matter: On the Discursive Limits of "Sex"*. New York: Routledge, 1993.

Judith Butler, *The Psychic Life of Power: Theories in Subjection*. New York: Routledge, 1997.

Judith Butler, *Undoing Gender*. New York: Routledge, 2004.

Judith Butler, *Frames of War: When Is Life Grievable?* London: Verso, 2009.

Judith Butler, *The Force of Non-violence*. London: Verso, 2020.

Judith Butler, *Who Is Afraid of Gender?* London: Allen Lane, 2024.

George Gordon Byron, *The Prisoner of Chillon*. London: Create Space Publishing, 2016, originally published in 1816.

Georges Canguilhem, *On the Normal and the Pathological*. Princeton, NJ: Springer, 1978.

Ray Carney, *Cassavetes on Cassavetes*. London: Faber, 2001, p. 65.

Michel de Certeau, *The Mystic Fable: The Sixteenth and Seventeenth Centuries*, ed. Luce Giard, trans. Daniel Smith. Chicago: University of Chicago Press, 2015.

Aimé Césaire, *Discourses on Colonialism*, trans. Joan Pinkham. New York: Monthly Review Press, 2001.

Claire Colebrook, *Death of the Posthuman: Essays on Extinction*. London: Open Humanities Press, 2014.

Claire Colebrook, *Who Would You Kill to Save the World?* Lincoln, NE: University of Nebraska Press, 2022.

Muriel Combes, *Gilbert Simondon and the Philosophy of the Transindividual*. Boston, MA: M.I.T., 2013.

Tom Conley, 'A Plea for Leibniz', in Gilles Deleuze, *The Fold: Leibniz and the Baroque*. London: Continuum, 2006.

Tom Conley, 'Singularity', in *The Deleuze Dictionary*, ed. Adrian Parr. University of Edinburgh Press, 2010.

Joseph Conrad, *Heart of Darkness*. London: Penguin, 2007. Originally published in 1899.

S. Crasnow and K. Inteman, eds., *The Routledge Handbook of Feminist Philosophy of Science*. London: Routledge, 2015.

C. Z. Cremer and L. Kemp, *Democratising Risk: In Search of a Methodology to Study Existential Risk*. Internet file, 2021.

Pierre Dardot, Christian Laval, Haud Guéguen, and Pierre Sauvêtre, *Le Choix de la Guerre Civile: Une Autre Histoire Néolibéralisme*. Lux: Montréal, 2021.

Joe P. L. Davidson, 'Extinctiopolitics: Existential Risk Studies, the Extinctiopolitical Unconscious, and The Billionaires' Exodus from Earth', *New Formations*, No. 107–108, 2022.

William Davies, 'Stay away from Politics', *London Review of Books*, Vol. 45, No. 18, 21 September 2022.

Gilles Deleuze, *Masochism*. New York: Zone Books, 1991.

Gilles Deleuze, *Desert Islands and Other Texts 1953–1974*. Los Angeles, CA: Semiotext(e), 2004.

Gilles Deleuze, *The Fold: Leibniz and the Baroque*. London: Continuum, 2006.

Gilles Deleuze, *Nietzsche and Philosophy*, New York: Columbia University Press, 2008.

Gilles Deleuze, *Difference and Repetition*. London: Bloomsbury Academic, 2014.

Gilles Deleuze and Claire Parnet, *Dialogues*, trans. Hugh Tomlinson and Barbara Habberjam. New York: Columbia University Press, 1987.

Jacques Derrida, *Writing and Difference*. London: Routledge, 2005, p. 110. Originally published in 1967.

Peter Dews, 'Adorno, Post-Structuralism and the Critique of Identity', *New Left Review*, Vol. I, No. 157, 1986, pp. 28–44.

Charles Dickens, *Our Mutual Friend*. Ware, Herts: Wordsworth Editions, 1997.

John Donne, *Death's Duel. Or, A Consolation to the Soul Against the Dying Life and Living Death of the Body*, 1631.

Anne Dufourmantelle, *In Defense of Secrets*, trans. Lindsay Turner. New York: Fordham University Press, 2021.

Lee Edelman, *No Future: Queer Theory and the Death Drive*. Durham, NC: Duke University Press, 2004.

Caroline Elkins, *Legacy of Violence: A History of the British Empire*. London: Bodley Head, 2022.

Frantz Fanon, *The Wretched of the Earth*. Preface by Jean-Paul Sartre. New York: Grove Press, 1963.

Frantz Fanon, *Black Skin, White Masks*, trans. Charles Lam Markmann. London: Pluto Press, 1986. Originally published in 1952.

Frantz Fanon, *Toward the African Revolution*, trans. Haakon Chevalier. New York: Grove Books, 1994.

Justin Farrell, *Billionaire Wilderness*. Princeton, NJ: Princeton University Press, 2020.

Anne Fausto-Sterling, *Sexing the Body: Gender Politics and the Construction of Sexuality*. New York: Basic Books, 2000.

Shon Faye, *The Transgender Issue: Trans Justice for All*. London: Verso, 2022.

Andrew Feenberg, *Technosystem: The Social Life of Reason*. Cambridge, MA: Harvard University Press, 2018.

Jessica Fern, *Polysecure: Attachment, Trauma and Consensual Nonmonogamy*. Vancouver, BC: Thornapple Press, 2020.

Aaron Fogel, *Coercion to Speak: Conrad's Poetics of Dialogue*. Cambridge, MA: Harvard University Press, 1985.

Michel Foucault, *Madness and Civilization*. London: Vintage, 1988. Originally published in 1961.

Michel Foucault, *Discipline and Punish*. London: Penguin, 1991. Originally published in 1975.

Michel Foucault, *The Birth of the Clinic*. London: Vintage, 1994. Originally published in 1963.

Michel Foucault, *Society Must be Defended*. London: Picador, 2003.

Michel Foucault, *The Birth of Biopolitics*. Basingstoke, Hants: Palgrave Macmillan, 2008.

Henri Foucillon, *The Art of the West*, :2 vols. London: Phaidon, 1970.

Nancy Fraser, 'Climates of Capital: For a Trans-Environmental Socialism', *New Left Review*, Vol. 127, January/February 2021, pp. 94–127.

Sigmund Freud, *Group Psychology and Other Writings*. London: White Press, 2004.

Samir Gandesha, *Identity Politics: Dialectics of Liberation or Paradox of Empowerment?* 4th Gillian Rose Memorial Lecture. Centre for Research in Modern European Philosophy, 19 October 2023, UCL.

Édouard Glissant, *Poetics of Relation*. Ann Arbor: University of Michigan Press, 1995.

Kurt Goldstein, *The Organism*. With a foreword by Oliver Sachs. New York: Zone Books, 2010.

David Graeber, *Bullshit Jobs: A Theory*. London: Allen Lane, 2018.

Jonathan Greenaway, *A Primer of Utopian Philosophy: An Introduction to the Work of Ernst Bloch*. London: Zer0 Books, 2024.

Melissa Gregg and Gregory J. Seigworth, *The Affect Theory Reader*. Durham: Duke University Press, 2020.

Marjoree Grene, 'Authenticity: An Existential Virtue', *Ethics*, Vol. 62, No. 4, 1952.

Leonid Grossman, *Dostoevsky*. London: Allen Lane, 1974.

Félix Guattari, *Lines of Flight: For Another World of Possibilities*. London: Bloomsbury, 2015.

Stuart Hall, *Selected Political Writings: The Great Moving Right Show and Other Essays*. Lawrence & Wishart, 2017.

Yuval Noah Harari, *Sapiens: A Brief History of Mankind*. London: Vintage, 2015.

Donna Haraway, *Simians, Cyborgs, and Women: The Reinvention of Nature*. New York: Routledge, 1991, p. 13.

Sandra Harding, *Sciences from below: Feminisms, Postcolonialities, and Modernities*. Durham: Duke University Press, 2008.

G. W. F. Hegel, *Phenomenology of Spirit*. New York: Oxford University Press, 1977, p. 240.

Eric Hobsbawm, *Interesting Times: A Twentieth Century Life*. London: Abacus, 2002.

Edmund Husserl, *The Paris Lectures*, trans. Peter Koestenbaum. The Hague: Martinus Nijhoff, 1967.

Fredric Jameson, 'World Reduction in Le Guin: The Emergence of Utopian Narrative', *Science Fiction Studies*, Vol. 2, No. 3, The Science Fiction of Ursula K. Le Guin, 1975, pp. 221–230.

Fredric Jameson, *The Antinomies of Realism*. London and New York: Verso, 2013.

Fredric Jameson, *Allegory and Ideology*. London and New York: Verso, 2019.

James Joyce, *Finnegans Wake*. London: Faber & Faber, 1975.

Carl G. Jung, *On the Nature of the Psyche*. Abingdon, OX: Routledge, 2001.

Franz Kafka, *The Complete Stories*. New York: Schocken Books, 1971.

Naomi Klein, *The Shock Doctrine: The Rise of Disaster Capitalism*. London: Penguin, 2008.

Jacques Lacan *Écrits: A Selection*. New York: Norton, 1977.

Jean Laplanche, *New Foundations for Psychoanalysis*. London: Blackwell, 1989.

Jean Laplanche, *The Unfinished Copernican Revolution: Selected Works, 1967–1992*. New York: Unconscious in Translation, 1989.

Jean Laplanche, *Essays on Otherness*. London: Routledge, 1999.

Bruno Latour, *Down to Earth: Politics in the New Climatic Regime*, trans. Catherine Porter. Cambridge: Polity, 2007.

Lesley Le Grange, 'What Is Postqualitative Research?', *South African Journal of Higher Education*, Vol. 32, No. 5, 2018, pp. 1–14.

Ursula Le Guin, *The Left Hand of Darkness*. London: Gollancz, 2018. Originally published in 1967.

Noa Levin, 'Spectres of Eternal Return: Benjamin and Deleuze Read Leibniz', *Filozofski vestnik*, Vol. XLII, No. 2, 2021.

Emmanuel Levinas, *Existence and Existents*. The Hague: Martinus Nijhoff, 1978.

Lisa Lowe, *The Intimacies of Four Continents*. Durham, NC: Duke University Press, 2015.

Jean-Francois Lyotard, *The Postmodern Condition: A Report on Knowledge*. Manchester University Press, 1984. Originally published in 1954.

C. De Magalhaes Gomes, 'Genero como categoria de analise decolonial', *Civitas*, Porto Alegre, 2018, pp. 65–82.

Clarence Major, *Juba to Jive: A Dictionary of Afro-American Slang*. New York: Viking, 1994.

Karl Mannheim, *Ideology and Utopia: An Introduction to the Sociology of Knowledge*. Eastford, CT: Martino Publishing, 2015.

Herbert Marcuse, *One Dimensional Man: Studies in the Ideology of Advanced Industrial Society*. London: Routledge, 2002.

Karl Marx, *Capital*, Vol. 1, trans. Ben Fowkes. London: Penguin, 1976.

Karl Marx and Friedrich Engels. *On Religion*. Mineola, NY: Dover Publications, 2008.

Brian Massumi, 'The Autonomy of Affect', in *Deleuze: A Critical Reader*, ed. P. Patton. Oxford, OX: Blackwell, 1996.

Achille Mbembe, 'Necropolitics', *Public Culture*, Vol. 15, No. 1, Duke University Press, 2003, pp. 11–40.

Jerome McGann, *Byron and the Poetics of Adversity*. Cambridge University Press, 2022.

Maurice Merleau-Ponty, *Signs*. Evanston, IL: Northwestern University Press, 1964.

Maurice Merleau-Ponty, *The Primacy of Perception*. Evanston, IL: Northwestern University Press, 1964.

Maurice Merleau-Ponty, *Phenomenology of Perception*. London: Routledge, 2012.

Jacques-Alain Miller, 'Perversion', in *Reading Seminars I and II: Lacan's Return to Freud*, ed. Richard Felstein et al. Albany: State University of New York Press, 1996.

A. Mitchell and A. Chaudhury, 'Worlding Beyond "the" "End" of "the World": White Apocalyptic Visions and BIPOC Futurisms', *International Relations*, Vol. 34, No. 3, 2020, pp. 309–332.

Adelaide Morris, ed., *Sound States: Innovative Poetics and Acoustic Technologies*. Chapel Hill, NC: University of North Carolina Press, 1997.

Clark Moustakas, *Heuristic Research: Design, Methodology and Application*. Newbury Park, CA: Sage, 1990.

Iris Murdoch, *Under the Net*. London: Vintage, 2002.

F. Neyrat, 'The Biopolitics of Catastrophe, or How to Avert the Past and Regulate the Future', *South Atlantic Quarterly*, Vol. 115, No. 2, 2016.

Friedrich Nietzsche, *Ecce Homo*. London: Penguin, 1979.

Ovid, *Metamorphoses*, trans. Arthur Golding. London: Penguin, 2002.

O. Oyewumi, 'Conceptualizing Gender: The Eurocentric Foundations of Feminist Concepts and the Challenge of African Epistemology', *JENdA: A Journal of Culture and African Women Studies*, Vol. 2, No. 1, 2002, pp. 1–9.

Tim Parks. 'Reading against the Novel', *New York Review of Books*, 18 July 2024, pp. 41–43.

Jan Patočka, *Heretical Essays in the Philosophy of History*. Chicago, IL: Open Court, 1999.

Adam Phillips, 'On Getting the Life you Want', *London Review of Books*, Vol. 46, No. 12, 20 June 2024.

Darryl Pinckney, 'Black Talk on the Move', *New York Review of Books*, 20 July 2023, pp. 15–17, 16.

Ben Pitcher, 'The Popular Culture of Extinction and the Racialization of Survival, 2022', *New Formations*, No. 107–108, 2023, pp. 84–100.

Plato, *Timaeus and Critias*, trans. Robin Waterfield. Oxford University Press, 2008.

Plato, *Phaedo*, trans. David Gallop. Oxford Classics, 2009.

Jasbir K. Puar, *Terrorist Assemblages: Homonationalism in Queer Times*. London and Durham: Duke University Press, 2007.

Ronald Purser, *McMindfulness: How Mindfulness Became the New Capitalist Spirituality*. London: Repeater, 2019.

Anibal Quijano, *Coloniality of Power, Eurocentrism and Latin America*. London and Durham: Duke University Press, 2000.

Otto Rank, *The Double: A Psychoanalytic Study*. New York: Meridian, 1971.

C. Riley Snorton, *Black on Both Sides: A Racial History of Trans Identity*. Minneapolis: University of Minnesota Press, 2017.

Bruce Robbins, 'Museum of Difference', *The Baffler*, No. 53, September 2020.

Camille Robcis, *Disalienation: Politics, Philosophy, and Radical Psychiatry in Postwar France*. Chicago, IL: University of Chicago Press, 2021.

Andrew Robinson, 'Bakhtin: Dialogism, Polyphony, and Heteroglossia', *Ceasefire*, 29 July 2011.

Carl R. Rogers, *Client-Centred Therapy*. London: Constable, 1951.

Richard Rorty, *The Rorty Reader*, ed. Christopher J. Voparil and Richard J. Bernstein. Hoboken, NJ: Wiley-Blackwell, 2010.

Gillian Rose, *Marxist Modernism: Introductory Lectures on Frankfurt School Critical Theory*. London: Verso, 2024.

Jacqueline Rose, *Proust among the Nations: from Dreyfus to the Middle East*. Chicago, IL: Chicago University Press, 2011.

Jacqueline Rose, 'The Analyst', *New York Review of Books*, Vol. LXX, No. 14, 21 September 2023.

Leon S. Roudiez, ed., *Desire in Language: A Semiotic Approach to Literature and Art*. New York: Columbia University Press, 1980.

Douglas Rushkoff, *Survival of the Richest: Escape Fantasies of the Tech Billionaires*. London: Scribe, 2022.

Jared Russell, *Nietzsche and the Clinic*. New York: Routledge, 2016.

Leopold von Sacher-Masoch, *Venus in Furs in Masochism*. New York: Zone Books, 1991.

Edward Said, *Reflections on Exile and Other Literary and Cultural Essays*. London: Granta, 2012.

Avgi Saketopoulou, *Sexuality beyond Consent: Risk, Race, Traumatophilia*. State University of New York Press, 2023.

Joan W. Scott, *Gender and the Politics of History*. New York: Columbia University Press, 1988.

Sandy Sela-Smith, 'Heuristic Research: A Review and Critique of Moustakas's Method', *Journal of Humanistic Psychology*, Vol. 4293, 2002, pp. 53–88.

Martin Seligman, *Flourish: A New Understanding of Happiness and Well-Being and How to Achieve Them*. Boston, MA: Brealy, 2002.

Stephen Shapin, 'The Superhuman Upgrade', *London Review of Books*, Vol. 39, No. 14, 13 July 2017.

Adam Shatz, 'Rapping with Fanon', *New York Review of Books*, 22 January 2019. https://www.nybooks.com/online/2019/01/22/rapping-with-fanon/, retrieved 19 March 2021.

Tamsin Shaw, 'Invisible Manipulators of Your Mind', *New York Review of Books*, Vol. LXIV, No. 7, 2017, pp. 62–65.

Gilbert Simondon, *Individuation in Light of Notions of Form and Information*, trans. Taylor Adkins. University of Minnesota Press, 2020.

Hortense Spillers, 'Mama's Baby, Papa's Maybe: An American Grammar Book', *Diacritics*, Vol. 17, No. 2, 1987.

Baruch Spinoza, *Ethics*. Princeton, NJ: Princeton University Press, 1996.

B. Stawarska and A. Ring, 'Black Speaking Subjects: Frantz Fanon's Critique of Coloniality of Language in Merleau-Ponty's Phenomenology', *Open Editions Journal*, Vol. 45, No. 1, 2023.

J. Fitzjames Stephen, *The Writings of James Fitzjames Stephen: On the Novel and Journalism*, ed. Christopher Ricks. New York: Oxford University Press.

Bernard Stiegler and Irit Rogoff, 'Transindividuation', *e-flux Journal*, March 2010.

Kathleen Stock, *Material Girls: Why Reality Matters for Feminism*. London: Fleet, 2021.

Nicholas Thoburn, David Bennett, Jeremy Gilbert, and Mandy Merck, 'Extinction and the Anthropocene: To End or Mend the World? A Conversation with Claire Colebrook', *New Formations*, No. 107–108, 2023, pp. 198–214.

G. Thomas, *The Sexual Demon of Colonial Power: Pan-African Embodiment and Erotic Scheme of Empire*. Bloomington, IN: Indiana University Press.

Alberto Toscano, *Late Fascism: Race, Capitalism, and the Politics of Crisis*. London: Verso, 2023.

Alberto Toscano, 'Shifting Currents', *New Left Review*, Vol. 140/141, March/June 2023.

Iana Trichkova, 'What Gets in the Way of Working with Clients Who Have Been Sexually Abused? Heuristic Inquiry', in *Critical Existential-Analytic Psychotherapy*, ed. Del Lowenthal. Abingdon, OX: Routledge, 2021.

Marina Tsvetaeva. *Art in the Light of Conscience*, trans. Angela Livingstone. Cambridge, MA: Harvard University Press, 1992.

Richard Von Krafft-Ebing, *Psychopathia Sexualis*. London: Forgotten Books, 2019.

Norman Waddell and Masao Abe, *The Heart of Dōgen's Shōbōgenzō*. New York: State University of New York Press, 2002.

Immanuel Wallerstein, 'Reading Fanon in the 21st Century', *New Left Review*, No. 57, May/June 2009.

Ben Ware, *On Extinction: Beginning again at the End*. London and New York: Verso, 2024.

McKenzie Wark, *Capital Is Dead: Is This Something Worse?* London: Verso, 2019.

Mckenzie Wark, *Love and Money, Sex and Death*. London: Verso, 2023.

Jessica Whyte, *The Morals of the Market: Human Rights and the Rise of Neoliberalism*. London: Verso, 2019.

Frances Wilson, *How to Survive the Titanic: The Sinking of J. Bruce Ismay*. New York: Harper Perennial, 2002.

S. Winter, *Freud and the Institution of Psychoanalytic Knowledge*. Stanford, CA: Stanford University Press, 1999.

Michael Wood, 'Yeats and Violence', *London Review of Books*, Vol. 30, No. 16, 14 August 2008.

Index

Note: Page numbers in *italics* indicate figures.

For Product Safety Concerns and Information please contact our EU
representative GPSR@taylorandfrancis.com
Taylor & Francis Verlag GmbH, Kaufingerstraße 24, 80331 München, Germany